Apostle of Culture

Apostle of Culture

Emerson as Preacher
and Lecturer

David Robinson

University of Pennsylvania Press
Philadelphia 1982

Library of Congress Cataloging in Publication Data

Robinson, David, 1947–
  Apostle of culture.

  Includes bibliographical references and index.
  1. Emerson, Ralph Waldo, 1803–1882.
  2. Preaching—Massachusetts—History—19th century.
  3. Authors, American—19th century—Biography.
  4. Unitarians—Massachusetts—Biography. 5. Massachusetts—Biography. I. Title.
  PS1631.R6   814'.3   81–16228
  ISBN 0–8122–7824–0   AACR2

Printed in the United States of America

To Gwendolyn

Contents

Acknowledgments

I have accumulated many debts in the course of writing this study, some of which I would like to acknowledge here. To begin with, I was greatly helped by a National Endowment for the Humanities Summer Stipend, and by grants from the College of Liberal Arts Research Program, the General Research Program, and the Humanities Development Program, Oregon State University. I also benefited from work that I was able to do under the auspices of the Institute on Freedom and Causality at the Center for Advanced Study in the Behavioral Sciences at Stanford, California. I have had support and encouragement at key points from Richard Astro and Robert Frank, whom I would also like to thank.

William Gibson and Sargent Bush read an earlier version of this study at the University of Wisconsin, and offered helpful commentary, and I was helped at later stages by Lawrence Buell, Robert Jones, and Andrew Delbanco. I am very indebted to Merton Sealts, who generously shared his own work on Emerson with me and offered indispensable help during the formulation of the book.

I have had much aid from the staff of the Houghton Library, Harvard University, and from that of the Boston Athenaeum. I want to thank both those libraries, and the Ralph Waldo Emerson Memorial Association, for permission to quote from manuscript sources variously documented in the study. I also want to thank Doris Tilles and the staff of the Interlibrary Loan Department at Oregon State. My debt to all those involved in the Harvard editions of Emerson's Journals and Early Lectures is enormous. In quoting from the new edition of the Journals, I have at some points omitted canceled passages that are preserved in that edition, and editorial symbols used in the edition, in the interest of the readability of the quotations themselves. Earlier versions of parts of the material presented here were published in *Philological Quarterly*, *ESQ: A Journal of the American Renaissance*, and the *Journal of the History of Ideas*.

xi

At earlier stages in the preparation of this book I had valuable help from Patricia Nametz, Robert Vorlicky, and Robert Winston, and I would also like to thank Betty Brose for her help. My greatest debt is to Gwendolyn Robinson, who not only made the study possible, but made it worthwhile.

Abbreviations

The following abbreviations are used throughout this study in parenthetical documentation. Where appropriate, such citations have been grouped within the text.

CEC   *The Correspondence of Emerson and Carlyle.* Ed. Joseph Slater. New York: Columbia University Press, 1964.

CW   *The Collected Works of Ralph Waldo Emerson.* Ed. Robert E. Spiller et al. 2 vols. to date. Cambridge: Harvard University Press, Belknap Press, 1971–.

EL   *The Early Lectures of Ralph Waldo Emerson, 1833–1842.* Ed. Stephen E. Whicher, Robert E. Spiller, and Wallace E. Williams. 3 vols. Cambridge: Harvard University Press, 1959; Harvard University Press, Belknap Press, 1964–71.

J   *The Journals of Ralph Waldo Emerson.* Ed. Edward Waldo Emerson and Waldo Emerson Forbes. 10 vols. Boston and New York: Houghton Mifflin, 1909–14.

JMN   *The Journals and Miscellaneous Notebooks of Ralph Waldo Emerson.* Ed. William H. Gilman et al. 14 vols. to date. Cambridge: Harvard University Press, Belknap Press, 1960–.

L   *The Letters of Ralph Waldo Emerson.* Ed. Ralph L. Rusk. 6 vols. New York: Columbia University Press, 1939.

Life   Ralph L. Rusk. *The Life of Ralph Waldo Emerson.* New York: Charles Scribner's Sons, 1949.

W   *The Complete Works of Ralph Waldo Emerson.* Ed. Edward Waldo Emerson. Centenary Ed. 12 vols. Boston and New York: Houghton Mifflin, 1903–4.

YES   *Young Emerson Speaks: Unpublished Discourses on Many Subjects.* Ed. Arthur C. McGiffert, Jr. Boston: Houghton Mifflin, 1938.

Introduction

Emerson himself realized the truth of a remark by Margaret Fuller, which he recorded in his journal, that the best of him was in his lectures (*JMN*, 7:301). Even though Fuller's insight was intended partially as a comment on her somewhat unsatisfactory relationship with Emerson, it does raise a central problem in Emerson studies. The man who has come to be seen in this century as the fountainhead of American literary symbolism and the father of the American poetic tradition was, through the most important phase of his career, devoted primarily to oratorical rather than literary endeavors. His ambition was geared to the spoken word, and his style nurtured by an oral tradition. Harold Bloom's observation is apt: "The primary Emerson is this confident orator."[1] Yet in our century, the fate of Emerson's reputation has fallen with the literary critics, those who are not only committed to the study of the written word, but forced by history to interpret Emerson only through his written texts. Surely this accounts in part for the uneasy feeling among historians of American thought and literature that Emerson's influence outdistances his achievement, or the bafflement which Joel Porte has noted among Emerson's interpreters, who feel that they have not gotten to the essential Emerson.[2] The force of an orator dies with him in part, and this has been the case with Emerson.

But to take the oratorical Emerson seriously, and inquire into the impact of his dozens of public addresses, raises a further problem. It becomes clear rather quickly that Emerson was not an artist who was working in a difficult and now unpopular medium, but rather a preacher who would insist that his value lay not in his expression but in his vision. As a critic, although keenly sensitive to language, he more often responded to the vision of the writers with whom he dealt, and he valued his own work less for its artistic polish than for the truth he tried to make it hold forth. To look at his oratorical side, therefore, is to look at his religious side as well, for the roots of all his great lectures and essays are in the sermon, the form through which he learned his craft of words. When we return to that source of his expression, we confront Emerson as a Unitarian preacher— not only a preacher at the outset of his career but, in curiously instructive ways, a preacher throughout his career. We see, as his friend Frederic Henry Hedge remarked, that Emerson was "always a preacher in the higher, universal sense."[3]

That Emerson began as a minister and always maintained a theological vision is a historical commonplace, but in part because of its familiarity, the notion has been comparatively little explored. The sermons remain the major grouping of unpublished manuscript material, and despite Arthur C. McGiffert's selection of them, they have been comparatively neglected in the criticism and are almost never anthologized.[4] James E. Cabot, whose *Memoir* of Emerson was the standard biography until Ralph L. Rusk's definitive study, offers a good example of critical attitudes toward the sermons. He characterizes them generally with the remark that "all is within the conventions of the Unitarian pulpit," but adds in passing that the key ideas of the essays "appear more and more as time goes on, but in general they are presented in Scriptural language, as if they belonged to the body of accepted doctrine."[5] It seems not to have occurred to Cabot that perhaps Emerson was preaching an accepted version of Unitarianism, that there are positions as "radical" in the sermons as in the revolutionary addresses and lectures of the late 1830s. Howard Mumford Jones, looking at the sermons some years later for clues to Emerson's development, came away puzzled to find there only "a younger and lesser Channing,"[6] but he did not pause to consider that in this comparison there was indeed a key to Emerson's impact. For Emerson was the most influential inheritor of the liberal theological tradition which Channing represented, and all his strikingly original work is an extension of that tradition.

Although McGiffert's work on the sermons has still not had the impact on Emerson studies that it should, the publication of the Harvard edition of Emerson's journals and early lectures, whose richly informative nature is bringing the Emerson of the early 1830s to light, is beginning to have an impact.[7] The lectures make it clear that even in this period of intellectual ferment, Emerson was compelled to deal with the theological questions he had preached on in his pulpit. Moreover, they suggest that his new vocation of lecturer was really a version of his own concept of the Christian ministry, which for a number of reasons he was never able to realize within the church.

Aside from this wealth of new source materials, two trends in recent criticism have helped to clarify Emerson's career and have made a study like this one possible. To begin with, "a revolution in American Unitarian historiography is currently in progress," to quote one of its leaders, Conrad Wright.[8] This revolution promises to illuminate Emerson precisely because it refuses to see nineteenth-century Unitarianism as Emerson saw it—or rather, as the rebelling Emerson saw it when he was struggling inwardly to free himself from his ministerial vocation, or after he found that he no longer needed any denominational identity. The characterization of Unitarianism as "corpse-cold" in some of Emerson's remarks proved to be an attractive enough description to discourage a thorough examination of that tradition until recently. Now there is evidence to suggest that Unitarianism was diverse and lively enough to accommodate even its chief rebel, Emerson.[9]

While this trend has clarified Emerson's context, another new approach, represented most importantly in the work of Stephen E. Whicher and Jonathan Bishop, is helping to clarify Emerson himself. As Porte characterizes it, this second trend is predicated on the assumption that beneath the public Emerson "there lies a finite consciousness troubled with a tragic sense of contingency and loss."[10] For both Whicher and Bishop, Emerson's tragic sense is rooted in his private experiences. Whicher stresses the importance of Emerson's inability to square his early dream of greatness with experience, and Bishop attributes the fade of the earlier radical Emerson specifically to "interior causes," primarily the death of his son.[11] The sense of complex and constant change in Emerson's career has been convincingly established by these studies, but to see Emerson from the perspective of his theological context sheds a somewhat different light on the change. Both Whicher and Bishop run the risk of portraying Emerson as a man whose philosophy was no more than the compensating reflection of his personal inadequacies and disappointments. Each study pushes so deeply at the Emersonian psyche that it overlooks Emerson's almost austere absorption

in the play of the mind, and his tenacious commitment to transform-
ing ideas into a relevant moral message for a specific audience.
However eloquent the private Emerson could be in his journals, no
writer ever needed an audience more, or assumed an audience more
completely. He always wrote with the orator's sense of an audience
immediately before him. What the early lectures show is that the
tempering of his optimism arose from his realization of an underlying paradox in his intellectual stance and the message he was preaching. Although he was committed to the idea of self-culture, which
he saw as the evolving of the soul toward an ultimate perfection, he
realized that he was calling for the pursuit of an unattainable end.
But the realization was not the product of any skepticism about the
possibility of the soul's growth; it arose instead from his perception
that growth itself awakened a further need for growth. The pursuit
of perfection which he urged on his hearers was therefore con-
demned to failure by its own nature. Without a concept of the
better, self-culture was impossible; but with such a vision, it could
never be completed.

It was the notion of individual growth that guided Emerson's
thinking almost from the first. The journals he kept before he under-
took his Divinity studies record it, his sermons return to the idea
repeatedly, and *Nature* is his most prolonged early attempt to clarify
the process of this self-cultivation. The lectures of the late 1830s
record his increasing struggle with what he came to see as a paradox
of achievement. Certainly personal tragedy in his early years, and his
son Waldo's death in 1842, added to his later skepticism, but the
seeds of it were in the intellectual task he set for himself as an apostle
of self-culture. That was a task he had inherited from his Unitarian
predecessors.

It is these interwoven strands in Emerson's early career that I
hope to trace in this study: the shape that his oratorical ambition
gave to his career, the corresponding dependence of that career on
his Unitarian background, and the nature of the inherent paradox
of self-culture that he discovered in following Unitarian assumptions
to their logical conclusions. To begin, however, we must assess the
nature of the Unitarian theology that nurtured him.

PART ONE

Emerson as Preacher

American Unitarianism
and the Theological Foreground
of Self-Culture

A Theology of Self-Culture

The theological battle lines which were drawn after Emerson's Divinity School Address have left us with one pervasive historical distortion, the ironic fact that the Unitarianism of that period gained a reputation as a negative movement, the complacent if not reactionary remainder of the final unraveling of Calvinist orthodoxy in New England. The irony is that the Unitarians themselves saw their movement as revolutionary in essence, and unknowingly bequeathed to their intellectual descendants, the Transcendentalists, much of the ardor that resulted in what we recognize as the rebellious spirit of that later movement. History does justify part of the popular conception of these groupings—certain of the Unitarians were, after all, the first to point with horror at the heresies of Emerson and his followers, and there is no doubt that some of the Transcendentalists themselves were convinced that Boston Unitarianism was one of the chief obstacles to the reform of the human spirit that they were attempting.

The scattered comments on Unitarianism left to us by Emerson disclose the frame of mind that is largely responsible for the creation of the negative historical conception of Unitarianism. In a late essay, "The Sovereignty of Ethics," published long after the Divinity School controversy would have been of great emotional importance to him, the by then revered Emerson put the point flatly: "Luther would cut his hand off sooner than write theses against the pope if he suspected that he was bringing on with all his might the pale negations of Boston Unitarianism" (*W,* 10:204). Elsewhere he searingly referred to "the corpse-cold Unitarianism of Brattle Street" (*W,* 10:552). But perhaps more revealing is a journal entry of 1835, at the time when Emerson was changing courses from preaching in a Unitarian pulpit to lecturing independently. He records without comment, but, one suspects, with a measure of approval, a remark by the visiting Harriet Martineau on some leading Unitarians: "Miss Martineau says that Mr Ware is sanctimonious, Mr Gannett popish, Unitarians in a twilight of bigotry, and that Mr Furness has a genius for religion" (*JMN,* 5:47). The passage bristles with biographical connotations when placed in the context of Emerson's tenuous relation with his ministerial profession at the time, and when we remember that the "sanctimonious" Henry Ware, Jr., had been Emerson's senior colleague at his first pulpit and had not been reticent in offering Emerson pointers on improving his style of preaching (see *L,* 1:257, 273). It was also Ware who, three years later, would offer the most searching, and emotionally painful, criticism of the Divinity School Address.[1] But what is perhaps more important about the remark is the sense it gives us of a younger generation passing judgment on its elders, and condemning or praising them with both the social sensitivity and the underlying idealism of youth. To call someone "sanctimonious" or "popish" in this case is to comment on the social manifestation of his religion in a way that inextricably fuses personality and abstract theology. It gives us both the provincial feel of the Transcendentalist movement and the movement's fervor of purpose, which, because of its expression by a few persons of talent, gives it a claim to our attention now. The final remark on William Henry Furness's "genius for religion" touches the central aspiration of almost every member of the movement.

While we must not lose the sense of immediacy that such candid remarks can lend to the Transcendentalist revolt, the color of Emerson's language, combined with his stature in American letters, has given this picture of Unitarianism more weight than a balanced understanding of the period can support.[2] The harder we look at the concerns of both Transcendentalists and Unitarians, the more difficult it becomes to establish the differences between them. Words like "revolt" and "rebellion" become increasingly problematic as the hard lines of intellectual division melt away; we are forced to think in terms of germination, development, and growth instead, and to appeal to a set of organic images that would have pleased either of the two camps. What each group shared at bottom was the desire to foster a certain growth or natural development in the individual. Emerson made his sense of this task clear in a sermon on his last day as minister of Boston's Second Church: "It is thought that juster views of human nature are gaining ground than have yet prevailed. Men are beginning to see with more distinctness what they ought to be." It was the duty of the age, therefore, to continue "the higher and holier work of forming *men*, true and entire men" (*YES*, p. 180). This call for the development of the individual, though it was given its most memorable expression by Emerson, would have been echoed by almost any of the Unitarians who preceded him. They were themselves fighting a pitched battle with the Calvinists over the issue of human capacity, and though that controversy had many points of contention, it resolved itself essentially into a debate over the possibility of affirming human potential against the conception of original sin. Compelled both by the logic of their rationalist inheritance and by an emotional revulsion at the Calvinist conception of man and God, the Unitarians had begun to formulate an affirmative religion whose core was, in the words of Henry Ware, Jr., "the culture of [man's] own spiritual nature."[3]

The repeated turn to the word "culture" or "cultivation" in Unitarian sermon and devotional literature reveals a conception of the soul based upon the organic analogy of germination, development, and fruition. "Culture," as it was used by Ware and other Unitarians, still carried most of the horticultural associations originally connected with the word. The more common modern connotations of culture as high art and social refinement or as the activities of a social grouping often bypass the set of organic references that gave it such force in the nineteenth century. Just as a plant needed direct and careful culture in order to grow and be productive, the human soul required a constant attention to bring it to its full capacity. Moreover, the development of both the living plant and the soul seemed to be directed by an inner potential, a force which, if it were not hindered or altered, would assure a well-proportioned and continuing process of growth.

The analogy between the culture of the plant and that of the soul broke down, however, at one crucial point, and here was created the major burden of Unitarian theology. Even though a plant grows by laws of its own nature, it must be cultivated by a force outside itself. Man, however, was responsible for the culture of his own soul. In this sense, the faith in the almost limitless capacity of human nature implied by Unitarian thought produced a correspondingly severe moral responsibility for the fostering of self-development. Thus the moral life was transformed from a sign, or an adjunct, of the religious life, into a religion in itself.[4]

One of the clearest statements of the assumptions of this religion of moral culture is William Ellery Channing's *Self-Culture* (1838), in which Channing relies on the organic conception of the soul to define the process of self-culture.

To cultivate any thing, be it a plant, an animal, a mind, is to make grow. Growth, expansion, is the end. Nothing admits culture but that which has a principle of life, capable of being expanded. He, therefore, who does what he can to unfold all his powers and capacities, especially his nobler ones, so as to become a well-proportioned, vigorous, excellent, happy being, practices self-culture.[5]

This use of the organic metaphor was not, of course, unique or original with the Unitarians; it was in fact one of the touchstones of Romanticism generally. But their direct application of the assumptions implicit in the metaphor to essential issues in American religious thought was unique. Given the theological nature of the history of American thought, the development of the organic metaphor of culture is most profitably seen in a theological, rather than a literary, context. Only from such a perspective does it become clear that the study of the rise of Romanticism in America is equivalent, at many points, to the study of the secularization of the American mind.

Self-Culture and the Unitarian Movement

Emerson referred to Unitarianism as a theology of "pale negations" because he understood the extent to which the movement was a denial of Calvinism. In their own eyes, the Unitarians felt that their position was affirmative, that they were denying what they perceived as Calvinism's original denial of human dignity. But in pursuing such a task, they forced upon themselves a rhetorical stance based in large part on the rebuttal of "false doctrine." Often this meant that they were either on the attack or on the defensive in their writing and preaching, and some of their most forceful and eloquent productions are polemical.[6] But even their most affirmative and uplifting writing, toward which they consciously strived, is haunted by the specter of Calvinism never very far in the background, and the doctrinal disputation in which they felt obliged to engage absorbed much of their intellectual energy.

Unitarianism began to coalesce as a theological movement in 1805 when the liberal Henry Ware, Sr., was elected Hollis Professor of Divinity at Harvard, after a contest in which liberals and orthodox Calvinists alike had realized that much was at stake.[7] Ware's election was chiefly important for the institutional stronghold, and thus the social legitimacy, that it gave liberal theologians. The intellectual roots of Unitarianism extend much further back into the tradition of Arminian thought which developed in the New England Churches of the Standing Order in the eighteenth century.[8] In that tradition, under the leadership of Charles Chauncy and Jonathan Mayhew, a critique of strict Calvinism had begun, centering on a modification of the notion of innate depravity.

The Arminian movement, however, only approached from a different angle a problem with which New England Calvinists themselves had struggled. Almost from the first, there existed in the Calvinist system a tension between the demand that salvation be understood as a gift of grace given entirely by God and the desire that human action should somehow find a place in the most crucial of human experiences. The Calvinist response to this tension re-

sulted in a tradition of "preparationist" thought, which preserved
God's place as the source of grace, but emphasized the duty of man
in preparing for the reception of that grace, should it be extended.
Already a strong tradition in the old world, preparationist thought
flourished in New England after the Puritan migration among such
leaders as Thomas Hooker, Thomas Shepard, and Peter Bulkeley.
While a definite historical connection between Unitarian ideas of
self-culture and preparationist thought seems doubtful, it is clear
that both schools of thought show the same pattern of reaction to
the implications of the doctrine of innate depravity.[9] The attempt,
in both cases, was to make a place for a human contribution to the
salvation experience.

We do well to remember that what was at stake for the partici-
pants in these theological controversies was not adherence to a set
of metaphysical abstractions, but the answer to the fundamental
question of individual salvation. As the tenets of Calvinism were
increasingly strained in meeting this vital question in the changing
contexts of the eighteenth century, the liberal tradition responded
with a doctrine of conversion which was a major departure from
Calvinism, but which also provided an alternative to the rising evan-
gelicalism that did not sit well in Boston and its environs. That
alternative consisted of seeing conversion not necessarily as a single
intense experience, but rather as a continuing process of character
formation and cultivation. Daniel Walker Howe has labeled this
conception a "doctrine of salvation through gradual growth,"[10] and
it had enormous consequences for the way men approached the
religious life.

To begin with, such a doctrine rendered the notion of a "conversion," in the sense of a dramatic change of heart, much less crucial.
Such an experience was not ruled out, but neither was it essential.
Henry Ware, Jr., clarified this point in a discussion of the religious
experience of children, answering the question, "How, then, shall
the infant become a Christian?": "I answer, in the first place, by
instruction and education. He is *now* of the kingdom of heaven; why
should he ever leave it?" In such a case conversion is unnecessary,
because the child can be successfully nurtured as a Christian and can
thus avoid the sinful or complacent life that makes a dramatic
change necessary. Ware was careful to note that such a life does not

make repentance unnecessary, for that is distinct from conversion: "Many imagine it to be essential that a man be converted. But they seem not to consider the distinction between *conversion* and *repentance*. Every man must repent. But I do not see that it is possible for such a one as I have described to be converted, in the proper sense of that term."[11]

But even for those without the advantage of such early cultivation, the experience of conversion could take many forms other than a sudden emotional change. Because human nature, according to the Unitarians, was not essentially corrupt, salvation came to be seen as the developing and unfolding of a potential inner virtue, rather than a wrenching inner change from corruption to righteousness. In further explaining the case of those who had not had the necessary early cultivation to be Christians by education, Ware insisted on the necessity of conversion, even though he realized that such language made some of his hearers uneasy: "Many, indeed, have a settled dislike to all language of this sort; and when you speak to them of conversion or regeneration, they at once suspect you of fanaticism, and shut their ears to all that can be said." But when Ware finally specified what such terminology entailed, he probably put his hearers more at ease: "I speak of nothing arbitrary, mysterious, or fanatical; but of a change in dispositions, affections, and character, to which any man is competent in the use of his natural powers, assisted by the means which the religion of Christ puts within his reach, and by those divine influences which are bestowed upon all who need."[12]

Such a change, as Ware and other Unitarians conceived it, was less in the nature of the soul than in the course of life through which the soul expressed itself. Outward acts of virtue were thus not merely possible signs of salvation, but the essential ingredients of salvation itself. Thus Ware could offer assurance of conversion to his hearers by pointing to Christ's injunction: " '*Ye are my friends,*' said our Lord, 'IF YE DO WHATSOEVER I COMMAND YOU.' "[13] For Joseph Stevens Buckminster, one of the Unitarian leaders of the generation before Ware, the "means" of conversion were similarly the "exhibition of the truths & motives of the gospel." Buckminster argued that such a change in life was necessarily a gradual process, and could be trusted much more than the sudden conversion experiences of Calvinists or evangelicals.

But as long as it is easier to fall down in swoons[,] to start in convulsions, & to groan in distress than to renovate the heart, as long as it is possible to gain belief to professions of instantaneous change without showing the gradual operation of the spirit in the progressive reformation, increasing holiness & goodness of character, so long will the cause of [Christ] be dishonoured.

The result of the renovation of the heart, then, was the "progressive reformation . . . of character," but it was an effect so closely linked to its cause as to be indistinguishable. Even the dramatic conversion of Paul, which was a favorite Calvinist example, could not sway Buckminster. It was, he noted, "a solitary instance, & in an age too abounding with miracles."[14] Perhaps the most eloquent testimony to this conception of conversion is that of William Ellery Channing, intellectual and spiritual leader of the Unitarian movement. Even though he seemed to undergo a "change of heart" at about age twenty, he preferred later to see his entire life as an unfolding conversion. When asked by an orthodox friend "whether he had not at some time experienced conversion," Channing replied, "I should say not, unless the whole of my life may be called, as it truly has been, a *process* of conversion."[15]

The conception of conversion as a process resulted in a view of the nature of human life as a period of probation or trial. Our state on earth, according to Ware, is "a state of trial, preparatory to a final state." The purpose of such a trial is the development of character, for the implication of the doctrine of gradual conversion is that the converted soul must exhibit itself in a virtuous character:

For, whether slight or momentous, [any action] affects our character; and character is the one thing essential. On character the judgment is passed, on character the fate of eternity is suspended. Character, therefore, it is which is tested, proved, cultivated, by the discipline of life; by the discipline of every hour of life; improved or deteriorated by every event.[16]

Ware's insistence on the "discipline of life" struck a responsive chord in most Unitarian thinkers, and as Howe has demonstrated, there was a pronounced strain of devotionalist pietism in the movement, despite its reputation for rationalism. This element of devotionalism can be detected in Buckminster's insistence that "a conscientious obedience to his [God's] will, habitual and persevering, is the grand constituent of a religious character."[17] John Emery Abbot, Howe's major exemplar of Unitarian pietism, preached in a similar vein that "to acquire a love of God, we must often and deliberately contemplate his character, . . . with devout and docile minds. All this requires deliberate, continued, and frequent attention."[18]

The emphasis on the discipline of life in the formation of character meant that the task of religion was, in Channing's words, "to ennoble human nature" and offer "every encouragement and aid to the pursuit of perfection."[19] In the trial or probation of life, religion thus became a positive counter to the potentially negative influences of both the outer world and humanity's inner weakness. It was out of this context that Unitarian polemicists turned with full force on the Calvinists, defending their position by pointing to the superior moral usefulness of Unitarianism in helping the soul through the trial of life.

Channing, the most eloquent and effective supporter of the claim for Unitarianism's superior moral conduciveness, based his argument largely on a moral revulsion against the wrathful God of Calvinism.[20] This point crops up persistently in Unitarian writing, mainly because the concept of an angry God was thought to endanger the moral life. Even in the midst of his biographical sketch of Abbot, Ware could find a place for similar slashes at Calvinism: "He [Abbot] was a Unitarian upon principle and from inquiry. . . . He had no belief that He [God] . . . suffers men to come into existence subject to a corruption which they cannot remove. . . . He, on the contrary, believed that all men are placed on an equal footing, to be tried with an impartial trial." Abbot himself bears out Ware's characterization when he describes the devout man as one who "rejoices in approaching to God, as the being in whom he lives, and moves, and enjoys, the healer of his infirmities, and the forgiver of his sins."[21]

While the emphasis of much of the Unitarian polemic was on the nature of God, its underlying implications were for the nature of man. The benevolence of God and the dignity of man were inextricably linked, as were the dignity of man and the possibilities of continuing growth of the soul. Fear of God, which Unitarians saw as the cornerstone of Calvinism, tended to thwart the full expression of human nature, the very thing necessary for continuing moral growth. The idea of a benevolent God, fair rather than arbitrary in his dealings with his creatures, also implied creatures who were similar to him in their moral nature.

Self-Culture and Self-Examination

While much of what the Unitarians said about self-culture arose from the more abstract context of Christian dogmatics, they did not neglect to offer detailed descriptions of that process and practical advice on the pursuit of it. Channing prefaced his *Self-Culture* lectures with an appeal to the possibility of culture: "Self-culture is something possible. It is not a dream. It has foundations in our nature. Without this conviction, the speaker will but declaim, and the hearer listen without profit. There are two powers of the human soul which make self-culture possible,—the self-searching and the self-forming power."[22] Considered in the fullest sense, these two "powers of the human soul" indicate the nature of the process of self-culture, by offering a view of the two vital directions into which the soul's energy can be channeled: inward to self-examination and outward to character formation. The turn inward, however, necessarily precedes the outward expression, for the proper expression of the soul depends upon a prior knowledge of the soul.

Here the Unitarians faced a paradox, in that self-examination, the first step in a process that affirmed human nature, was found to contain a pronounced element of the negative in it. This paradox emerges in a sermon of Buckminster's entitled "Sincerity": "Every principle of real virtue is an active and a progressive principle. It cannot leave a man satisfied with his present attainment. . . . He who carefully examines himself, cannot avoid discovering his imperfections, and he who is afraid to discover or negligent in the search has no sincere disposition to correct them."[23] Buckminster begins by stressing as the basis for virtue an "active and progressive principle" similar to the "principle of life" which Channing had used as the basis of his definition of culture. But this progressive principle quickly leads Buckminster to the fact that the "imperfections" in the soul underlie its active principle. The need for progress, in fact the very possibility of progress, logically implied an existing imperfection. But this logical implication was fully borne out by the experience of the limitations of the self in the practice of self-examination. Buckminster warned his congregation of the difficulties of embarking on a process of self-examination in no uncertain terms: "You may, at first, find the investigation difficult. You will, no doubt, make many unpleasant discoveries. Entering on a region, which you have never explored, a full prospect of your heart, if it could be presented at one view, must surprize and appal you."[24] The very fact that the extent of human weakness can be surprising suggests how far Buckminster and his hearers are from Calvinism. But that emotion of surprise becomes one of fearful discovery as the delving into the self continues.

An interesting case in point in this respect is again William Ellery Channing, whose sensibility was a touchstone for the Unitarian mind, so that he became, in Emerson's words, "a kind of public *Conscience.*"[25] Contemporary accounts of him often refer to his "saintliness," but hint at his reserve; and his preaching, though fervent and eloquent, was also almost coldly rational at points. Beneath the public figure of the man, and even beneath his private reserve, there was an intense self-consciousness that became almost self-consuming during the crisis of his "change of heart."[26] Channing's nephew and biographer, William Henry Channing, comments on a paper recording his act of self-consecration, which "marks the transition-point in the development of his character." Although too "personal" in nature to publish, the document is "chiefly remarkable for the sincerity with which its writer lays bare the morbid action of his soul." He adds that "an on-looker may be inclined to mourn that conscientiousness so strictly rules an originally buoyant genius." Yet seen from Channing's own eyes, at the distance of some years, the incident takes on enormous importance: "If I ever struggled with my whole soul for purity, truth, and goodness, it was there. There, amidst sore trials, the great question, I trust, was settled within me, whether I would obey the higher or lower principles of my nature." It was during "this great conflict," he says significantly, "that my mind was then receiving its impulse towards the perfect."[27] The struggle Channing fought with that part of himself which restrained him from the pursuit of perfection was one example of the struggle that, in the eyes of most Unitarians, a sincere self-examination would initiate in any heart. Character was the end for which they strove, and the means for its attainment were internal, as Ware argued: "The spring is within. The happiness and woe are within. Within, therefore, is the arena on which the contest for character and immortality is to be waged."[28]

It was out of this experience of sin that the responding impulse to self-cultivation was born. While frank about the actual limitations of human nature, the Unitarians were also secure in their sense of the potential for human improvement. In fact, the experience of limit was the major counter to complacency and spiritual stagnation. Thus Buckminster could pointedly ask, "Are you satisfied with the religious progress you have made? . . . Can you take pleasure in the progress of the divine life in your souls?" If satisfaction existed, that was a problem, for it implied that the delving into the self had not gone far enough, and that the development of character was being correspondingly stunted. "If," he said in another sermon, "you have ever found yourself long stationary in your religious characters, the probability is that you have been retrograding."[29] Ware echoed this warning by arguing that "he who is not gaining ground in a virtuous character and Christian preparation, is losing ground." Thus what is ultimately the most positive religious view of man usually begins, according to Ware, with "a sense of personal unworthiness" or, more explicitly, the "sense of sin, the feeling that [man's] life has not been right."[30] With this state of mind as the impetus to improvement, self-culture becomes possible.

There is, of course, little that is unique in this aspect of Unitarian self-examination aimed at revealing to man his sins and short-comings as a Christian. New England Calvinism, against which the Unitarians consciously arrayed themselves, had put heavy emphasis on self-examination as part of the process of preparation for grace. The difference between Unitarian and Calvinist ideas of self-examination lay in how the results of self-discovery were interpreted. As a Calvinist one prepared the soul to receive the gift of grace, a gift whose origin was completely outside the self and whose presence was unrelated to the "worthiness" of the self. Yet the Unitarian discussions of self-examination repeatedly stress the discovery of an inner power of the soul, the realization of which is the basis of their affirmation of the human character. In these cases, the unpleasant task of confronting the limits of the self is transformed into an experience of joy and renewal. Continuing his metaphor of exploration in explaining self-examination, Buckminster assures his congregation that

though you will find, at first, many dark and narrow defiles, many hidden and dangerous pit-falls, many spectacles of unexpected deformity, yet, if you regularly, carefully, and perseveringly pursue the investigation of yourself, the prospect will, at last, brighten, the region will become more open and level, and your progress, at last, smooth, easy, and delightful.[31]

It is the "delightful" aspect of self-examination that Ware expands upon in his own discussion of the relation of meditation to self-examination. At certain times, during this process, he says, the mind "whether in the body or out of the body it can hardly tell, soars, as it were, to the third heaven." Such an experience, he is quick to remind us, "is rarely to be expected," but it is one of the indications of "the joy of heart which is one of the genuine fruits of the Spirit." Ware is, of course, eager to emphasize the power unleashed by contemplative self-examination without appearing too close to revivalist enthusiasm; his final recommendation is that the Christian should seek "a calm and composed state of the affections, an equanimity of spirit, a serenity of temper."[32] Even this frame of mind, which seems relatively tame when compared with the experience of soaring "to the third heaven," is a positive step in self-conception from the "sense of personal unworthiness" which began the process of self-examination.

The change in self-conception which the Unitarians were convinced would take place in the process of self-examination is both an interesting phenomenon in itself and part of an important phase in the development of American thought. One clue to the basis of that change can be found in one of Emerson's journal entries of 1830 —a period before personal tragedy, intellectual dissatisfaction, and vocational crisis had led to his break with the church. "God is the substratum of all souls" (*JMN*, 3:213), he wrote, and this notion of the God within was to be repeated and amplified as Emerson's work developed. But even at this relatively early point in his thought, he

expressed the conviction which had assumed a prominent place in
Unitarian thought. The proper emphasis of the religious life was on
human power and potential, primarily because human power, in its
deepest sense, is divine. While it is certainly the case that this
realization moved Emerson in more dramatic and historically important ways than it did his colleagues, it is also important to remember
that in 1826 Channing pleaded for his hearers to follow "the
promptings of the divine monitor within us"[33] in pursuit of moral
perfection.

Yet if the concept of the underlying divinity of the soul, or of the
God within the individual, helps to explain the positive experience
the Unitarians linked with self-examination, the concept itself raises
another important question. Is it accurate to regard this concept as
based upon the kind of experience of the divine which Western
thought has usually regarded as mysticism? What may give pause at
this idea is, of course, the long historical association of Unitarianism
with rationalism. The Unitarians were, after all, the exponents of
German rationalist techniques of biblical interpretation; and in what
is usually considered the central document of Unitarianism, Channing's "Unitarian Christianity," we find him pointedly saying, with
his Calvinist opponents clearly in mind, that "the existence and
veracity of God, and the divine original of Christianity, are conclusions of reason, and must stand or fall with it."[34] Reason notwith-
standing, there is an undeniably experiential basis to Channing's talk
of the "divine monitor within," or Ware's description of the ecstasy
of the soul in contemplation of itself. Champions of rationalism, the
Unitarians were also champions of religious experience.[35] It is this
uniquely complete merger of reason and experience in theology that
both sets Unitarianism apart historically in American religion and
explains, to an extent, the brevity of its vitality. The synthesis it
attained could not hold together long in the ferment of the early
nineteenth century.

Once we recognize the presence of private experience in a system
of thought, such as this conviction of the ability of self-examination
to reveal an inner presence of God, we set a limit to the extent of
an intellectual inquiry into the system. Such an experience can be
asserted, described, or compared, but never fully explained. Even so,
there are revealing instances in which Unitarian thinkers, them-

selves intent on communicating with their hearers, offer a clearer picture of one of the components of such an experience. Channing's insistence on the progressive or dynamic nature of the soul, discussed earlier, can, in the context of this discussion, help establish one important distinction: for the Unitarians, the experience of divinity within was less a moment of static fulfillment than a hint of unrealized potential. It served, therefore, as an impetus to the effort to attain moral perfection. The Unitarians saw self-examination not as a means of discovering the perfection of human nature, but rather as a means of discovering the potential for perfection. This distinction clearly links the process of self-examination to the larger process of self-culture, in that the progressive realization of the potential perfection of the soul was in fact what the Unitarians referred to as culture. As Ware put it, man's goal in life "is, and can be, nothing less than to arrive at the full perfection of the nature with which God has endowed him. . . . These [intellect and character] are to be cultivated for the sake of their permanent continuance and undying value. This cultivation is the great business to be accomplished upon earth."[36] The divinity within man is thus the revelation of the potential perfectibility of human nature, and it is at this point that the Unitarians break most explicitly with their Calvinist predecessors. Channing, therefore, classed self-examination or self-searching as part of the process of culture because of the encouragement that the process could give to what he called the "self-forming power" of the soul. It revealed to man not only what he lacked, but what he could strive to become: "We are able to discern not only what we already are, but what we may become, to see in ourselves germs and promises of a growth to which no bounds can be set, to dart beyond what we have actually gained to the idea of perfection as the end of our being." Again, Channing appeals to an organic analogy of the "germ" of potential divinity in man, but the implication is clear that the growth of that germ is dependent on human commitment to perfection, rather than to any development determined by the nature of his soul. Thus the "self-comprehending power" is that part of us by which "we are distinguished from the brutes," and more importantly, that power "without [which] there would be no self-culture, for we should not know the work to be done."[37]

Self-Culture and Self-Discipline

Considering the foregoing discussion of human potential as the Unitarians conceived it, one might fairly question whether "theology" is an appropriate label for Unitarian thought. Certainly the movement was humanist in impulse, and Howe has gone as far as to say that "Christian humanism summed up the Unitarian sense of values."[38] But this humanism, it must be stressed, was indeed Christian humanism, essentially because the Unitarians accepted the biblical revelation as the basis of their faith. More specifically, however, in the debate with the Calvinists over the nature of God which gave Unitarianism its name, the Unitarians developed a conception of Christ which came to be a central referent for their conception of the culture of the soul. That they rejected the notion of the triune nature of God did not mean that they excluded an important role for Christology from their thinking. Channing could argue that "the doctrine that this Jesus was the supreme God himself, and the same being with his Father, . . . seems to us a contradiction to reason and Scripture so flagrant, that the simple statement of it is a sufficient refutation," and go on, in the same sermon, to affirm that "life conformed to the precepts and example of Jesus is the great end for which faith in him is required, and is the great condition on which everlasting life is bestowed."[39] The key phrase in Channing's discussion is the "example of Jesus," for in this concept the Unitarians were able to link the humanistic thrust of their thinking with their Christian heritage. Rather than seeing Christ as the figure who made salvation possible, as a God assuming the form of man, the Unitarians saw him as a man who, through his exemplification of the perfection of human nature, made it possible for man to become Godlike. The culture of the soul, therefore, had a more definite aim when it was considered in terms of Christ's example, and the notion of human perfection was grounded, to an extent, in his concrete person.

The process of self-examination, the first step toward the soul's culture, implied a standard by which man could judge himself. Buckminster emphasized the unique quality of Christ's example in preaching "The Practicableness of the Example of Our Savior," a recurrent topic of Unitarian sermons:[40] "The moral character of Jesus is distinguished from that of every other teacher's upon record, by this peculiar circumstance, that it united excellences which are usually thought irreconcilable or which are very rarely found conjoined in any individual."[41] Ware echoed this sentiment in stronger terms, insisting that "the world has seen but one perfect exemplification of this character; and that in the person of Jesus Christ. . . . Him we are to imitate."[42] Each Unitarian minister might urge his hearers to imitate a different set of attributes which he felt Christ exemplified, but this pattern of thought about Christ forms an essential part of Channing's description of the process of culture. Christ, as the perfect example of conduct, reveals to man his shortcomings, but also inspires him to a higher level of moral conduct. It was the second part of this formula that, because it was most clearly at variance with orthodoxy, was given the greatest attention by the Unitarians. Channing lamented the fact that "multitudes—I am afraid great multitudes—think of Jesus as a being to be admired rather than approached";[43] it was a problem that lessened the influence of his example. Just as they insisted on the potential improvement of man, the Unitarians insisted that Christ was indeed approachable and imitable. Buckminster preached that "no man can rise from the study of this [Christ's] character and say, 'It is very sublime and perfect; but what is that to me?' "[44] Channing, always intent on emphasizing the positive in human nature, assured his hearers that "though so far above us he [Christ] is still one of us, and is only an illustration of the capacities which we all possess."[45]

The Unitarian conception of the exemplary nature of Christ was a point of reference for each of two powers of the soul, the self-searching and the self-forming, which Channing presented as the basis of self-culture. Christ as the figure who perfectly realized human potential not only provided a standard of self-judgment, as noted above, but also stood as a realizable example for the formation of the soul. The process of self-formation which followed the initial examination of the self, however, was a more problematic issue for the Unitarians, and became a problem for Emerson himself during the formative years of his association with Unitarianism. The problem lay in a basic conflict in Unitarian thought: the radical individuality of the potentially divine soul against the authority of the example of Christ. Certainly it is not difficult to see how the Unitarian stress on man's essential goodness, based as it was on the germ of divinity within, could establish a predilection for radical individual freedom. To the extent that the Unitarians were struggling against Calvinist restraints on such freedom, the doctrine served its intended purpose. But the question which plagued the Unitarians was exactly where to draw the line—how far could the sense of individual power be taken without threatening its overriding goal of the cultivation of the soul toward perfection? Ware put the question most directly in a sermon on the problem of liberty and authority: "Many of the young, ardent, speculative, or enthusiastic, fancy they, too, are called upon to manifest their spirit of independence, and assert their liberty. . . . In their restless sympathy with this insatiable spirit of independence, they are tempted to inquire, whether they should not be independent of *Christ,* as well as of men?"[46] As might be evident from Ware's tone in the passage, such a departure from the biblical authority of Christ was feared deeply by the Unitarians, who were extremely sensitive to charges that they were abandoning the Bible in their attack on Calvinism.[47] In another sermon, Ware warned against exalting "a frail man to the seat of judgment, where God has placed his Christ."[48]

It was Emerson's Divinity School Address in 1838, with its rejection of the authority of the past, which finally forced the issue of authority into a major dispute. But the controversy of the address is only the climax of the question of individual authority versus traditional authority with which the Unitarians had struggled for some years. In theoretical terms, the problem was illusory, for the dichotomy lent itself to ready synthesis. Channing, in further explanation of the meaning of his term "self-forming power," offered an example of both the problems and the possibilities of such a synthesis:

But self-culture is possible, not only because we can enter into and search ourselves. We have a still nobler power, that of acting on, determining, and forming ourselves. This is a fearful as well as glorious endowment, for it is the ground of human responsibility. We have the power not only of tracing our powers, but of guiding and impelling them; not only of watching our passions, but of controlling them; not only of seeing our faculties grow, but of applying to them means and influences to aid their growth.[49]

The problem Channing brings to the surface here is the relation between the process of "impelling" human powers, a term that suggests growth, and the process of "controlling" human passions, a term that suggests limitation. Philosophically considered, these contrasting processes are grounded in the dualism of flesh and spirit. It is the spiritual or ideal part of man which contains the potential for development, and this part alone must therefore be cultivated. Such cultivation, to the Unitarians—including Emerson, it should be noted—necessitated a corresponding control of the flesh and passions.

Buckminster, for example, preaching a sermon entitled "Self-Government," argued that no man has "complete rule over his own spirit, who has not under his habitual control the tenour of his thoughts, the language of his lips, the motions of lust and appetite, and the energy of his passions."[50] Such an attitude toward self-control and self-denial was certainly typical among the Unitarians. Superficially at least, they admitted no conflict between this stress on self-control and the doctrine of spiritual liberty which they espoused. Channing emphasized "that spiritual and inward liberty which his [Christ's] truth confers on its obedient disciples." His resolution to the dichotomy of freedom and authority was itself a paradox: a "freedom" won by "obedience." In his definition of spiritual freedom he again merged control with freedom: "It consists in moral force, in self-control, in the enlargement of thought and affection, and in the unrestrained action of our best powers."[51] The authority by which one determined the need for "self-control" and, conversely, the path of "unrestrained action" were to become central issues in the Transcendental revolt.

The practical result, however, of the idea of control as a means to freedom was a tendency to recommend discipline as the method of culture. Ware faced the issue directly in a work whose title, "Religion a Restraint and an Excitement," aptly summarized the tension of Unitarian moral thinking. Even though the religious life may ultimately become a positive incentive to virtue, Ware argued, its initial phases require a constant and vigilant discipline of the self.

"Undoubtedly the first aspect in which religion presents itself to man, is that of restraint. Its office is that of prohibition. Its commandments run in the language of denial—Thou shalt *not*. . . . It is thus a universal and ever-present restraint."[52] The restraint which Ware presents as an integral part of the religious life echoes what Buckminster, concluding his sermon "Self-Examination," called "a new career of more effective obedience."[53] In another sermon, Buckminster justified the rigorous discipline that the Christian religion demanded by calling it "absurd and impious to suppose, that such rewards are to be attained without a sacrifice."[54] Channing himself, despite many instances of impassioned defense of man's power for good, concluded a discourse entitled "Self-Denial" with this warning: "Place no trust in your good propensities, unless these are fortified, and upheld, and improved by moral energy and self-control. . . . [The Christian] must deny himself, he must take the cross, and follow Christ in the renunciation of every gain and pleasure inconsistent with the will of God."[55] Few preachers, even among the orthodox, could have offered a sterner view of the necessity for Christian discipline.

Thus the idea of the constant growth of the soul, the metaphor of the seed of divinity within man which could be cultivated to fuller growth, came to be intimately tied to more traditional views of the Christian life as one of self-sacrifice and vigilance. The "self-forming power," though it was affirmative in conception, contained within it a self-denying aspect arising from the dualism of body and spirit in Unitarian thought. Perhaps the best example of this form of thought is the concluding chapter of Ware's *On the Formation of the Christian Character*, entitled "The Religious Discipline of Life." Here Ware stresses that "watchfulness and self-discipline belong to all times and occasions," and goes on to recommend particular care in the regulation of thoughts, feelings, appetites, and conversation, in that order. But Ware himself realized that to stop the religious life at restraint alone "would be a most absurd and pernicious error,"[56] and he, like the other Unitarians, urged positive measures as an essential part of the self-forming process of culture. Yet a close examination of these recommendations suggests that the Unitarian belief in human power was essentially a belief in the ability of man to conform himself to the example of Christ—the power to obey.

Practically, there was little difference between these Unitarian recommendations and the long tradition of Puritan moral philosophy in New England. Howe has noted that "Harvard Unitarians could not reconcile themselves to the loss of Puritan piety,"[57] and their struggle against that loss was manifested in the intensity of their moral watchfulness. One result of this watchfulness was to stress the necessity of constant prayer as a positive means of conforming the mind and affections to God, and we find Emerson preaching his first sermon on the text "Pray without Ceasing," an excellent example of Unitarian devotionalist thinking. The Unitarians also stressed devotional reading, pious meditation, and decisive moral action as constituting the path which one followed in self-cultivation.[58] Considered strictly in the realm of moral action, the Unitarian expression of faith in self and the Puritan expression of self-distrust generated remarkably similar results.

The Unitarians saw the building of such moral character as a solution not only to the problem of life on earth, but to the question of eternal life as well. The reward of such moral rigor was not, as one might have expected, an eternal rest, but was instead an opportunity to continue the quest for moral growth eternally. Buckminster preached that the regenerate Christian "appears a being, whose existence has but just commenced. Death is only a boundary, a line, which marks off and distinguishes the first and shortest portion."[59] Thus when we press Unitarian thinkers to answer the question to what end this process of cultivation tends, we find that the process becomes an end itself.

Christian teleology had traditionally emphasized a salvation that promised deliverance from human nature with its limitations and resultant suffering. But in a system of thought which questioned those very limitations, a new teleology was required, one which stressed fulfillment rather than deliverance as the goal of human existence. The Unitarians recognized that the logical end of any process of cultivation must be perfection, and turned repeatedly to the idea of the perfected character as the goal of the religious life. Channing's important sermon, "Likeness to God," stresses "perfection of the soul" as the aim of religious instruction,[60] and Ware exhorts his readers in the same vein that "the scriptural word is *perfection.* Strive after that. Never be satisfied while short of it, and

then you will be always improving."[61] In Ware's exhortation, however, one can sense a hint of doubt. Even though he urges perfection
as a goal, he guarantees only constant improvement—not the
achievement of a state of perfection. Elsewhere he admits that the
example of Christ "is in a sense so perfect, that we may not hope
to equal it. But this should be no discouragement. It should rather
animate us the more."[62] Progress itself, rather than an achieved
perfection, comes to be an inspiring and uplifting force.

In devising a theology whose aim was to free man's latent spiritual
powers, Unitarianism had burdened man with a goal which, even
though it was his nature and duty to pursue, he could never attain.
Regardless of the paradox, the Unitarians embraced this impossible
ideal with a conscious consistency that at times approached celebration. As Ware put it, concluding a discussion of the necessity for the
Christian to strive for nothing short of perfection, "Happy they who
are so filled with longings after spiritual good, that they go on
improving to the end of their days."[63] As this remark might indicate,
the theoretical teleology of static perfection existed side by side with
a practical teleology of continual growth.

In this light, it was possible for the Unitarians to argue that the
"germ of divinity" within man realized itself not as the fulfillment
of human potential, but as the constant striving for that fulfillment.
This continual process of upward striving did not end at death but
was indeed eternal. Ware explained, for example, that "improvement is the universal law of God," and when this law was applied
to the soul, the result was a process of culture beginning on earth,
but continuing through eternity: "[Man's] soul may grow—not like
his body, which is to perish in seventy years, and therefore becomes
perfect in twenty; but, as it is never to perish, it never reaches a
perfection beyond which it may not pass."[64] In Ware's view, there
was no rest even for the righteous. Channing clearly saw the nature
of life after death as one of process. "Heaven is sometimes described
in a manner which excludes the idea of improvement, of progression," he noted, but such a view seemed "a most discouraging and
melancholy one." Instead, he argued that heaven should be seen "as
a state which will offer far greater means of improvement than the
present . . . and give continually increasing energy and splendor to
all the virtues which ennoble our nature."[65]

When its teleological implications are noted, then, the concept of "culture" comes full circle: a means to an end that becomes an end in itself. As a tool for the realization of human power, it also becomes a focus for the realization that such power is never perfected. Few men struggled as deeply with the polarities of this concept as did Emerson in his early career as a Unitarian minister and then as a lecturer. A believer in unity who still recognized duality, he was also a believer in perfection who saw his own imperfections with painful clarity. While much of his early preaching stressed the possibilities of moral and spiritual progress, his journal entries in the same period recorded many passages of frank and unflattering self-analysis, or of despair at what he felt was personal failure—a failure always heightened by his counterpointing faith in human progress through the culture of the soul.

II

Emerson's Ministry

Self-Culture and the Unitarian Ministry

The development of a theology of self-culture inevitably led to changes in the role of those who were most directly responsible for popularizing it, the Unitarian clergy. Since self-culture demanded, as we have seen, an intense commitment to piety among its adherents, it made particularly heavy demands of those ministers whose job it was to foster that piety among their parishioners. These demands resulted in increased emphasis on the minister's duties as a pastor, counselor, and teacher, as opposed to those of the traditional role of preacher. While this emphasis did not, theoretically, lessen the value of pulpit oratory, in practice it channeled the limited energy of a minister toward pastoral duties rather than preaching. This was a significant change for a tradition that had developed a pride in, and a reputation for, pulpit eloquence, and had produced preachers like Buckminster and Channing. But it is even more significant when we realize that Emerson, whose first ambition was for pulpit eloquence, began his career in the midst of this change and under the guidance of its major proponent, Henry Ware, Jr.

This change was by no means the first that had transpired in the position of the New England clergy since the early settlements. The immense authority they had assumed in the Puritan theocracy of the seventeenth century had taken several dramatic turns in response to the evolution of that society, the most dramatic of which arose from the direct challenge to ministerial authority engendered during the Great Awakening in the first half of the eighteenth century. During the Awakening, itinerant preachers and inspired laymen threatened to come between the settled ministers and their congregations with a new and dynamic style of preaching, and even went so far as to accuse settled ministers unsympathetic to revival techniques of being "unconverted," and thus holding their spiritual authority unworthily and ineffectually. There was a complex response to this challenge within the liberal ministry, the major result of which was a reassertion of the value of literate and learned ministers and, of course, literate and learned preaching.[1]

Yet the emphasis on learned preaching did not necessarily mean an emphasis on rational preaching, if this is taken to mean a rationalism that excluded appeals to the affections or artful use of metaphor, illustration, and other poetic and rhetorical devices. Learned preaching came closer to being literary preaching, with ministers like Buckminster and Channing using the sermon as an art form. This meant that they avoided both what they felt were the irrational excesses of revivalism, with its danger of degenerating into formless ranting, and the extremes of rationalism, with its danger of contracting into arid logic. The pulpit thus became, in the best hands, one of the major vehicles for the development of the art of eloquence, which held such a high place among the arts for so many of that era.

There is a certain irony in pointing to Henry Ware, Jr., as a key figure in the beginning of a trend away from this development of a literary clergy. As a preacher he was one of the very best of his denomination, "second only to Dr. Channing in popular esteem."[2] He was, moreover, much given to the pursuit of literature, and produced a considerable amount of poetry and fiction besides his theological writing. The prose style of his sermons is clear, vigorous, and at points moving, and he remains one of the most readable of the Unitarian writers. But despite these literary talents, Ware's chief distinction lay in his skills as pastor rather than preacher. He was "the ideal type of the parish minister,"[3] and he apparently enjoyed a remarkable ability for cultivating sympathetic relations with his parishioners. His successes in these pastoral endeavors are borne out in the impact he made on Boston's Second Church, where he preceded Emerson as the minister and was his senior colleague for a period, and at Harvard, where he carried on a remarkable ministry to its students as Professor of Pulpit Eloquence and the Pastoral Care. He had done an impressive job of reviving Boston's Second Church, ushering in what a later successor to that pulpit, would call "another golden age, like that which it had enjoyed under the first

of the Mathers."[4] At Harvard he was a professor of unusual influence, and many of the ministers who were trained there were
touched by his intense devotionalism, which even involved an evangelical element of soul winning.

Ware's position at Harvard had been created for him, partially in
the hope, largely mistaken, that a professorship would be less wear-
ing on his frail health than the pastorate of a large church had been.
But more importantly, the creation of Ware's chair at Harvard was
a sign that the Unitarian denomination was increasingly aware of the
theological importance of "the pastoral care" to its religious identity.
The theological school at Harvard had been established only recently, in 1819; the first official gesture of denominationalism, the
formation of the American Unitarian Association, had occurred in
1825; and Divinity Hall had been erected in 1826.[5] Ware's move
to Harvard was of a piece with these other steps toward denominationalism, because his approach to the ministry exemplified in a
professional sense many of the ideals of the theology of self-culture.

It is not surprising to find that Ware not only was committed to
"the pastoral care," but also was the greatest early popularizer of the
theology of self-culture. One of the indications of his importance is
the enormous popularity of his *On the Formation of the Christian
Character*, "the classic exposition of Unitarian religion conceived as
a method of personality development."[6] Published two years after
he had assumed his duties at Harvard, it was "a fitting manifesto and
rationale for his new position,"[7] that of teacher and minister to
future ministers. The book is closest in form to a devotional manual,
offering, as we have seen, practical advice about the Christian life
based on the premises of self-culture.

While Ware was making his theology felt to a general Christian
audience through that work, he was making a perhaps greater impact
on Unitarianism in his writing and preaching about the Christian
ministry. His *Formation* may have been his most important theological manifesto, but his most important homiletical manifesto, and his
most direct statement of his purposes at Harvard, was his introductory address to the Theological School, *The Connection between the
Duties of the Pulpit and the Pastoral Office.*[8] Ware saw clearly that
his position implied a double duty—teaching "pulpit eloquence"
and also teaching "the pastoral care." He was emphatically commit-

ted to the idea that neither of these duties should be slighted, and his introductory address is a prolonged argument that the two duties are inseparable. He argues for the inseparability of the two duties on the basis of their interdependence: "The minister is the better preacher for having his heart warmed by intercourse with his hearers in private; and he goes to them in private with the greater influence and effect, because he carries with him the sacredness and sanction of the pulpit."[9] The fundamental assumption here, one which indicates Ware's sense of the direction preaching was to take, is the notion that a man is a better preacher because of his contact with his hearers. Clearly this is a rationale for preaching to the affections; moreover, it suggests a possible restriction on the art of literary preaching. Such art is permissible only within the bounds of its appeal to the affections of the hearers. Theoretically, literary preaching and preaching from the heart are not exclusive, but practically and historically, they have been manifested in differing traditions.

Ware's assumptions about preaching are the natural outgrowth of his conception of religion as a process of character formation. The connection between duties of pulpit and the pastoral care, he argues, "may be discerned, first, *in the nature of the object to be accomplished by the ministry.*" That object is not to give "instruction in religion" or to gain "assent to the doctrines of revelation," goals which are too palely intellectual for Ware, but rather "to act on the characters of men," that is, to change their way of living. Given this goal, he is realistic enough to see the limitations of preaching: "Now, character is a very complicated thing, dependent on a vast variety of circumstances and influences. Of these the pulpit can never furnish but a small proportion."[10] Preaching must, therefore, be enlivened and supplemented by the individual contact of the minister and his congregation; it must take its place as one of a variety of means to self-culture.

Ware's skeptical realism about the power of preaching is based not only on the psychology of the hearers, but also on the talents of the preachers. Eloquence in the pulpit, he asserts, does not mean "that high and singular gift . . . of the orator" because such gifts are so rare. Genuine masters of eloquence "are but few in an age, and the church, if it must depend on them, would soon perish for want of advocates." Ware's skepticism about the possibility of pulpit oratory, however, overlays an even deeper skepticism about the value of such oratory. "But so far from being necessary," he argues, "it is not certain that this highest eloquence is advantageous, or even desirable, in the pulpit." His point is in large part a pedagogical one. Who, after all, could object to a genuine oratorical genius in the pulpit? But when the aspirations of ministers are turned in that direction, the results are usually disastrous. Ware himself rises to heights of eloquence in his attack on what he considers the false eloquence engendered by such aspirations, condemning "the flashy common-places of flowers, and rivers, and clouds, and rainbows, and dews," or "the empty music of periods which are rounded only to be harmonious, and the tricks of speech which perform no office for the sense." Preaching of this kind, which Ware calls "miserable foppery," is the result of the separation of the pulpit from the pastoral care, and "could never have been committed by a man who walked faithfully among his people, caring for their actual wants."[11]

Ware's definition of pulpit eloquence is thus severely restricted, but it is a definition, he insists, which is "capable of being learned." It is no more than "the power and habit to select judiciously, arrange clearly, and express forcibly and fervently, the topics suited to the pulpit, and to utter them in a distinct, correct, and pleasant elocution."[12] Whatever pedogogical advantages his position has, it is not one calculated to satisfy a thirst for oratory, or to be a suitable outlet for essentially literary ambitions. Ware's emphasis on judicious selection, correct elocution, and suitable choice of topics are all forms of restraint, aimed at eliminating possible oratorical excesses rather than inspiring oratorical flourishes. Such restraint is tied directly to the minister's pastoral duties, which he saw as the true foundation of pulpit practice in providing both the nature of the subject and its appropriate mode of treatment.

The foregoing discussion of Ware's homiletical theories may make him appear more conservative about preaching than he really was. In an earlier work, he was interested enough in pulpit innovation to recommend extemporaneous preaching rather than reading from set texts—a practice dangerously close to revivalist techniques, as he well knew.[13] He recommends the extemporaneous preaching in this work because he feels it will discourage the kind of style-conscious preacher who "is more anxious for correctness than impression" and who "fears to . . . have more motion than the very letters on his manuscript." It may even lead, Ware feels, to a beneficial "forgetfulness of self" and an "unconstrained following the impulse of the affections,"[14] which is the most powerful kind of preaching. If this sounds like a different position from the one he took in his initial discourse at Harvard, it should be noted that the underlying target of criticism is the same—the preacher who fails to remember that a sermon is only part of his larger pastoral relation.

It may be difficult to measure Ware's impact on the entire Unitarian denomination, although the evidence indicates that it was considerable. But it is possible to gauge his effect on the young minister who came, in 1828, to take over Ware's pastoral duties at Boston's Second Church. The two men shared many concerns and assumptions, and certainly shared a respect for one another. But their ambitions, their temperaments, and their conception of the duty of the minister were vastly different.

The Vocation of Eloquence

The period after his college studies that Emerson devoted to keeping school was not unusual for a young man preparing for the ministry. There was often a financial reason for such a pause, as was the case with Emerson, and the period might also be the beginning of an advanced course of study that would lead to ordination—then a much more individual process than now.[15] But for Emerson this was much less a pause than a period of groping indecision and personal crisis. His chronically poor health as a young man, the very real danger of death that consumption posed for him, accounts for much of his indecision and professional hesitation. Whicher has brilliantly related the fundamental connections between his struggle for health and his developing philosophy, and Bishop has called this period of indecision after graduation Emerson's first "crisis," even suggesting that in his dread of a career as a minister we may find the psychosomatic cause of part (though not the most serious part) of his illnesses.[16] No one who reads the letters and journals can fail to sense Emerson's doubts about entering the ministry, and while such

doubts deserve attention, we should not overlook the fact that there
was also an enormously strong positive motivation for his choice of
this vocation. He saw it as the best avenue for pursuing his interest
in, and talent for, public speaking, which was in his youth the form
his deep-rooted literary ambitions took.

Emerson was therefore struggling with indecision that went
deeper than any doubts about his health. Part of the indecision arose
from his own frank recognition of the limits of his talents and
personality; part of it arose from what Henry James referred to as
"the terrible paucity of alternatives"[17] provided him by New England culture; but a third part, ultimately more positive in nature than
these other two, arose from his burning ambition for "eloquence,"
which ran so deeply in him that it seemed to outstrip any available
mode of pursuing it in the established professions. This latter reason for his indecision reveals less the paucity of New England cultural alternatives than the religious scrupulousness with
which Emerson measured his career options. Even though he was
"born into a ministerial family and educated virtually as a matter of
course for the ministry,"[18] he prolonged his decision long enough
to suggest that he did not feel it inevitable. Tradition, the advice of
his elders and brothers, personal talent and interest, and sheer feasi-
bility all pointed him to the ministry, but he balked at this choice
until he felt assured that his career in the pulpit would not interfere
with his calling to eloquence.

We can gather something of the sense of Emerson's attitude
toward his career choice from some scattered comments he made
during his period of school keeping following graduation. The remarks are surprisingly few, considering his unsettled state, but it is
clear that at best, he merely tolerated teaching, and that he envied
somewhat the scholarly life of the divinity student, but had little to
say about the profession to which studying theology would lead. In
a series of letters in 1822 and 1823 to a Harvard classmate who had
enrolled at Andover Seminary, he lightly laments his own situation
as a schoolmaster, and queries his friend about the use of the Andover library "when time shall suffer me to go to the schools and
open the Divinity folios."[19] In 1823 he tells another classmate, "My
sole answer & apology to those who inquire about my studies
is—I keep school.—I study neither law, medicine or divinity, and

write neither poetry nor prose." Yet he goes on to refer to the future, "when I have been to Cambridge & studied Divinity" (*L*, 1:127, 128). At times he gives the impression that the inevitability of his ministerial vocation is being postponed, but these are letters to college acquaintances and only partially revealing. A genuine spark of enthusiasm, however, seems to be ignited by his comments on oratory. He promises to send a friend an essay on oratory,[20] and in a letter to his aunt he refers to his hearing of Channing's "sublime sermons" (*L*, 1:138). While much external evidence points, if somewhat tentatively, toward the choice of the ministry, as the opportunity to begin his Divinity studies approaches, he confides much deeper doubts in the privacy of his journal.

On April 18, 1824, Emerson records his decision to enter the ministry with an ostentatious flurry that signals it as a personal turning point for him. "I am beginning my professional studies," he writes, "and I deliberately dedicate my time, my talents, & my hopes to the Church." The key word is "deliberately," and the deeper significance of this journal entry is that, finally, *he* has made the decision of a career that others and even he himself at times may have thought inescapable. "So solemn a step" should not be made, he says, "without some careful examination of my past & present life" (*JMN*, 2:237), an examination which quickly turns into self-analysis.

He realizes, first of all, his intellectual weaknesses and strengths, admitting that his "reasoning faculty is proportionately weak" and that he could never "write a Butler's Analogy or an Essay of Hume." Clearly he is measuring himself by only the most exacting of standards. But theology is still an appropriate outlet for his talents, because as he sees it, "the highest species of reasoning upon divine subjects is rather the fruit of a sort of moral imagination, than of the 'Reasoning Machines' such as Locke & Clarke & David Hume" (*JMN*, 2:238). His "model" of such a "moral imagination" is Channing's Dudleian Lecture, which he had heard some three years before as an undergraduate.[21] Here he feels that he may have an outlet for his talent: he remarks that "the preaching most in vogue at the present day depends chiefly on imagination for its success, and asks those accomplishments which I believe are most within my grasp" (*JMN*, 2:238).

This curious blend of self-deprecation and ambition is only a prelude to a much deeper series of remarks, which center less on the presence or absence of certain talents than on Emerson's sense of the limits of his very personality. He recognizes in himself, especially in comparison with others, "a signal defect of character which neutralizes in great part the just influence my talents ought to have." Though he is unsure whether the defect arises from a superficial lack of easy manner and form, or is "deeper seated in an absence of common *sympathies,*" he knows its effect: "a sore uneasiness in the company of most men & women, a frigid fear of offending & jealousy of disrespect, an inability to lead & an unwillingness to follow the current conversation" (*JMN,* 2:238). While this self-doubt may seem to be primarily an admission of social awkwardness, Emerson concentrates on its implications for a choice of career.

He notes that "the profession of Law demands a good deal of personal address" and that medicine "makes large demands" for "a seducing Mannerism." Such requirements only complicate the difficulties of one who frankly admits, "I am ill at ease . . . among men." The remaining profession, the ministry, is his final option, and he realizes that this office is "twofold," encompassing "public preaching & private influence." But the private influence that a minister must exert is largely a moral question, he feels, rather than a question of manners and social graces. In fact, there is even "a decent pride which is conspicuous in the perfect model of a Christian man" (*JMN,* 2:239–40)—a requirement that may well convert Emerson's personal reserve into a professional asset.

The foregoing discussion may give the false impression that Emerson chose the ministry for the negative reason that his other options were ruled out. In fact, there was a singularly strong positive motivation for the choice, a motivation so fundamental that Emerson calls it an inherited trait. He notes that while he inherits his father's "formality of manner & speech," he also derives from him "a passionate love for the strains of eloquence" and feels, in his best moments, that he himself has "those powers which command the reason & passions of the multitude," the powers of oratory. Again he returns to the pulpit as a possible outlet for his interests and talents: "My trust," he says, "is that my profession shall be my regeneration of mind, manners, inward & outward estate," but more to the point he adds, "for I have hoped to put on eloquence as a robe" (*JMN*, 2:239, 242). The ministry, then, represents for him the necessary means to the pursuit of eloquence, and it is by this standard that he will eventually judge it when he leaves the profession.

Having made his decision, Emerson's greatest burden was maintaining the patience of resolve through his constant struggles with ill health. But while he certainly had no regrets about leaving the schoolroom, there are hints that he valued another course of life, that of private and independent study. The youths who are trained in the colleges, he writes in August 1824, "are speedily divided in the study of the three liberal professions"; others become schoolmasters or "enter the Compting house." But Emerson is more interested in those who "leave the College for solitary study," realizing that the others "are very soon ingulphed in the great vortex of a busy world" which kills their private literary ambitions. He realistically knows that "only a very small minority" of those who pursue letters independently can "reasonably expect eminent success" (*JMN*, 2:270–71), but the difficulty of the task and the power of self-mastery it demands make it all the more appealing.

This lingering indecisiveness about not only his own vocational choice, but the problem of vocation in general, is a clear symptom of the birth pangs of the literary life in America. Emerson was undergoing his own version of Hawthorne's struggle for a career as a writer in a culture that had placed severe restrictions on that career. Though Hawthorne's struggle required a more dramatic break with the past, Emerson's was in a sense more difficult because of the complex nature of the New England literary tradition. As a writer of fiction, Hawthorne was exploring entirely new possibilities for the life of letters in New England. But as a preacher and moral philosopher, Emerson was attempting to realize fully the literary aspects of a tradition that was only partially given to literary enterprise.[22] Much of the tension that we sense in his unsettled early years arises from the tension within the ministerial profession itself, which was the major channel for literary talent, but which could not be taken entirely as a literary vocation. The most eloquent of the preachers, Channing, risked being "styled selfish and inactive by many, because he was not a bustling parish minister."[23] This very charge was what Emerson hazarded in entering the ministry.

Emerson's continuity with his tradition was solidified, moreover, by one element not of interest to Hawthorne or most other authors of that generation—the element of public speech, as embodied in the sermon. The ministerial profession was "literary" if we make the important qualification that the labor of creating texts was overwhelmingly directed toward an oral form. This is not, of course, to say that much non-oral writing was not done, but to note that such writing was an adjunct to, or a support for, preaching. Even the reading of sermons required an act of imaginative reconstruction of the spoken event itself: "I have been at an Ordination hearing maxims on eloquence till I burned to speak," Emerson noted in 1825, adding, "I have been reading Everett's rich strains at Plymouth,—gazing at the Sun till my eyes are blurred" (*JMN*, 2:318). To *read* Everett—or Channing, Buckminster, or Webster, to name Emerson's oratorical ideals—was clearly to *hear* their "rich strains." The power and immediacy of eloquence, then, served both as present motivation and as a vital link with the past as Emerson entered his ministerial vocation.

The Christian Minister

Just before his ordination on March 11, 1829, Emerson wrote his brother William that he was "very well but casting many a lingering look at my chamber as the execution day approaches" (*L*, 1:264). He was, of course, making light of his own case of nerves before this public ceremony, but beneath the humor we can detect the attitude of trepidation with which he entered his profession. Some weeks later, by then immersed in the duties required of a new minister, he sent his grandfather Ezra Ripley, the minister at Concord, this report: "I have been exceedingly busy the last week in making my introductory visits in the parish. It is a new labour & I feel it in every bone of my body. I have made somewhat more than fifty pastoral visits and am yet but in the ends & frontiers of my society" (*L*, 1:267). Knowing what we do about Emerson's self-professed shyness, it is safe to surmise that his exhaustion was as much emotional as physical. But the more lasting impact of these visits was not fully revealed until almost seven years later, in a journal entry in which he meditated his message for the young ministers he will address at the Divinity School. It begins with an insistence on the futility of imitating even the best models for the profession, among which Emerson includes his own predecessor, Ware. The approach of one man is successful because "it was natural to him & so in him it has a charm," but if another attempts the same, he "dooms himself to mediocrity." As the passage continues, the references become more specifically tied to Emerson's personal experience: "The young preacher comes to his parish & learns there are 300 families which he must visit each once in a year." Rather than "groping to get exactly the old threads of relation" which had been established by his "venerable predecessor," he should "cast all this nonsense of false expectation . . . behind him," strike his own path, and "acquaint them at first hand with Deity." Not only should he "not be anxious to get out to see in civil sort his 300 families," but "perhaps it is mere folly for him to visit one" (*JMN*, 5:500–501).

The passage suggests that much of Emerson's message in the Divinity School Address had its origin not only in his frustration with his Concord pastor, Barzillai Frost, but in his own impatience with his career as minister.[24] Emerson could express his impatience much more unreservedly in 1837, when he was largely free of the profession, but much of his ministry was a struggle to resolve the tension between duties such as pastoral visits and what he called the "poetic" and "exhilarating" aspects of his work (*JMN*, 5:500). The presence of Ware did not make this struggle any easier for Emerson, for despite his genuine respect for Ware, he did not aspire to the vision of the ministry that Ware both preached and embodied.

Ware's gift for the pastoral care placed a burden on Emerson which is readily discernible in his introductory sermon, the customary occasion on which a new minister made his own hopes and goals for his pastorate known to his congregation. Emerson broke his discourse into two parts, which reflected his recognition of the two branches of ministerial service, "public ministrations and . . . pastoral visits." Although the first of these duties includes both public prayers and preaching, it is preaching, "a high and difficult office," which receives most of the attention in the first sermon. As we might expect, the duty of preaching brings to Emerson's mind a vision of the power of eloquence. He calls it "the mightiest engine which God has put into the hands of man to move man," and appeals directly to his hearers for confirmation: "I believe there is not one of us, my brethren, whose opportunities have been so abridged, living in this free state, as never to have witnessed its prodigious effects." These effects increase "especially when it rises to topics of eternal interest," for when the preacher deals effectively with the soul, "the speaker and the hearer become the pipes on which a higher power speaketh." To make the sanctity of such moments unquestionable, he adds, "It is like the breath of the Almighty moving on the deep." The power of preaching, therefore, lies in its potential to foster an almost mystical absorption of speaker and hearer into a unity that overshadows their private selves. Emerson sees the source of a preacher's power as beyond the preacher himself, in his ability to make his personal voice a tool through which a universal voice may speak. Emerson believes strongly enough in the universal nature of oratory to assert that "every man who gives himself wholly up to a just sentiment which he lives to inculcate, will be eloquent"; the key to the power is in the surrender, and the obstacle to its achievement is essentially a moral one: "sloth and disuse." "God keep me," the young preacher pleads, "from this frigid indifference" (*YES,* pp. 24–26). Even taking into account the differing occasions of their remarks, it is plain that Ware and Emerson differ fundamentally on the nature of pulpit oratory. Emerson's "breath of the Almighty moving on the deep" is a far cry from Ware's recommendation of judicious selection and arrangement and "distinct, correct, and pleasant elocution."[25] Emerson is calling for a constant attempt at the kind of oratorical genius that Ware regards as much too rare even to attempt. More importantly, in Emerson's essential faith in the availability of eloquence to those who can pay the moral price of self-surrender, we can detect the foundation for his entire aesthetic, both of the spoken and of the written word.

Emerson's more specific remarks about the nature and style of preaching will concern us later, but it is enough at present to note the tone of confidence he sets in discussing this duty. There is a much more tentative tone in the second sermon, on pastoral duties, which even becomes a plea for patience and understanding when Emerson broaches the topic of the relation of congregation to its pastor. He recognizes that his duty is not to establish spiritual guidance where none has been, but to "help . . . the spiritual progress of those who have loved their spiritual guide as he deserved to be loved." That guide, of course, is Ware, whose virtues "need no praise" and whose "counsel and sympathy are not withdrawn" from the congregation. The problem, as Emerson frankly puts it, is that "there is an expectation that will operate unfavorably on my inexperience arising from the very signal merits which have created among you so warm a sympathy in your minister." His plea for lower expectations reflects his shrewd sense of the role he might be expected to perform, based not only on his consciousness of his own limits, but on his recognition of Ware's talents. "I must beseech you," he says, "to consider that no man can suddenly be a good pastor" (*YES*, p. 37).

The evidence suggests that Emerson was right to feel that he was in the difficult position of trying to replace a very much beloved pastor. In his farewell address to the church in October 1830, Ware had noted the "strong, deep, fervent affections" involved in "the bond between minister and people" and, referring to the circumstance of health that caused him to leave, added that "*our* separation . . . has not been sought or desired on either side."[26] More pointedly, Ware returned to his conviction that "private duties of personal and pastoral intercourse are, at least, as important as the public exercises of the pulpit, and in fact necessary to their efficiency and success," adding that he had concentrated his energies in that direction: "If I have done any good, I attribute it almost entirely to the opportunities and power which I have in this way gained."[27] Such a ministry would surely leave a congregation with high expectations of the next minister, expectations which a younger man would feel keenly.

Seen in this context, Emerson's first sermons on the ministry indicate his mixed emotions as he entered his new career: a confident determination to use the pulpit as a vehicle for inspiring eloquence, and an insecure apprehensiveness about the pastoral duties at which his predecessor so excelled. But that conflict seems even deeper when we consider one journal entry, written before or shortly after those sermons. It begins with a direct question, "What is the office of a Christian minister?" to which Emerson offers a catalogue of responses, all dealing with the perception and communication of truth. But as the entry continues, his observations become more personal: "I please myself with fashioning in my retired thoughts the Idea of the Christian Minister." The description which follows is singularly notable for its vision of detachment: "a man who is separated from men in all the rough courses where defilement can hardly be escaped; & who mixes with men only for purposes that make himself & them better; aloof from the storm of passion, from political hatred, from the jealousy & intrigue of gain, from the contracting influences of low company & little arts" (*JMN*, 3:152). Here, in his conception of his ministerial vocation, is the beginning of the "polished . . . aloofness" which James sees as a key to his character.[28]

Emerson at the Second Church

Emerson was never able to resolve satisfactorily the conflict he felt between preaching and pastoring. Preaching a sermon of retrospective analysis of his first year as a minister, he noted that the two roles of preacher and pastor are "often in some measure incompatible" and pointedly added that "the minister who makes it an important aim to convey instruction must often stay at home in search of it when his parishioners may think he would be more usefully employed in cultivating an acquaintance with them" (*YES*, pp. 70, 71). This is an example of rather plain speaking from the pulpit, which may indicate, as McGiffert surmises, some dissatisfaction among the congregation with the new minister's comparative aloofness (*YES*, p. 227). But if there was such dissatisfaction, it was apparently slight.[29] The real question was not the congregation's satisfaction with Emerson as minister, but Emerson's satisfaction with the ministry itself.

The recognition of this essentially professional, or vocational, dissatisfaction goes far in providing a corrective to what earlier students of Emerson have seen as intellectual dissatisfaction. However appealing in dramatic terms, it is misleading to refer to the events leading up to Emerson's resignation of his pulpit in 1832 as, in Whicher's terms, a process of being "launched out from the slavish shore into the open seas of the mind" from the "land-bound faith" of Unitarianism.[30] This is not to overlook the intellectual development Emerson was experiencing during his years as a minister, or the emotional stresses of the loss of his wife Ellen. But it is to argue that his development is best understood as a gradual following of Unitarian assumptions rather than a rebellion from them. And if he took those assumptions further than many of that denomination did, he was not alone in doing so. In 1844, well after he had established himself as an independent thinker and leader of the Transcendental movement, Emerson returned to tell his old church, "I do not find in the years that have elapsed since I stood here to teach, any new varieties of thought, but rather an accumulation of particular experiences to establish, or should I rather say, to illustrate, the leading belief of my youth."[31] The real rebellion for Emerson was vocational rather than intellectual; it was less what he wanted to say than how he wanted to say it, and to whom, that led to his break with the church.

While we can attribute Emerson's resignation of the pulpit largely to a building frustration with his profession in general, there were immediate causes which, superficially at least, triggered his move. He objected to the necessity of administering the Lord's Supper, which was part of his prescribed formal duties, on the grounds that it falsely gave authority to Jesus. While not opposed to others' partaking of the ceremony, he explained, "It is my desire, in the office of a Christian minister, to do nothing which I cannot do with my whole heart" (W, 11:24).

Beneath the theological doubts which he displays here, which did have a central part in his intellectual development, there is evidence of a radically democratic concept of the ministry, a response which in some ways anticipates the sociological fact that the authority of the profession was being undermined. If Ware had counted on the authority of the pulpit to increase the effect of the pastor's performance, Emerson was set firmly against a reliance on any authority which derived from an office and not from the person who held that office. Ministerial authority did, after all, have the damaging side effect of setting a minister apart, and thus falsifying his relations with others. Channing complained that "courtesy to ministers—or rather to their *cloth*—checked a frank sincerity to them,"[32] and the result of this barrier was likely to be a fundamental insecurity in relations with others. Thus, in the Divinity School Address, Emerson memorably describes the village blasphemer who "sees fear in the face, form, and gait of the minister" (*CW*, 1:87).

Formal authority was too often false authority in Emerson's eyes, and false authority was finally no authority at all. In a journal entry following the preaching of one of his later sermons in 1834, he noted that "when there is any difference of level felt in the foot board of the pulpit & the floor of the parlor, you have not said that which you should say" (*JMN*, 4:294). He reached this conclusion from his own experience in the ministry, and it is not surprising that it was an issue of formality in worship that prompted his resignation from the Second Church. His career as preacher would continue, in different forms, throughout his life.

But in appraising Emerson's resignation, we should overlook neither the real pain that arriving at the decision caused him, nor the signs of relief that followed the decision. In July 1832, when he retreated to the White Mountains to contemplate taking this step, he worried about its possible adverse consequences: "Let me not bury my talent in the earth in my indignation at this windmill. But though the thing may be useless & even pernicious, do not destroy what is good & useful in a high degree rather than comply with what is hurtful in a small degree" (*JMN*, 4:30). Emerson's concern was that what he saw as the relatively trivial matter of Communion might distract him from the high calling to truth which he continued to feel. In resigning his pastorate, which had been the avenue of his pursuit of that truth, he wanted to caution himself against abandoning his calling entirely. It was not, after all, the actual celebration of the Lord's Supper that Emerson objected to, but rather his own role in the celebration, one which in his judgment compromised absolute honesty. In a sermon from 1829 he made it clear that he considered the purpose of the Lord's Supper to be self-improvement: "I believe the whole end and aim of this ordinance is nothing but this, *to make those who partake of it better*" (*YES*, pp. 57–58). By 1832, he was still far from ruling out the value of the observation:

The Communicant celebrates on a foundation either of authority or of tradition an ordinance which has been the occasion to thousands,—I hope to thousands of thousands—of contrition, of gratitude, of prayer, of faith, of love, & of holy living. Far be it from any of my friends,—God forbid it be in my heart—to interrupt any occasion thus blessed of God's influences upon the human mind.

But he was still troubled by the stigma of the uniformity of mind and soul which he felt was erroneously associated with the ordinance, and he followed this expression of faith in the Lord's Supper by a reservation which became part of his explanatory sermon to his congregation in September:

I think Jesus did not mean to institute a perpetual celebration, but that a commemoration of him would be useful. Others think that Jesus did establish this one. We are agreed that one is useful, & we are agreed I hope in the way in which it must be made useful. viz; by each one's making it an original Commemoration.   [*JMN*, 4:30]

Such a position transformed the Sacrament into a mode of private devotion, a step too radical for his congregation to make.

But after the decision was made, we can sense his own feeling that different possibilities could now begin to open for him. Soon after, he wrote his brother William that the "severing of our strained cord that bound me to the church is a mutual relief," and then spoke of "the projects that sprout & bloom in my head, of action, literature, philosophy," even mentioning the founding of his own magazine (*L*, 1:357–58). Clearly he felt that the resignation, however painful, was a clearing of the field for other projects, some of a literary nature. Such embryonic plans would be nurtured by his European journey of 1833, and by his opportunity to speak from the lecture platform as well as the pulpit upon his return.

III

Emerson's Preaching

The Preaching of Culture

Given Emerson's vocational goal of eloquence, we can now ask how successful he was in pursuing that goal in the mode of the sermon. When he entered the ministry, the sermon had been for two centuries the major channel for American thought and literary expression. It would be, along with his journal, the genre in which he established the contours of both the content and the form of his mature expression. Sermon form was in a state of rapid transition during Emerson's ministry, in large part because of the intellectual ferment which accompanied the rise of the theology of self-culture. The close connection between ideas and form in this period stems from the fact that the sermon was an ideally suited mode of expression for the philosophy of self-culture. The immediacy of its oral presentation, the authority of its homiletic context, and most importantly, the tradition of moral persuasion that it embodied made the sermon an essential tool for a movement whose touchstone was moral perfection.

By the time Emerson began to preach, the move away from the structures of the Puritan sermon had been accomplished within Unitarianism, just as Calvinist dogma had been abandoned. The text-doctrine-application form had been "largely discarded" by the nineteenth-century liberals, but elements of all of these sermon parts continued to be present in their preaching in a much-altered form.[1] The text often served as a poetic or metaphoric point of departure for the sermon, a kind of literary epigraph, rather than a dominating influence on its form. Scriptural texts were often supplemented by references to current or historical events, questions, or moral problems as the beginning points of sermons. A remark in Emerson's journal seems typical of the prevailing attitude: "A text is the hat of a sermon. Who buys a hat before a head is made?" (*JMN*, 3:122). Although it was his habitual practice to offer a text with his sermons, these texts were rarely explicated at length, and often were not even mentioned in the sermon. Moreover, the journal entries from which many of his sermons were drawn show little if any concern with scriptural interpretation. Because of the antidogmatic stance of the Unitarians, the doctrine of Calvinist sermons was replaced with what might be called an inspirational ideal for the congregation, imaginative in nature rather than logical.[2] And the application of the sermon, which dealt most directly with moral action, was greatly magnified in importance. In a sense, the liberal sermon became one long exercise in moral application and exhortation.

It was this preoccupation with moral persuasion that lay behind Emerson's assertion that the office of a Christian minister was "to explain the theory of a perfect life" (*JMN*, 3:152). The very fact that such a life was a "theory," however, called upon all the imaginative resources of the preacher, not to argue logically for the details of such a life, but to depict it symbolically. "Eloquence is best inspired by an Infinite Cause" (*JMN*, 2:319), Emerson wrote in 1825. The expansive dynamism of self-culture demanded that the preacher give his congregation an ever-enlarging image of the potential self. Such a task may have had moral ends, but it required the use of literary means. After hearing Emerson lecture in 1836, Mary Channing, daughter of the famous preacher, wrote this excited comment to Elizabeth Peabody: "Oh, Miss Peabody! When one hears one of these lectures of Mr. Emerson, one feels one can never do wrong any more!"[3] This might well be regarded as the ideal response to a Transcendentalist discourse, given its blend of emotion and moral resolve. Yet while accepting Channing's moral sincerity, we can recognize her response as an aesthetic one as well. If she was moved by a moral vision, it is also important to remember that the vision itself was an aesthetic product. Art and morals, though never easily separable, rarely exist together without some tension. The tension Emerson faced was that of keeping the tools of aesthetic creation subordinate to the ends of moral persuasion.

The concept which served as the focus for both the moral and the aesthetic impulses of Emerson's preaching was that of human perfection. We find him returning to it repeatedly in his journals, always with the confidence that "preaching is only an exposition of our human nature" (*JMN*, 3:197). "A Religion is a theory of human life," he preached in 1829; yet that life is not the one which we know from day to day, but instead one which we feel impelled toward. "Religion," he added, "provides for the good by the culture of the soul acting on the belief that this child of God will be seen as its powers are bro't out to inherit the self-existence of its Sire."[4] As in Channing's "Likeness to God," the stress was placed not only on the likeness between man and God, but on the process which brought that likeness into being, culture. But behind the similarities between the two, which are indeed real, there lies an important historical distinction. Channing worked toward his perfectionist theology over a lifetime, beginning from a context of Calvinism. Emerson began, in a sense, where Channing left off, and was extending Unitarian assumptions almost from the first of his ministry. This is not to argue that Emerson's work is derivative or that Channing's is incomplete, but to stress that Emerson's preaching should be seen as both an expression of Unitarian theology and a prelude to Transcendentalism. Seen from the perspective of intellectual history, Transcendentalism is less a rebellion from Unitarianism than its logical culmination.

From Moral Sense to Universal Man

In an 1826 journal entry Emerson observed that even though "our perception of moral truth is instinctive . . . we are not born to any image of perfect virtue." Thus while we may recognize "with faithful readiness the virtue & the vice of actions presented to us," this recognition is not the work of an informed intellectual faculty, and it leaves a need for "a learned experience to enumerate all the particulars that make the whole of virtue" (*JMN*, 3:21). The entry marks out both the assumptions which Emerson had accepted at the beginning of his preaching and the direction in which he hoped to expand them. The "instinctive" recognition of moral truth was the product of the "moral sense," a concept which he inherited from eighteenth-century moral philosophy as it was transmitted through Unitarian theology. The "image of perfect virtue" was the goal toward which he would strive in his sermons.

As students of Emerson have increasingly come to realize, his belief in the "moral sense" or "moral law" was the basis of his faith in human nature. Under the influence of Dugald Stewart and Richard Price, Emerson held man's ability to make moral judgments to be both innate and universal.[5] In a journal entry early in 1823, he recorded the depth of his commitment to the idea that man was innately equipped with the faculty of judging right from wrong. For Emerson, the implications of this fact were enormous:

But it is in the constitution of the mind to rely with firmer confidence upon the *moral principle,* and I reject at once the idea of a delusion in this. This is woven vitally into the thinking substance itself so that it cannot be diminished or destroyed without dissipating forever that spirit which it inhabited. Upon the foundation of my *moral sense,* I ground my faith in the immortality of the soul, in the existence & activity of good beings, and in the promise of rewards accommodated hereafter to the vicious or virtuous dispositions which were cultivated here. [*JMN,* 2:83]

As this passage reveals, Emerson held the mind to be inescapably moral, moral in its very essence. The act of perception itself, as a product of the mind inextricably a part of a moral universe and having as part of itself a moral principle, was an act of moral discrimination. In a thinker who prided himself on flexibility and change, Emerson maintained this idea with tenacious consistency, holding it, in Bishop's words, "at a depth below the reach of criticism."[6] Even though he may never have questioned the existence of the moral sense as part of the human soul, Emerson did alter his definition of it. It would perhaps be more accurate to say that he gradually changed his emphasis on the function of the moral sense—a change which his journals reflect and which is apparent in his sermons. In short, Emerson moved from an early position in which he felt the moral sense to be a simple discriminator of right and wrong actions, not unlike what we might now call the conscience, to a more dynamic conception of it as that power by which man was inspired to the good by an ideal of perfection. Though he continued to call it the "moral sense" or "moral law," and always thought of it in moral terms, the concept as it evolved took on connotations which we might today associate with the imagination. For Emerson conceived of the moral sense as a power by which man was able to perceive a perfection which transcended the world ordinarily available to his senses.

In 1822 Emerson set down a definition of the "moral law" which can be regarded as a point of departure in his development of the concept: "It is not necessary to describe that law, otherwise than by saying that it is the sovereign necessity which commands every mind to abide by one mode of conduct, & to reject another, by joining to the one a perfect satisfaction, while it pursues the other with indefinite apprehensions" (*JMN*, 2:5). The moral sense as it is presented here is the power to choose correctly between two possible actions, one of which is morally right. Emerson states the idea more succinctly, and with a fervor not present in the formality of the earlier entry, some eighteen months later, in February 1824: "I am glad to find at least *one* unfading essential beneficent principle in human nature—*the approval of right*" (*JMN*, 2:221). In an age like ours, which rarely questions the notion that moral decisions are at best complex and many-sided, if not impossibly muddled, Emerson's notion of an innate moral sense can seem to us, as Bishop writes, "a kind of enormous illusion."[7] It can also strike us as automatic and lifeless in the extreme. When, however, we find Emerson giving himself the room to explore his own feeling about the moral law, as he proceeds to do later in the 1822 entry quoted above, there is an unmistakable sense of dynamism communicated: "It [the moral law] has no taint of mortality in the purity & unity of its intelligence; it is perfectly spiritual. It sometimes seems to sanction that Platonic dream, that the soul of the individual was but an emanation from the Abyss of Deity, ↑and about to return <thither>↓ whence it flowed."[8] Emerson's "Platonic dream" may in fact be closer to Neoplatonism, but his technical use of the term is unimportant here. What is crucial is the association of the moral sense with a level of more perfect forms, toward which the soul is tending. His addition of the phrase depicting the soul's return to its origin, preserved in the recent edition of the journals, gives an even firmer sense of his attempt to depict the moral law in dynamic rather than static terms. Through the power of the moral law, the soul is directed toward its original perfection and unity, and is thus kept in a continual process of flowing toward that unity and away from individual isolation. This image simply bursts with implications that will eventually become central axioms for Emerson: that idealism functions as a means of moral guidance, that moral rightness consists in acting universally rather than individually, and that the moral soul is dynamic, always in flux and process.

The association of the moral sense with ideal forms, on which the above passage hinges, was to receive greater emphasis in Emerson's continuing thought on the subject. Later in 1822 he insisted that the moral sentiment "clearly partakes of another world than this and looks forward to it in the end." Its power, he went on to add, lies in its ability to link man to that other world:

Its dictates are never blind, are never capricious, but however they may seem to differ, are always discovered on a close and profound examination to point to a faultless and unattainable perfection. They seem to refer to a sublime course of life and action which nowhere exists or to which we are not privy; and to be an index of the Creator's character lent to mankind in vindication or illustration of the command—"Be Ye perfect as He is perfect."   [*JMN*, 2:49–50]

Although his terminology may differ slightly, Emerson's moral sentiment at this point is extremely close to the "divine monitor within us" which Channing urged as a guide to the soul's moral perfection.[9]

However firmly he held the existence of the moral sense, Emerson never committed himself to a rigid formula for its definition, as an 1833 journal entry suggests: "Yesterday I was asked what I mean by Morals. I reply that I cannot define & care not to define. It is man's business to observe & the definition of Moral Nature must be the slow result of years, of lives, of states perhaps of being" (*JMN*, 4:86). Although we must keep in mind Emerson's own admission that such definitions evolve gradually with life and experience, it is illuminating to examine the form morality and the moral sense took for him in the years of his ministry. "What is God?" he asked in 1830: "The most elevated conception of character that can be formed in the mind. It is, the individual's own soul carried out to perfection" (*JMN*, 3:182). The entry again shows the unmistakable influence of Channing, who had preached that "God is another name for human intelligence raised above all error and imperfection, and extended to all possible truth."[10] The relation of this conception of God to Emerson's developing conception of the moral sense is an important foundation of his strategy as a preacher. The ideal world revealed by the moral sense was, when translated into moral terms, the ideal individual referred to as God. Emerson's ideal man is therefore a version of the moral sense, as it took form for him in the late 1820s and early 1830s. His sermons suggest that the ideal man was a norm by which the characters of others, and of the self, could be measured. It was in essence imageless, but took a human form from the individual which was measured against it, revealing itself in man's ability to project further perfection on any given human quality or any particular human character. Its regulative function, therefore, grew out of the inspirational quality it lent to the human mind. While Emerson may, by associating the moral sense with ideal forms, have linked it with Platonism ontologically, its ethical implications were Platonic as well, in that evil was interpreted as the failure to realize fully the capacity for good which the moral sense revealed in the ideal man. Evil, or sin, was thus an absence of possible good. In the sermon "Trust Yourself," Emerson referred to the "image of God in human nature which has placed a standard of character in every human breast, which is above the highest copy of living excellence." A better sense of this standard can be obtained from his description of its function:

Every man has an idea of greatness that was never realized. Take the history of a great and good man, of Newton, or Franklin, or Washington, and explain all its details to the most obscure and ignorant wretch that wears the human form, you shall find that whilst he understands all its elevation he will be able to put his finger upon imperfections in that life. Which shows that in his heart there is a greater man than any that has lived in the world.   [*YES*, p. 110]

Emerson's point here is that man's ability to recognize the imperfection of his fellowmen indicates an existing standard of perfection within him. Thus, paradoxically, the recognition of failure is positive because within it is the seed of further attempts at perfection. The absence of such a recognition of limitation produces the greatest of sins: apathy.

Emerson's insistence on the necessity of pursuing the ideal man within us was his own statement of the Unitarian concern with the culture of the soul. In his sermon "Self-Culture," he referred to the moral sense in yet another guise, as a "Divine eye" within the soul convincing man that "it is in his power to obtain a degree of participation (I speak it with reverence) in the attributes of God." This power of the soul manifested itself, as we have noted, in "an unceasing effort at self-culture," which, when Emerson explained it in greater detail, proved to be the aspiration to a higher nature than our present one: "We are endowed with the power of voluntary action and taught to turn our freedom to this end [self-culture]. Our present condition, is one extreme form which we are to depart, and this height of a divine nature the other extreme towards which we are to aspire" (*YES*, pp. 100, 101). The divine nature he refers to here is the ideal man referred to earlier. In "Trust Yourself," he reminded his hearers that "there are in each of us all the elements of moral and intellectual excellence, that is to say, if you act out yourself, you will attain and exhibit a perfect character." But the fact is that such a character is never actually encountered in this world. Emerson's response is that "wherever there is manifest imperfection in his [man's] character, it springs from his own neglect to cultivate some part of his mind" (*YES*, p. 106). His characteristic habit of thought is again revealed in this passage: limitation or failure is taken as a point of departure rather than a final judgment on human nature.

Jesus and Emerson's "Universal Man"

The complex theological issue of Christology lay behind Emerson's emphasis on human perfection. No theological doctrine was in greater flux in the early nineteenth century than the nature of Jesus, and no religious symbol carried greater emotional overtones. We have seen that Emerson's reasons for resigning his pastorate in 1832 went far beyond the issue of the Lord's Supper, but that sacrament does indicate a point of increasing doubt for him in the early 1830s. What was the place of Christ in a philosophy of self-culture? In their

preaching Channing and Ware had made Christ a central emblem
of perfected, and therefore perfectible, humanity. But as Emerson
confronted the same issues, the crucial role of Jesus began to give
way to what we might call a stance of prospective humanism, which
placed an image of perfected humanity in the future rather than in
the history of Christianity. The "brighter age" (*YES,* p. 180) to
come which Emerson predicted in his 1832 sermon "The Genuine
Man" still seemed a real possibility in 1836, when he noted, "The
Revival that comes next must be preached to man's moral nature,
& from a height of principle that subordinates all persons. It must
forget historical Christianity and preach God who is, not God who
was" (*JMN,* 5:126). This entry looks forward to the opening lines
of *Nature,* completed later that year, and the boldness with which
Emerson eliminates "historical Christianity" and "all persons" (including Christ, presumably) from the coming revival indicates the
distance which has arisen between his developing views of the means
of culture and those of the Unitarians. Channing and Ware, always
conscious that they were in opposition to the Calvinists, who denied
man's inherent capacity for good, had countered this position by
using Jesus as an example of human capability. Emerson, however,
subtly turned Unitarianism around by eventually concluding that
Jesus did not establish a philosophy of human potential, but rather
served as one of its several teachers through history. The humanistic
thrust of Unitarianism was based on Christology, but the radical
humanism drawn from that Christology paradoxically gave Emerson
a rationale for relegating Jesus to a role of no greater relative importance than numerous other figures of history. Summarizing the tenets of his "First Philosophy" in 1835, he wrote, "Jesus Christ was
a minister of the pure Reason" (*JMN,* 5:273). His use of the indefinite rather than the definite article is a significant measure of his
development.

The story of Emerson's eventual rejection of Unitarian Christology begins, however, with the recognition of his rather complete
immersion in Unitarian attitudes toward Christ during his earlier
years. There is ample evidence, in both his private journals and his
public sermons, of a reverence for Christ which is basically a formulation in his own terms of the Christology of Ware and Channing.
Preaching in 1830, a year after his ordination, he explains the claims

of Jesus in these terms: "For all men are at all times drawing insensibly a moral from what they see doing around them; and with this moral (as it appears to those who have deduced it most clearly) the precepts of Jesus strictly coincide" (YES, p. 69). The passage, in its association of Jesus with man's moral perception, or what Emerson here calls man's constant effort to draw a moral from all that happens around him, makes Jesus the exemplar of the moral sense. When we remember the previous discussion of the close connection between the moral sense and Emerson's conception of the universal man, it is also apparent that Christ embodies, at this point in Emerson's thought, the concept of the universal man. Through an association with a moral sense which functions through aspiration, Christ assumes the role of a moral ideal. The idea that Christ embodies the potential perfection of each individual makes this position indistinguishable from that of Channing or Ware.

In a sermon of May 1830, "The Authority of Jesus," Emerson deals explicitly with the basis of Christ's claim to authority, and close attention to his position in this sermon helps to set the stage for his later qualification of that authority. His argument is that Jesus's claim for man's devotion is justified by his embodiment of the moral law available to every human. Christ thus derives his authority from a preexisting law; he does not, by his authority, establish that law.

A great error to which we are liable on this subject, is, that we are apt to separate the truth taught by Jesus from his office, and suppose that it was his divine authority, his peculiar designation to the office of Messiah that gives authority to his words, and not his words that mark him out as the Messiah. The utterance of that truth is his office. It is his truth that made him Messiah.   [YES, p. 96]

It should be stressed here that the young minister does not, in this sermon, question the authority of Jesus, even though he does establish a principle by which that authority could be criticized. Nevertheless, it was not out of character for Emerson to be seeking authority elsewhere than in the founder of Christianity, considering his wide reading in secular sources at this time. That reading is revealed clearly in the liberal use of secular sources and allusions in his sermons, a fact Ware had noted with apprehension.[11] So, not surprisingly, in November 1830, five months after the sermon on

Jesus, we find Emerson, in his journal, beginning to use the principle of criticism he set out previously.

Smother no dictate of your soul, but indulge it. There are passages in the history of Jesus which to some minds seem defects in his character. Probably a more full apprehension of his history will show you these passages in a more agreeable light. Meantime count them defects & do not stifle your moral faculty & force it to call what it thinks evil, good. For there is no being in the Universe whose integrity is so precious to you as that of your soul.   [*JMN,* 3:212]

While he does not admit it directly, it is a safe assumption that Emerson's was among those minds who saw defects in Christ's character. The entry seems self-directed, a kind of exercise in building self-confidence and self-reliance. The conflict is between Jesus and the moral faculty, and true to the doctrine he preached in "The Authority of Jesus," Emerson elevates the moral sense over Jesus in this instance. Already we can see the beginnings of a necessary choice between a method of self-culture guided by the authority of historical Christianity as embodied in Jesus, and a self-culture not only aimed at the self, but directed by the self—the self, it must be remembered, which is acting universally, or as one with God.

   Time would, of course, make Emerson's problem with Christology more acute, and by 1832, the year of his resignation, we find even stronger indications of his tendency to prefer individual guidance to historical authority. A journal entry of October 1, 1832, castigates the teacher who discovers a great truth, but "turns up the ends of it at last with a cautious showing *how* it is agreeable to the life & teaching of Jesus—as if that was any recommendation. As if the blessedness of Jesus' life & teaching were not because they were agreeable to the truth. Well this cripples his teaching." He concludes the entry with an imagined dialogue indicating the direction of his thought at this period—a powerful affirmation of the self: "You must be humble because Christ says, 'Be humble.' 'But why must I obey Christ?' 'Because God sent him.' But how do I know God sent him? 'Because your own heart teaches the same thing he taught.' Why then shall I not go to my own heart at first?" (*JMN,* 4:45). The dialogue ends here, with the question unanswered by

Emerson's orthodox strawman, but undoubtedly answered within Emerson's own heart.

By July 1835, his process of rejection of the exclusive authority of Jesus had completed itself, as his most explicit journal entry on the subject reveals. Here, at last, Emerson explains some of his reservations about Jesus, and again he seems to be addressing a representative of orthodoxy, giving his entry the form of an imagined dialogue:

You affirm that the moral development contains all the intellectual & that Jesus was the perfect man. I bow in reverence unfeigned before that benign man. I know more, hope more, am more because he has lived. But if you tell me that in your opinion he has fulfilled all the conditions of man's existence, carried out to the utmost at least by implication, all man's powers, I suspend my assent. I do not see in him cheerfulness: I do not see in him the love of Natural Science: I see in him no kindness for Art; I see in him nothing of Socrates, of Laplace, of Shakspeare. The perfect man should remind us of all great men. Do you ask me if I would rather resemble Jesus than any other man? If I should say Yes, I should suspect myself of superstition.   [*JMN*, 5:71–72]

Emerson is careful to temper his rejection of Christ's absolute authority with a protestation of respect for him, which is undoubtedly sincere. But it is clear at this point that Emerson is much more interested in the varieties of human greatness than in any exclusive reverence for Jesus, particularly with the connotations of conformity, orthodoxy, and even "superstition" that such a reverence implies. His attitude might best be summarized in a journal entry of August 1837, in which he stresses the importance of Jesus' ability to call forth the potential divinity of each individual rather than inspire a reverence for his own person: "If Jesus came now into the world, he would say—You, YOU! He said to his age, I" (*JMN*, 5:362).

This struggle with Christology was part of a process of secularization in Emerson's thought that was based upon the elevation of the nature of man. It can be seen as a further step toward the complete humanizing of Jesus begun by the Unitarians. The aim of this humanizing, of course, was to bring the faith in the spiritual potential of every individual into line with the more general acceptance of the spirituality of Jesus. The God Incarnate in Christ was also in every other individual; this made Jesus a "fellow worshipper" (*JMN*, 5:231), rather than an object of reverence. The difference between Jesus and the ordinary man, to the extent that it could be perceived, was in the degree to which the "God within" had been cultivated. Yet the idea that Jesus perfectly embodied the moral sense, which Emerson preached as late as 1830, continued to have ramifications in his thought long after the assumption of Christ's perfection was abandoned, or judged irrelevant. We see it emerging in Emerson's search for a hero or great man who embodied in one way or another the moral perfection universally available to man. In the early 1830s Emerson could no longer be content with a single historical figure as a guide to his own potential, even if that figure were Jesus. But he was not content, either, that the process of self-culture could be carried on without the presence of any exemplary ideal.

The Culture of "The Genuine Man"

The sermon entitled "The Genuine Man" is the most prolonged attempt among Emerson's sermons to define the ideal man who had come to embody the moral sense for him during his years as a minister. Preached on his last Sunday as minister of the Second Church, and twelve times thereafter into 1837, the sermon in its composition and use spanned a transitional period for Emerson, and the sermon therefore has both biographical and intellectual importance for his development in these years. He took as his theme the idea which we have seen repeated in different contexts in many of his previous sermons, the recognition that "there is a man in us, we have not seen executed out of us" (*YES*, p. 181). Pointedly referring his remarks to "any young person engaged in the formation of his character" (*YES*, p. 184), Emerson combined theme and structure into a vehicle designed to foster self-culture. The immediate personal circumstances of the sermon remind us that, in these remarks, Emerson was justifying his own resignation to his congregation, and the stress on self-reliance points unmistakably toward Emerson the Transcendentalist. But we should also remember that this sermon is as much the culmination of his preaching of his own version of Unitarianism as it is the justification of his withdrawal from the Unitarian church. His change of professional roles and his disaffection from the institution of the church do not affect the continuity of his concern with self-culture as the process of making the moral sense more consistently and integrally a part of his life and of the lives of those for whom he preached or wrote.

The thematic importance of "The Genuine Man" is supplemented, however, by its artistic qualities, for it provides a representative example of the extent to which the sermon served as a literary vehicle in nineteenth-century America, particularly among the Unitarians. Lawrence Buell has argued that "up until 1850, the best American sermons were still on the whole the best literature that America was producing," and he has noted the Unitarians' transformation of the dogmatic sermon into an "inspirational oration."[12] It is clear that Emerson, with his deep distaste for theological dogma and his tendency to use a wide range of secular sources and examples in his preaching, was part of this movement, but this point has rarely been explored in detailed critical analyses of his sermons, which take into account not only his theological and philosophical positions, but also his use of the sermon form as a medium of expression.

The extent to which we judge Emerson successful in this sermon depends upon our perception of his purpose. His presentation of an ideal of humanity as a "Genuine Man" falls under Buell's designation of an "inspirational oration." His purpose is moral inspiration, grounded in the conviction that the moral sense is best cultivated through an appeal to man's sense of the better. His own discovery of the universal man as a manifestation of the moral sense is therefore translated into this sermon, which attempts to inculcate in his hearers a mood of moral aspiration. There is, however, an autobiographical element in the sermon. When it is read in the context of Emerson's resignation of his pulpit, its insistence upon total honesty and complete openness, or what Emerson calls the necessity of *"truth of character"* (*YES*, p. 188), can be seen as forms of self-explanation and self-justification. In the wake of his own decision to make no compromise with his integrity, even at the expense of his profession, Emerson stresses self-direction as the key to the necessary truthfulness of the genuine man. This is most forcefully apparent when he discusses vocational choice, an issue which was at this point much on his mind.

It is plain to all observers that some men have been formed for public life, for the management of general affairs, of a robust fabric of soul that needs the rough discipline of hot contention, of deep stakes, of great antagonists, and a vast theatre. Others as manifestly are born to benefit men by the advancement of science. . . . Others embrace the mechanical arts and find no pleasure like that of exercising their own ingenuity to valuable ends. Others delight in the bustle of commerce. Others have quieter yet scarcely less effectual means of serving their fellow men in gentle offices of compassion or instruction. But to each his own mode and the genuine man finds his way to that for which he is fitted.   [*YES*, p. 187]

Emerson is not excusing himself, or even explaining himself, as much as he is preaching to himself in the sermon. He seeks not only to inspire his congregation, but to remind himself that there is a "calling" for him, even if it is not the Christian ministry.

The purpose of moral inspiration dictates the formal structure of the sermon. There is a "text" but, typically, it serves primarily as a literary epigraph, with Emerson making little attempt to explicate it at length. As for the sermon's "doctrine," it is certainly not a logical treatise, but rather the kind of imaginative construct of an ideal of virtue characteristic of such preaching. As such the "doctrine" and "application" are practically indistinguishable, though Emerson closes with a peroration that attempts to apply the idea of the human ideal to the daily lives of his congregation. The important point is that the structure of the sermon is dictated by the necessity of an appeal to the moral imagination of his audience. The resulting structure can be described as a presentation of the universal man on three ascending levels. He begins with an impersonal portrayal of the genuine man and translates that portrayal into personal, and then into universal, terms: he moves from "man" to "self" to "God." The sermon's structure thus reinforces its inspirational purpose by guiding the imagination of the hearer to increasingly higher levels of spirituality.

The sermon's opening also introduces the first of a series of visual metaphors, the major literary device of the sermon, important both as a unifying device and as a focus of meaning.[13] "Men are beginning to see with more distinctness what they ought to be," Emerson

argues, and such vision is necessarily of the imagination—the product of a mind's eye straining to envision an ideal. Thus Emerson
portrays his age by means of a similar metaphor: "We stand on
tiptoe looking for a brighter age" (*YES*, p. 180). As he moves on to
describe his "genuine man," Emerson stresses the idea that it is not
the "circumstances" of the great man which are important, but
rather "the soul of him," and this distinction, crucial to his attempt
to delineate the "perfection of human nature" (*YES*, p. 181), is
again dependent upon the visual imagery of the sermon. The outward manifestations of greatness, Emerson argues, tend to divert our
attention away from that which is essential to human greatness; only
a deeper vision which penetrates these outward circumstances can
reveal the genuine man.

> We meet a prosperous person. The imagination is first excited and the
> judgment a little shaken by the renown of his name. Then he is announced
> by all sort of cheerful and respectful attentions. Then every word comes
> loaded with the weight of his professional character. Then there still is
> another fence of fine plausible manners, and polished speech, and the men
> are very few who have the firmness of nerve to go behind all these inclo-
> sures, and with an undazzled eye penetrate unto and measure and weigh
> the man himself; and the men are fewer still who can bear the scrutiny.
> [*YES*, p. 182]

Emerson's point, of course, is that social life and particular social
situations make any true encounter between persons rare, and the
power of this particular passage is the clarity and immediacy with
which he deals with the phenomenon of social life itself. We become
the one about to meet a famous man; we remember our own tendency to be dazzled by all that surrounds him; we confirm, from our
own experience, the superficiality that makes such meetings awk-
ward formalities. This direct appeal to experience is supplemented
by the imagery of "inclosures" or successive "fence[s]" or barriers
which the "undazzled eye" must break through in order to scrutinize
the only important aspect of greatness—the man himself, "the soul
of him."

Having already appealed through imagery to the personal experience of his listeners, Emerson can then put the question to them
directly:

Is it not true in your experience, brethren, that thus the man is the least part of himself? Arts and professions, wealth and office, manners and religion are screens which conceal lameness and imperfection of character. The eye is so entertained with the outward parade that rarely does anybody concern himself with the state of the real person that moves under all. The whole world goes after externals and the soul, God's image and likeness, is overlooked.

Again the question is supported with the complementing images of the "eye" and the social "screens" which prevent vision. But most importantly, this appeal to experience, strengthened by the use of the rhetorical question, allows Emerson to move the focus of the sermon away from this exterior image of both superficial and genuine greatness to the source of that greatness, man's individual soul, which is "God's image and likeness." Again Emerson turns to a question to make his point both direct and immediate, asking, "Is it not true that men do not think highly, reverently of their own nature?" (YES, p. 182). With this question, he makes the transition from the impersonal to the personal; he moves from his opening consideration of "man" to his concentration on "self," thus translating his ideal for humanity into personal terms directly related to his hearers and, of course, to himself.

In order to make this transition to the personal intelligible, he defines the "self" to which he speaks with extreme care, distinguishing between a common usage of the word and a usage he wants to establish as normative: "There are two ways of speaking of self; one, when we speak of a man's low and partial self, as when he is said to be selfish; and the other when we speak of the whole self, that which comprehends a man's whole being, of that self of which Jesus said, What can a man give in exchange for his soul?" (YES, p. 182). The distinction between the "partial" and the "whole" self transcends speech usage, of course, but Emerson emphasizes the difference by illustrating one with a common expression and the other with a reference to the language of Jesus. It is "the whole self" that is important to the concept of the genuine man, for in that self which transcends limits we find the basis of "the perfection of human nature." This higher self expresses the potential state of man rather than his actuality, but as an image of potential, it serves the purpose of moral inspiration. Thus Emerson locates his ideal image of man, the genuine man, within the individual rather than outside him.

Emerson culminates his discussion of the "whole self" with another visual metaphor. He had earlier asked his congregation to survey "the whole circle of your acquaintance" to locate the ideal man; he now asks them to look to themselves for the same ideal: "It seems to me, brethren, as if we wanted nothing so much as a habit of steadily fixing the eye upon this higher self, the habit of distinguishing between our circumstances and ourselves." The distinction that social life makes so difficult, that between a person's outward circumstances and his true self, is now put in the context of the self, where it remains a difficult distinction. We need, he insists, "the practice of rigorous scrutiny into our daily life to learn how much there is of our own action and how much is not genuine but imitated or mercenary" (*YES*, pp. 181–83).

The necessity and the difficulty of "steadily fixing the eye upon this higher self" are the concerns of the second part of the sermon, for after Emerson has associated the self with the genuine man, he must make that association a practical reality to his hearers by making the "self" a moral guide. A moral guide is presumably endowed with moral authority, and while there was a long tradition to support the moral authority of Christ, the location of authority in the self was problematic—ultimately the trigger of the "Transcendentalist" controversy which surrounded the Divinity School Address. Emerson at this point, however, is already asserting that the authority of self is based in God, a fact which suggests that it was less his own change than a change in social climate (and the temperament of a few individuals) that brought on the controversy. For in this sermon, he is unequivocal about the relation of the self to God: "And it [the development of the inward nature] is founded and can only be founded in religion. It can only prefer this self because it esteems it to speak the voice of God" (*YES*, p. 184). This is not to suggest that "The Genuine Man" is a radical departure into Transcendentalism. The point is, rather, that even though Emerson may sound in 1832 as he would sound in 1838, analogues to his position can be found among other Unitarians, including the leader of the denomination, Channing. Emerson does not change his position, then, as much as he changes emphasis: downplaying or ignoring the role of Jesus, stressing the divinity of human nature.

Emerson's most telling description of the genuine man is his assertion that "he is transparent" (*YES*, p. 185). We are reminded, of course, of the transparent eyeball experience in *Nature*, having the advantage of history to alert us to a phrase which will grow in significance. But the very image itself, apart from any associations with Emerson's later works, indicates the direction of his thought. Transparency, in the metaphorical context of this sermon, is the highest rung on the ladder of spiritual insight. The earlier imagery of barriers to vision has suggested a blinding of the self, and thus a denial of the source of spiritual power. The removal of those barriers has indicated spiritual "vision," based on a self that acts consistently and openly because it acts upon principle. Transparency indicates an even greater spiritual intensity, because it implies a state in which the self not only is unveiled and thus visible, but is really not a "self" at all. Just as one sees through a transparent object to all around it, one sees "through" a genuine man, realizing that the self one perceives is indistinguishable from the universe of which it is a part. The transparent self is thus the negated self, if we think of self in the low and partial sense. But in terms of the "whole" self, it is the self raised to the level of the universal.

To illustrate the "transparency" of the genuine man, Emerson turns to two exemplary men of great importance to him: George Fox, who would be the subject of one of his early lectures in the "Biography" series; and Emanuel Swedenborg, the representative mystic of *Representative Men*. Even though these examples illustrate Emerson's point by grounding it in human reality, they are ultimately unsatisfying. Transparency does not finally denote individual personalities, but rather the absorption of personality in a higher law. He comes closer to his intention in the following illustration:

It was happily said of a great man "that he was content to stand by, and let reason argue for him." That is precisely the impression left on your mind whenever you talk with a truth speaker, that it is not he who speaks, so much as reason that speaks through him. You are not dealing with a mere man but with something higher and better than any man—with the voice of Reason, common to him and you and all men.

This passage is central to the transition from the level of the personal to the level of the universal in the sermon, and it hinges on the term "Reason," which would grow in importance for Emerson. While the passage is couched in terms that attribute truth to another, rather than directly to "you" the hearer, Emerson follows it closely with this conclusion: "There is this supreme universal reason in your mind which is not yours or mine or any man's, but is the Spirit of God in us all" (*YES*, p. 186). The "genuine man" has become "you"; now "you" has become "God."

The formal transition of the sermon from the self to God is, we should remember, exactly the transition Emerson hopes to enable his hearers to make in their own lives. It is a transition made possible by an exacting truth to self rather than a conscious abandonment of self, for the proper devotion to self in its higher sense will mean an abandonment of self in its lower sense. Emerson calls this necessary devotion to self an attention to man's "inward voice": "By listening to this inward voice, by following this invisible Leader, it is in the power of a man to cast off from himself the responsibility of his words and actions and to make God responsible for him." We can, with very little strain, sense an edge of defensiveness in this affirmation, in that Emerson seems to be addressing himself to a possible orthodox objection: can the individual be entirely trusted with moral responsibility? Is there not a need for an authority outside the self? The answer, as he puts it, is that authority does transcend the individual in that it rests in God. With this point established, he can finally assert the superiority of his religion of self-trust over "historical" religion: "Finally in answer to any (if such there be) who shall say, 'This quality is good, but is there not something better?' I would add one remark, that the conviction must be produced in our minds that *this truth of character is identical with a religious life.*" As if this emphasis were not clear enough, he goes on to insist that this inward voice "is the direct revelation of your Maker's Will, not written in books many ages since nor attested by distant miracles but in the flesh and blood" (*YES*, pp. 188–89). This is as direct a challenge to historical Christianity as any of Emerson's later works, but it is especially interesting because of its context. Emerson challenges history while arguing for an effort at self-culture, for he sees the result of the devotion to self, the attention to the inward voice, as the fuller cultivation of the moral potential of the soul. Seen in this light, "The Genuine Man" stands as a statement pointing in two directions. As a prolonged argument for self-culture, it taps the vital center of American Unitarianism, and American liberal religion in general. But as an argument for the moral authority of the individual, and thus a rejection of tradition and history, it looks forward to the flowering of literary culture in New England, only a few years distant.

PART TWO

Emerson as Lecturer

IV

The Naturalist

From Preacher to Lecturer

Emerson benefited enormously from one sociological phenomenon in his lifetime—the rising popularity of the public lecture. He returned from his European trip in 1833 with no secure place or profession, having only a developing collection of ideas and a certain skill in presenting them, honed by his years in the pulpit. What he needed was an audience, which was there at his return in the beginnings of the lyceum movement in New England. The lyceum provided a rare opportunity for Emerson to embrace the more literary side of the ministerial vocation, leaving aside its pastoral aspects.

There is something anomalous about Emerson's considerable success on the lecture circuit. The map of his lecture engagements indicates a widening circle of popularity, centered in New England and spreading along the Eastern seaboard and into the Middle West, growing as both his own reputation and the strength of the lyceum grew.[1] Yet his appeal cannot be explained in ordinary terms, since he was neither dramatic nor sensational and can hardly be considered a humorist. As Henry James put it, commenting on Emerson's sometimes roughhewn Western audiences, "Certainly never was the fine wine of philosophy carried to remoter or greener corners."[2] William Charvat's comment on the paradox of Emerson's success makes the point well:

He was not popular in the ordinary sense: he did not draw the biggest audiences, and he was not offered the highest fees. But for some forty years he was invited everywhere, and was repeatedly invited back, by people who "understood" (in the ordinary sense) little of what he said; who often resented not understanding him; and who frequently were offended by what they did understand.[3]

71

What could have been the appeal of a lecture which was not fully comprehensible to a large part of his audience? Much of it lay in the blend of inspiration and comfort that even a minimally thoughtful person could glean from a great deal of Emerson's lecturing. Such qualities are always at a premium, but in a society torn by war and wracked with the conflict between religious doubts and a deeply ingrained religious heritage, inspiration and comfort were even more welcome. Appropriately, "Immortality" was one of Emerson's most popular discourses in his later career.[4]

The appeal of Emerson's air of comfort accounts primarily for his later success and even veneration as a lecturer, but to understand his early popularity we must look to a different appeal, his ability to articulate the alienation of "solitary, conscientious, and unhappy young people with a fair degree of education, a type the age produced in quantity."[5] In general, these were young people left with a religious sensibility the church could no longer satisfy, and an aesthetic hunger that American society could not answer. Finding no sufficient place in society, they welcomed Emerson's championing of solitude and self-reliance, and his posture against society. Emerson's own struggle with the problems of a social vocation and with his personal isolation were in a sense the problems of his age, writ large, and because these struggles found their way into his lectures, they found a ready audience.

For Emerson himself, the lectures form an invaluable bridge from the pursuit of preacher to that of essayist. Though the lecture was indebted to the sermon tradition, at least as he used it, it had many fewer restrictions than even the liberal sermon. Moreover, he improved upon the broad range of possible topics which lecturing afforded him by developing series or courses of lectures, which challenged him to a comprehensive treatment of the issues he chose. It was largely through his repeated use of the series of interconnected lectures that he molded something like a philosophical system. It was also a version of this form which gave shape to his major literary accomplishment, the collected series of essays of the 1840s and 1850s.

Even though his career as a lecturer began after a break with the past, the resignation of the church, and even though he began to explore relatively new topics in his first lectures, science and English literature, the underlying continuity of his concerns as preacher and lecturer is striking. The same themes of potential human perfection, and the vision of self-culture as its process of realization, characterize the lectures. Important clues to the direction of his lecturing can be found, in fact, in the European tour which he began soon after his resignation, with the loss of his wife Ellen still weighing on him.[6] His journals and letters suggest that the trip was not only for escape and revitalization, but part of a personal philosophical search beyond New England. He wanted further evidence that a "new age" was in fact dawning, bringing about humanity's realization of its inherent potential. Europe offered him three kinds of experiences which had been in some ways limited in New England: the presence of evidences of the past, contact with famous men, and encounters with the rising influence of science.

The expansive nature of travel agreed with Emerson physically and mentally, and he wrote his brother Charles from Rome, "I am in better health than ever since I was a boy" (L, 1:373). This must have been the case, since his travel letters and journals from Italy record an almost constant round of excursions, centering on ruins, historic architecture, museums, and other monuments of the past. "I go to see old Rome, not new" (L, 1:368), he wrote. He never seemed to share the opinion of Hawthorne and James that America's lack of a past was a handicap or a tragedy, but it is clear that the past as he experienced it in Europe, especially in Italy, affected him profoundly. It was not that the evidences of the past unsettled or surprised him—in fact just the opposite was the case, as he explained to George Sampson:

It [traveling] furnishes the student with a perpetual answer to the little people that are always hinting that your faith & hope belong to your village or your country, & that a knowledge of the world would open your eyes. . . . I am glad to recognize the same man under a thousand different masks & hear the same commandment spoken to me in Italian, I was wont to hear in English. [L, 1:371]

But the past, however impressive, was not completely satisfying to him because it awoke expectations for a humanity which could fulfill the potential the past suggested. After a long letter to Charles full of descriptions of his excursions in Rome, he pointedly added this lament: "Ah great great Rome! it is a majestic city, & satisfies this craving imagination. And yet I would give all Rome for one man such as were fit to walk here, & could feel & impart the sentiment of the place" (*L*, 1:374). Two days later, in much the same mood, he wrote his aunt Mary: "God's greatest gift is a Teacher & when will he send me one, full of truth & of boundless benevolence & heroic sentiments. I can describe the man, & have already in prose & verse. I know the idea well, but where is its real blood warm counterpart" (*L*, 1:376). Much of Emerson's trip, particularly his travels in England, was a search of this sort, in which he tried to find the men behind many of the literary voices he had heard. The results were usually disappointing to him, his friendship with Carlyle being the notable exception, but the result was not dispiriting. If the famous men he was able to see or meet did not privately fulfill the expectations which their public reputations raised, that fact seemed to be only further confirmation that self-culture was the next necessary step toward the new age. The "genuine man" of whom he had preached could not be affected by the shortcomings of the famous men whom he met.

The Ethics of the Creation

The impact of history and the continuing search for humanity which characterized Emerson's travel would manifest themselves soon in his lecturing. But the most immediate literary product of his trip was a series of lectures on science which were stimulated by his visit to the flourishing school of natural historians, botanists and zoologists centered around Paris's Museum d'Histoire Naturelle. Emerson's involvement with science in this period, and his apparent inclination to study it with some seriousness, are well known to students of his early development.[7] But the prevailing view of Emerson's relation with science has been established by Harry Hayden Clark's cautionary reminder that Emerson was not "an inductive scientist," that he instead "approache[d] natural history with a method essentially *a priori*, ethical, and deductive, like that of Plato, Schelling, Goethe,

Kant, and Coleridge."[8] Clark's point is well taken, and a reading of Emerson's writings on science certainly shows him to be no more than a dabbler in astronomy, geology, and natural history. But such necessary caution should not obscure the impact of science on his thought. If Goethe and Coleridge were finally more influential on him (as they were), and if Emerson in his pursuits more nearly resembles them than the actual scientists of his day, there is still much to be said about the contribution of pure science to the pattern of his development.[9] His experience at the Paris Museum is the clearest example of such influence in his early writings and stands as a significant turning point in his thought, culminating one phase of his thinking and initiating another. The impact of the experience lay in its forceful presentation to Emerson's mind of the implications of botanical and zoological classification, emphasizing as it did both the appeal of scientific procedure itself and its potential philosophical uses. He was not entirely ready to abandon revealed theology until his experience at Paris, and he had no clear vision of how nature might support the moral sense until he had worked through this experience.

Although we tend to look back on Emerson as one who championed truth as a form of intuition, it is important to remember that his early rationalistic tendencies were significant in his development, helping to free him from a biblically based religion and sustaining his interest in close scientific observation. "Is anything gained by depreciating our reason [?]" he asked his congregation in 1830. "Is not one God the author of reason & of revelation? The best[,] the indispensible evidence of revelation is its entire agreement with reason."[10] Even though Emerson could assert this "entire agreement" of reason and revelation in 1830, his commitment to revelation would become more and more qualified in the period that immediately followed. In the 1824 journal entry which records his dedication to the ministry, Emerson cites Channing's Dudleian Lecture as a model of the imaginative preaching to which he aspires, setting Channing off against "reasoning machines" like Locke and Hume (*JMN*, 2:238). The passage seems to express a young poet's contempt for rationalism, and a preference for the eloquence Channing represents. But the modern reader who actually goes to the

Dudleian Lecture will, I think, be surprised at the nature of the "higher flights of the fancy" to which Emerson refers.[11] The lecture's form is closer to a Thomistic theological argument than an inspirational oration or poem. Channing begins with a careful and systematic refutation of the objections to a belief in the possibility of the biblical miracles, including a direct refutation of Hume. He goes on to offer a point-by-point listing of the reasons that give a rational foundation to a belief in miracles. The lecture exemplifies the "supernatural rationalism," a synthesis of rationalism and credence in supernatural miracles, that Channing and his associates inherited from the theologians of the eighteenth century—an inheritance which reminds us that rationalism was not exclusively a method of the deists in the eighteenth and early nineteenth centuries.[12]

One appeal of Channing's Dudleian Lecture to the young Emerson was Channing's rather ingenious argument that miracles have a rational basis. Stressing that God's creation of an orderly universe was a means of proving his power and benevolence, and not an end in itself, Channing concluded that "nature clearly shows to us a power above itself, so that it proves miracles to be possible." The argument is a curiously circuitous one on close examination: reason tells us that an orderly universe establishes a creator; the existence of such a creator tells us that an orderly universe is not necessary. For Channing, there was no problem with belief in miracles; the difficulty for him was rather the opposite: "To a man who cherishes a sense of God, the great difficulty is, not to account for miracles, but to account for their rare occurrence."[13]

Emerson himself was preaching virtually the same doctrine a decade later. In his sermon "Miracles" (1831), he declares that "the existence of God is necessarily suggested to the reasoning man by what he now beholds and a miracle suggests no more." His elaboration of the argument, however, is interesting as an indication of his future development:

The ordinary course of nature indicates an intelligence capable of alleged works, for it can require no greater power to suspend than to originate the operations of nature. In other words, I can believe a miracle, because I can raise my own arm. I can believe a miracle because I can remember. I can believe it because I can speak and be understood by you. I can believe in a manifestation of power beyond my own, because I am such a manifestation. [*YES,* p. 122]

Emerson's equation of miracles with the normal processes of nature in this passage marks the beginning of his eventual rejection of any belief in miracles, stated most emphatically in the Divinity School Address. There he argued that Jesus spoke of miracles because "he felt man's life was a miracle," adding that "the very word Miracle, as pronounced by Christian churches, gives a false impression; it is Monster" (*CW,* 1:81). Even though the sermon "Miracles" was an attempt to lay a rational basis for the supernatural in Christian revelation, the eventual result of this attempt, as his stand in the Divinity School Address confirms, was to make such a belief irrelevant to true religion.

Emerson's impatience with revealed religion grew throughout the early 1830s, culminating finally in *Nature.* While arguments from the design of nature could easily establish the existence of God, they could not so easily serve as the foundation for moral action. Nature clearly indicated a creator, but to derive an elaborate moral code from it, or even the moral principles necessary for the conduct of life, was much more problematic. Channing commented upon the difficulty in his Dudleian Lecture, noting that "the laws of nature, operating as they do with an inflexible steadiness, . . . give the idea of a distant, reserved sovereign much more than a tender parent." In Channing's view, the result of the use of natural reasoning alone had historically been a failure to accept "the doctrine of one God and Father, on which all piety rests."[14] To Emerson, for whom moral perception was the essence of religion, the moral gap created when revealed religion was rejected posed a serious problem.

His concern about the moral problem left by natural theology is suggested in a sermon of July 1829. Here Emerson begins by explaining the assumption that the world indicates a creator, just as a watch indicates a maker, an argument used with great effect in William Paley's *Natural Theology.*[15] Even though he is glad to accept the argument as proof of God's existence, he is clearly worried about the assumption that naturally follows from it, that God is a withdrawn and uncaring technician, not related vitally to his creation. To counter this idea, Emerson is pushed back upon idealism, using the claim of "the pious Bishop Berkeley" that the *"material world exists only as it is perceived."* If we accept the assumptions of Berkeley, Emerson argues, we must conclude that we do not perceive independently existing things, but only their impressions stamped upon our mind by an act of God. Since these impressions are continually before us, God must sustain them continually, in which case he cannot be withdrawn. He thus concludes: "The artist who constructs a watch avails himself of powers perpetually afforded him by nature that is by God—as the force of gravity or the elasticity of the steel. If these powers shd. be withdrawn his machine wd. stop—But God has no such powers out of himself."[16] Emerson's argument may not be entirely convincing, though we can see some of its elements emerging more persuasively later in the "Idealism" chapter of *Nature*. But it is an interesting early instance of his attempt to extricate himself by rational means from what he considered a possible dilemma of natural theology.

This dilemma became increasingly bothersome as Emerson's reluctance to accept the biblical revelation grew. He had largely identified Christianity with morality in his early years, and his growing doubts about the supernatural foundations of Christianity thus robbed his "moral sense" of one important support. Nature increasingly became the factor to which he turned for confirmation of his own moral sense: if it could, with the aid of reason, establish God's existence, could it not, with close observation and enlightened perception, be transformed into a moral guide as well? In a journal entry late in 1826, Emerson notes that "the changes of external nature are continually suggesting to us the changes in the condition of man" (*JMN*, 3:50–51); this is a prelude, at least, to the position that nature leads to moral perception. Later in 1830, he is more explicit about man's ability to use nature morally: "Man is the interpreter of all the works[;] he draws the audible moral from all. His tongue should tell the ethics of the creation" (*JMN*, 3:186). If, in fact, man could discern "the ethics of the creation," then moral philosophy as well as cosmology could be based upon speculation about nature.

Toward a "Theory of Animated Nature"

The fact that Emerson was rendered receptive to a natural basis for moral truth by his background in natural theology and his growing rational doubts about the truth of revealed religion accounts in large part for the impact of the experience at the Paris Museum. The resulting intellectual consequences were twofold. In the first place, he gained new insight into a developing theory of nature itself, which he would begin to express in the scientific lectures and bring to completion in *Nature*. Emerson sensed that "nature is not fixed but fluid" (*CW*, 1:44), and this perception indicated his movement to what we might call a dynamic concept of nature rather than a static one. To use Emerson's phrase, he began to formulate a "Theory of Animated Nature" (*EL*, 1:83), in which he saw the possibility of the fulfillment of his earlier search for the "ethics of the creation."[17] In addition to this theory of animated nature, Emerson also attained a new respect for the scientific method which revealed it to him, classification. The intellectual procedure of classification clearly fascinated him epistemologically—his later attempt to write a *Natural History of Intellect*, in which he intended to apply the tools of scientific classification to the mental processes, indicates his life-long fascination with the methodology of classification. Yet it is also important to note that classification appealed to Emerson vocationally as well, if even for a brief period. It posed to him an alternative which he rejected only after a serious weighing of its potential to foster his expanding search for his proper intellectual work. His declaration "I will be a naturalist" (*EL*, 1:10) was a serious proposition, and should not be regarded merely as the poetic effusion of an impressionable young man. Emerson may not have known fully the implications of such an ambition, but he would soon set about finding them out.

Upon his return, Emerson found ready audiences for scientific lectures, and in the winter of 1833–34 he lectured on science four times, beginning with an account of the Paris Museum and an argument full of hope for the future of scientific study. "Every fact that is disclosed to us in natural history removes one scale more from the eye" (*EL*, 1:15), he says, in a metaphor that portrays the scientist as seer. The lecture is filled with biographical exempla from the history of science: Duhamel, Linnaeus, Buffon, Cuvier, Humboldt, Galileo, Reaumur, Huber, Newton, and Kepler are all referred to as representative of extraordinary vision and achievement. And, for Emerson, their pursuit itself, not only the results it obtains, is crucial. The life of the scientist, he says, "abounds with the narrative of sleepless nights, laborious days and dangerous journeyings." "This high unconditional devotion to their cause" (*EL*, 1:22–23) is valuable enough of itself to be worth all their actual discoveries.

The results of the scientific pursuit do have great importance, however, in that "the greatest office of natural science (and one which as yet is only begun to be discharged) [is] to explain man to himself." In a way that prefigures *Nature* strikingly, Emerson notes that "the power of *expression* which belongs to external nature" is based on "that correspondence of the outward world to the inward world of thoughts and emotions." The result of this correspondence is the realization that "the laws of moral nature answer to those of matter as face to face in a glass." He thus concludes the lecture on a note of expectancy: "I look then to the progress of Natural Science as to that which is to develop new and great lessons of which good men shall understand the moral" (*EL*, 1:23–26). It is clear at this point that Emerson has incorporated the study of science as a key tool in his search for "the ethics of the creation."

Emerson only hints in this lecture at the most impressive and useful fact that science was providing him, that of the dynamism or flux of nature. He appeals to geology to substantiate his assertion that "before the period when God created man upon the earth very considerable changes have taken place in the planet." Emerson is, of course, still bound to the teleological assumption of the primacy of man in creation, but we see here that his assumption of the design of nature is beginning to incorporate ideas of change and mutation. Natural forms, he realizes, must be seen from the perspective of their changes over time; or, as he puts it, "every form is a history of the thing" (*EL*, 1:15, 17).

Expanding on this idea in his next lecture, "The Relation of Man to the Globe," Emerson argues that the history of the development of nature is a progressive series of changes in preparation for the advent of man, who "is no upstart in the creation, but has been prophesied in nature for a thousand thousand ages before he appeared." Emerson uses the evidence of these changes to argue for the perfect adaptation of the earth for man's uses, suggesting a developing perfection of nature and a developing perfection of man's uses of nature: "With the progress of the cultivation of the species the globe itself both in the mass and in its minutest part, becomes to man a school of science." The development of nature puts man in the position, finally, of realizing the process of that development, and therefore of putting nature to use for his own further development. Emerson's enraptured conclusion to the lecture suggests that his exposure to science is indeed strengthening his sense that nature has a potential moral use: "I am thrilled with delight by the choral harmony of the whole. Design! It is all design. It is all beauty. It is all astonishment" (*EL*, 1:29, 46, 49).

Emerson's third lecture, "Water," differs from the first two in the restricted range of its subject matter, but it is an extended example of the dynamic quality of nature and its potential moral uses. The lecture, which is superficially a rather puzzling treatment of an equally curious topic, has elicited little comment from Emerson's critics, perhaps because, as Whicher and Robert E. Spiller note, it is the "most factual and least personal of his scientific talks" (*EL*, 1:50); it may even strike us as the driest of his lectures. The clue to understanding the lecture is Emerson's quotation from Playfair that "water everywhere 'appears as the most active enemy of hard and solid bodies.' " Emerson devotes an entire lecture to this single element because he sees it as a central illustration of the fact that nature is a process, not a static substance. The qualities of water demonstrate "how mighty a benefactor is this most flexible and active of created things." As the medium which dissolves the solider substances of the earth, such as the minerals, it acts as a constant unifier of the earth, changing otherwise solid and separate substances into fluid and unified ones. But because "the same power that destroys in different circumstances is made to reproduce," this dissolving action of water nourishes the plant and animal life of the planet. As he concludes, "We cannot help returning with new interest to the beautiful phenomenon of its eternal circulation through nature" (*EL*, 1:53, 68, 55, 63).

Water, therefore, most nearly exemplifies Emerson's contention that "the axioms of geometry and of mechanics only translate the laws of ethics." In its fluid and ever-changing state, it exemplifies the ideal condition of both nature and of the soul. In its ability to dissolve and rearrange the elements it contacts, it exemplifies the ideal of unity in diversity, which was a central moral axiom for Emerson. And in the sustenance of organic life which is its product, it metaphorically demonstrates the organic growth of the soul. Emerson's concluding remark in the lecture is well founded when all of these symbolic properties of water are taken into account: "It may exalt our highest sentiments to see the same particle in every step of this ceaseless revolution serving the life, the order, the happiness of the Universe" (*EL*, 1:25, 68). It is not surprising, in fact, to hear him describe an experience of God, some two years later, by saying, "The currents of the Universal Being circulate through me" (*CW*, 1:10).

The moral lesson that Emerson is beginning to see emerge from nature is one that he does not explicitly state until the end of *Nature*. When we correctly perceive that the creation is "fluid," we then know that its dynamic quality reflects the dynamic quality of the soul. The admonition "Build, therefore, your own world" (*CW*, 1:45) stresses not only the quality of self-reliance, but that of ongoing spiritual growth and expansion, of self-culture, as well. If the truth of nature is her progressive development for the culture of man, the moral truth to be drawn from that is the use of nature for the willed continuance of that process of self-cultivation.

The reader of the first three of Emerson's science lectures will be struck by the significant change of tone in the fourth and last, "The Naturalist." There are, of course, many obvious similarities to the first three—the same emphasis on the levels of usefulness of the study of nature and the same quality of awed devotion to natural beauty—but there is a note of skepticism about science which is not apparent in the earlier lectures. Quite early in the discourse, Emerson voices this skepticism in the following terms: "But the question occurs to a man mainly engaged in far different pursuits whether it is wise to embark at all in a pursuit in which it is plain he must content himself with quite superficial knowledge; whether it is no waste of time to study a new and tedious classification" (*EL*, 1:70). Although the passage is in the third person, there is little doubt that the "man mainly engaged in far different pursuits" is Emerson himself, who, almost a year after his visit to Paris, is coming to a recognition that his command of science will remain "superficial," and that further pursuit of the "tedious classification" could well be a "waste of time."

It should be remembered that the year 1834 is a significant one for Emerson's development of another calling, that of the poet, and this second calling, broadly defined, is surely the "far different pursuit" in which he now finds himself engaged.[18] But while the competing demands of this other activity can explain in part Emerson's change in attitude toward science, they cannot fully explain the note of warning sounded in the essay, best expressed in his remark that "we are not only to have the aids of Science but we are to recur to Nature to guard us from the evils of Science" (*EL*, 1:76). What lies behind such a statement is Emerson's personal investigation not only of scientific results, but of the method of scientific classification. His rejection of that method as a mode of work for himself is a revealing episode in his search for vocation and marks his emergence from his year-long flirtation with the exact sciences as a chosen form of intellectual work.

In the spring of 1834, Emerson began to dabble in botanizing and plant classification in the woods around Concord, noting in the midst of these activities that "Nat. Hist gives *body* to our knowledge. No man can spare a fact he knows" (*JMN*, 4:282). This Thoreauvian sentiment, though short-lived in actual practice for Emerson, was a sincere experiment in carrying out the full implications of his developing theories of nature. But Emerson lacked the patience and temperament of a true scientific naturalist, and began to find that the process of plant classification did not satisfy his need for a comprehensive understanding of nature as a moral entity. The detail of classification seemed to him to obscure the larger goal of philosophical understanding, and while he continued to respect the value and necessity of classification, he realized that it was not a role for him. A journal entry of June 1834 marks the end of his detour into scientific classification, an end at which he had hinted in "The Naturalist":

Every thing teaches, even dilettantism. The dilettante does not, to be sure, learn anything of botany by playing with his microscope & with the terminology of plants but he learns what dilettantism is; he distinguishes between what he knows & what he affects to know & through some pain & self accusation he is attaining to things themselves.   [*JMN,* 4:297]

Again, Emerson is putting frank self-analysis in impersonal terms, indicating that he has gained enough distance from the "pain and self accusation" of his superficial career as a natural scientist to see its place in his own development. "The Naturalist," which was delivered to the same group that heard his first excited lecture after his return from Europe, is the public testimony that corresponds to this private admission that his abilities and inclinations are not suited for the life of a scientist.

That Emerson was able to abandon the pursuit of science, yet maintain his commitment to natural philosophy, is in part attributable to the influence at this period of Goethe, who offered him an example of the natural scientist somewhat more poetic than that of the Paris naturalists. "The Naturalist" is filled with references to Goethe, whom Emerson sees as a figure of great enough vision to know and use the tools of science as a means to the larger pursuit of truth.[19] The moral drawn from Goethe's example is that the student's mind should be "in a natural, healthful, & progressive state," so that "in the midst of his most minute dissection" he will "not lose sight of the place & relations of the subject" (*JMN,* 4:288). Again the emphasis is on progress and perspective, and the two ideas are clearly related: if one loses the larger perspective, the study of nature loses its progressive quality, becoming dead and confining. In "The Naturalist," this notion becomes a plea for the proper proportion of means and ends: "The necessity of nomenclature, of minute physiological research, of the retort, the scalpel, and the scales, is incontestable. But there is no danger of its being underestimated. We only wish to insist upon their being considered as *Means"* (*EL,* 1:80).

The larger end toward which those means should be directed is indicated in a journal entry of May 1834: "We have no Theory of animated Nature. When we have, it will be itself the true Classification" (*JMN,* 4:288–89). Emerson's "Theory of animated Nature" is the clearest statement of his sense that "the ethics of the creation" are to be found in the dynamic quality of nature—a quality which classification pursues, but which is finally available through a unified vision that transcends the divisions pursued by science. "Integrate the particulars" (*JMN*, 4:288) is his advice to the naturalist, for the act of integration will serve as a progressive act as well, since the notions of unity and progress are inseparable in the larger view of nature. Emerson's realization of the moral possibilities of his theory of animated nature is underscored in the concluding words of "The Naturalist":[20] "No truth can be more self evident than that the highest state of man, physical, intellectual, and moral, can only coexist with a perfect Theory of Animated Nature" (*EL*, 1:83). Without a vision of nature's dynamism, we lose our vision of the dynamism of the soul, and thus our sense of human potential. Nature's ability to reflect man's moral nature "as face to face in a glass" has its most important implications in the shared progressive quality of both. By the time Emerson had worked through the last of his lectures on science, this idea was clear to him. Its origin we have seen in the search for fundamental ethical lessons available in nature, whose roots were in the questions posed by natural theology and whose development was fundamentally altered by Emerson's visit to Paris. Emerson would not fully formulate his own theory of animated nature until the final chapter of *Nature*, when his Orphic poet would sing of nature's fluidity and apply the lesson to a vision of the growth of the soul. But the story of Emerson's experience in Paris, and his emergence from that experience, explains why an Orphic poet, and not a natural scientist, is the hero of *Nature*.

Nature and Self-Culture

The importance of Emerson's *Nature*, both to his own development and to the history of American literature, has been widely recognized. Kenneth W. Cameron's *Emerson the Essayist* convincingly demonstrates its place in several important traditions of Western thought. Whicher calls the book Emerson's "most sustained and serious attempt to formulate his philosophical and religious position," and Bishop calls it simply "our primal book." Richard P.

Adams, even though he finds it "fundamentally unsatisfactory," notes that it was important to Emerson himself, "a clearing up and clearing away of Emerson's accounts with his teachers and his own journals to that point."[21]

The foregoing chapters have suggested how various those journal accounts were, and almost a half-century of criticism has established the enormity, and subtlety, of Emerson's debt to his many teachers. But it is worth noting that the most direct, and most fruitful, line of development behind *Nature* can be found in Emerson's inquiries into natural science, particularly as those inquiries had a moral end. In this sense, *Nature* is also central to Emerson's developing philosophy of self-culture, for it is an exposition of the role which the natural world plays in the process of self-culture. But by the end of the work, we have also learned something about that process itself, something which Emerson implies, but does not directly state: it is a process without a final product. At no single point can the development of the soul be regarded as complete, for the final moral lesson of a perpetually changing nature is that of a perpetually changing soul.

Nature represents a break from the oratorical pattern of Emerson's career in that it was the first of his literary productions, aside from poems, which was not meant to be delivered orally. But its essential continuity with the theological and semitheological character of his previous works can be noted in its affinities to the tradition of devotional literature. A journal entry of March 1836, a few months before the publication of *Nature*, reveals much about Emerson's state of mind during this period:

I thought yesterday morning of the sweetness of that fragrant piety which is almost departed out of the world, which makes the genius of A-Kempis, Scougal, Herbert, Jeremy Taylor. It is a beautiful mean[,] equidistant from the hard sour iron Puritan on one side, & the empty negation of the Unitarian on the other.   [*JMN*, 5:144–45]

The entry does reveal Emerson's impatience with the two religious traditions closest to him at the time, but it is also a significant indication that he had not lost admiration for the devotionalist tradition of Christian literature, for Thomas à Kempis, Henry Scougal, and Jeremy Taylor all distinguished themselves as writers of devotional manuals, and George Herbert expressed a devotionalist perspective in much of his poetry.[22] But even among the Unitarians, Emerson had a modern example of a devotional manual in Ware's *On the Formation of the Christian Character.* This latter work, which Howe calls an "heir of this long tradition" of "devotional manuals,"[23] is evidence that the devotionalist tradition could survive the changes of liberal theology. *Nature* is not a book which can or should be narrowly classified, and to argue for its heritage in devotionalist literature is not to argue that this one approach exhausts its generic or philosophical implications. *Nature* does, however, reveal a certain coherence from this devotionalist perspective, in that it places Emerson's concern with practical morality in the forefront.

Devotional literature can be distinguished by its emphasis on practical morality, its dedication to the methods for the day-to-day living of the religious life. In her study of the devotional literature of seventeenth-century England, Helen White stresses this characteristic of the devotional manual, noting that the book of devotion "concentrates its resources on the realization of that pattern of life which all religious effort strives to commend."[24] Though devotional literature may not necessarily ignore theological or philosophical controversy, it places such controversy in the secondary role of supporting the more important quest for fulfillment in the moral life. That this is Emerson's major concern in *Nature* is often overshadowed by the book's striking philosophy, but *Nature* begins by asking what is at bottom a moral rather than a philosophical question: "To what end is nature?" (*CW,* 1:7). The moral nature of the question is confirmed by the answer, which Emerson reaches in the chapter "Discipline": "This ethical character so penetrates the bone and marrow of nature, as to seem the end for which it was made" (*CW,* 1:26).

The structure of *Nature* can be seen to revolve around Emerson's attempt to answer that early question, "To what end is nature?" His initial attempt to formulate the answer comes in the first chapter, "Nature," which contains a direct and vivid account of man's actual experience of the natural world. Emerson records such a moment most memorably in his description of the "transparent eye-ball" experience: "Standing on the bare ground,—my head bathed by the blithe air, and uplifted into infinite space,—all mean egotism vanishes. I become a transparent eye-ball. I am nothing. I see all. The currents of the Universal Being circulate through me; I am part or particle of God" (*CW,* 1:10). The passage has drawn both censure and praise for its mysticism, and has provoked both delight and scorn for its literary qualities. Caricatured memorably by Christopher Pearse Cranch, it is also rarely forgotten by commentators on *Nature.* [25] While the passage deserves much attention, it is in fact only one part of a larger statement in the "Nature" chapter of man's experience of the natural world. It would perhaps be more accurate to say man's "experiences" of the natural world, because this occurrence is only one of several examples recorded in the chapter. Emerson begins by mentioning the stars, stating that the "rays that come from those heavenly worlds" give man "the perpetual presence of the sublime." He then speaks of "the flowers, the animals, the mountains" which reflect "all the wisdom of his best hour"; of the "charming landscape which I saw this morning"; of the "perfect exhilaration" felt in crossing "a bare common"; of "the distant line of the horizon" in which "man beholds somewhat as beautiful as his own nature"; of the "waving of the boughs in the storm" which "takes me by surprise, and yet is not unknown"; and finally of "a kind of contempt of the landscape felt by him who has just lost by death a dear friend." These experiences are varied in kind and intensity, and further differentiated by Emerson's varying use of the first or third person to recount them. In general, as intensity and meaning increase, he expresses himself in the more personal terms. We might even surmise that his use of the third person to describe "man laboring under calamity," who has "just lost by death a dear friend," is a masking device for his own grief over one of the several deaths that had touched him deeply. In this variety of natural occurrences, the "transparent eye-ball" does stand out both for its intensity and richness of implication, but it should not blind the reader to the profusion of other experiences, all of which contribute to the conclusion that "every hour and season yields its tribute of delight; for every hour and change corresponds to and authorizes a different state of the mind" (*CW,* 1:8–11, 9).

Emerson's portrayal of the sensation of becoming "part or particle of God" amidst this number of other natural experiences actually serves to heighten its impact. Though Bishop refers to "the notorious eyeball sentence" as a "parody" of Emerson's earlier feeling of exhilaration while crossing the common, it is in fact a totally different order of experience. The very range of reactions to nature which is presented in the paragraph suggests that, contrary to Bishop's argument, Emerson is not using "more or less synonymous ways of saying 'the same thing.' "[26] The transparent eyeball experience is unique and important precisely for the reasons Bishop censures it: its language, tone, and voice set it apart from the more low-keyed responses to nature elsewhere in the chapter. The mixed feeling of fear and gladness in the earlier description of crossing the common may help to prepare the description of the transparent eyeball experience, and we might speculate that the "fear" he speaks of in the earlier passage is related to the loss of ego depicted in the transparent eyeball passage. But what sets the latter experience apart is that Emerson describes it as an experience not only of nature, but of God. Individual personality vanishes momentarily in it and divinity is present. The "low and partial self," which he defined in "The Genuine Man" and now calls "mean egotism," gives way totally to the "transparent" or universal self. His use of the word "transparent" carries the implications of a mystical fusion of the self into a divine, all-pervasive unity.

Such an experience has enormous implications for Emerson's growing concern with the effort at self-culture. Culture's essential aim is to realize fully the divinity in human nature; and in the experience he describes, momentarily at least, that aim was fulfilled. In a sense, therefore, the transparent eyeball passage, which is properly described as mystical in its portrayal of the merger of the individual personality with the divine, can be regarded as the end of culture. Yet the strategy of *Nature* is to transform this experience from an end in itself to a means for the continued moral growth of the soul. One important reason for this is obvious: such experiences are both rare and unwilled. Emerson cautions that "it is necessary to use these pleasures with great temperance," going on to add that "nature is not always tricked in holiday attire" (*CW*, 1:10). Temperance is indeed necessary, primarily because we have little choice in the matter. The "harmony" of man and nature is not available at will, and must serve instead as an inspiration to a slower and more deliberate process of moral cultivation. Emerson tempers his mysticism, therefore, not because he finds it unsatisfactory or dangerous, but for the very practical reason that such occurrences are a less-than-dependable means for maintaining the connection between man and God, and man and nature. *Nature* thus begins with an experience of divinity, and devotes itself to recovering the results of that experience. The experience itself has come and may come again; but its results, the loss of man's "mean egotism" and the attainment of oneness with God, can be regained through the right use of nature—what Emerson will eventually call the use of nature as "discipline."

The structure of *Nature* is therefore a systematic demonstration of the moral uses of nature, which Emerson presents as an ascending scale of Commodity, Beauty, Language, and Discipline. It should be noted at the outset that throughout this ascending scale of value, nature is constant. Her increasing value is the product of an increasingly penetrating moral vision, an escalation of perception which Emerson was beginning to work through in his discussions of the "educated eye" of the naturalist in the lectures on science. Emerson precedes his discussion of the first level of the ascending scale, "Commodity," by reminding the reader that "nature always wears the colors of the spirit" (*CW*, 1:10), and follows the discussion of the highest level on the scale, "Discipline," with the well-known chapter "Idealism." His purpose, of course, is to remind us that it is mind and not nature that is ascending in power—to make it clear that nature is the object of perception, but that perception itself is the issue to be addressed. The chapter "Idealism" has a larger purpose as well, as we shall see later, but to understand that purpose we must first examine the ascending moral uses of nature.

Emerson treats "Commodity" most briefly among the uses of nature, but even this limited function, he argues, is a source of wonder and praise when one considers "this zodiac of lights, this tent of dropping clouds, this striped coat of climates, this fourfold year." He speaks of commodity, but his language foreshadows "Beauty," the next use of nature, and this pattern of foreshadowing is repeated in each of the four ascending uses. Beauty, which he explains as a product of the combination of man's creative perception and his active will, is "the mark God sets upon virtue." Best exemplified in the noble or heroic act, it is a form of beauty which refers back to the "work" of man mentioned in "Commodity" and which looks forward to the fuller discussion of moral action in "Discipline." Man's sense of the beauty of a noble action is dependent upon a sense of congruence with nature, which is the subject of "Language." The relation between word and fact which begins that chapter is, for Emerson, an instance of a "relation between mind and matter" which "stands in the will of God." This "miracle" of connection, when fully realized, means that "the universe becomes transparent, and the light of higher laws than its own, shines through it" (*CW,* 1:11, 15, 22). Again, transparency is Emerson's metaphor for the merging of the individual into the universal, but in this case it is nature, not man, which is termed "transparent." When read in conjunction with the transparent eyeball passage, this assertion of nature's transparency reaffirms the correspondence of man and nature: each in combination with the other can ultimately merge into the higher unity denoted by "Reason."

Even this perception of unity, however, is not the ultimate level in the ascending scale of nature's uses, though it foreshadows nature's ultimate end, discipline. As Emerson notes, the use of nature as discipline "includes the preceding uses, as parts of itself" (*CW,* 1:23), and as the chapter "Discipline" explains, discipline includes those preceding uses by translating them into moral action. In this chapter, the devotional character of *Nature* is clearest, for it is here that philosophy is subsumed under the category of practical morality.

Emerson divides his presentation of this morality into two parts, which can be thought of as man's capacity for virtue and the nature of that virtue. The "will" is central to the discussion of man's capacity for virtue, for "the exercise of the Will or the lesson of power is taught in every event." Nature's correspondence to spirit provides this "lesson of power," for if nature can be subsumed under the will of man, so can spirit. Just as man can prosper physically through his dominance of nature, he can grow morally through exercising his will in the spiritual world. But his exercise of will can take place only within limits; even will conforms to the laws of nature, just as it must to the laws of spirit, for though nature is "thoroughly mediate," she also "pardons no mistakes." Emerson's position is finally paradoxical: the highest exercise of will is the one which most closely conforms to natural and spiritual laws. The child, therefore, exhibits a mature will in learning to say " 'thy will be done!' "—an expression of humility which teaches him that he can "conform all facts to his character" (*CW*, 1:24–25).

Not only is man's capacity for virtue proven by his ability to merge his will with a universal will, but that same ability also indicates the nature of virtue, and is thus the discipline taught by nature. Human morality, therefore, consists of acting from universal rather than particular or selfish motives. This is no new idea for Emerson; his earlier distinction between the partial and the whole self in "The Genuine Man" makes much the same point. But it has greater impact in *Nature* because of Emerson's effectiveness in building his discussion of nature's uses to a unified climax. The universal or whole self demonstrably includes the whole of nature as Emerson completes his view of the ascending uses of nature. His analysis of human morality carries with it a confirmation of the morality of the universe: "The moral law lies at the centre of nature and radiates to the circumference. It is the pith and marrow of every substance, every relation, and every process. All things with which we deal, preach to us." The conclusion Emerson draws from this realization that the moral law is all pervasive is a familiar one: "The Unity of Nature, —the Unity in Variety,—. . . meets us everywhere" (*CW*, 1:26, 27). Unity can thus be identified as both the object of the ascending moral perception and the method of that perception.

What follows this discussion of the final and most important use of nature is Emerson's chapter "Idealism," a complex and sometimes misunderstood section of the book. What is the purpose, after all, of concluding a detailed analysis of the uses of nature by questioning its independent existence? Is this not, as one early reviewer argued, mere contradiction? Or can it be explained, as Porte has suggested, as proof of Emerson's skepticism about the physical?[27] The content of Emerson's discussion of idealism, and its placement in *Nature* as well, can be better understood by seeing it as part of a recapitulation of the transparent eyeball experience with which *Nature* began. In that instance, the experience of unity, the merging of man and nature in God, was expressed not only by denying the self—"I am nothing"—but by positing a larger self that contains within it all value. The result of such an experience, as Emerson puts it, is that "the name of the nearest friend sounds then foreign and accidental. To be brothers, to be acquaintances,—master or servant, is then a trifle and a disturbance" (*CW*, 1:10). Emerson's comment is not a denial of the value of friendship or brotherhood, but an assertion that the whole or universal self transcends the value of even the dearest of social relations, for by definition, the universal self contains all value. The "Idealism" chapter takes the same attitude toward outward nature as is taken toward social relations in the "Nature" chapter. The merging of the self into God made possible through discipline also gives that self ultimate value. The mind functioning on the level of discipline can therefore be said to contain all value and meaning, even to the extent of relegating nature to a part of itself. This is not to deny the value of nature, but rather to make that value part of the larger value of the self.

Nature's importance, therefore, is her contribution to the process of culture, a process which continually places the perception of spiritual truth above the perception of the appearance of the material world:

Culture inverts the vulgar views of nature, and brings the mind to call that apparent, which it uses to call real, and that real, which it uses to call visionary. Children, it is true, believe in the external world. The belief that it appears only, is an afterthought, but with culture, this faith will as surely arise on the mind as did the first. [*CW*, 1:36]

It is what Emerson calls the "vulgar view" of nature that can be overcome by culture. Indeed, culture can transform man's belief that truth lies in appearance to a higher belief that truth lies in the "visionary" realm. This visionary reality was the basis of the transparent eyeball experience, and Emerson argues that culture, the expansion of the soul, can help one to regain that sense of higher reality. Just as the mysticism of the transparent eyeball experience made the self perceive its unity with God, culture can expand the perceptions as well, revealing that the soul is universal.

This universal soul, revealed in the mysticism of the transparent eyeball experience and reconstructed in moral terms in the ascending scale of nature's uses, is the final goal of the process of self-culture. Faced with an essentially unreliable access to that self through passive mystical experience alone, Emerson makes it his underlying purpose in *Nature* to translate his growing idealism into a formula for practical morality that will make that self available at will. His final realization in the book, however, is that such a state of the soul is "progressive," and thus that he has no static goal to achieve. The insistence that "matter is a phenomenon" in the chapter "Spirit" and the Orphic poet's closing pronouncement that "nature is not fixed but fluid" (*CW*, 1:37, 44) are the indicators of Emerson's realization that the transparent soul is itself an ever-changing phenomenon. For nature, in revealing her own "progressive" character, shows us that we too must be progressive in our moral life. This realization of the dynamism of the soul, which manifests itself in Emerson's lecturing after *Nature*, results in a view of culture not as a process of reaching the goal of the moral life, but as a process which itself is the moral life. Emerson's sense of the moral life thus becomes like the vision of the ever-progressive heaven of his Unitarian predecessors, and like them he finds that vision satisfying, at least in 1836.

V

The Humanist

History and the Universal Man

Even while Emerson was contemplating the book on "Natural Ethics" that would become *Nature* (*L*, 1:447), he was in the midst of preparing a series of lectures on English authors, and he had completed, earlier that year, lectures on biography which included sketches of several famous men. His interests in natural history and in human biography, both of which had roots, as we have seen, in his preaching, were now beginning to deepen in his lecture career; the two sets of interests, though in some senses antithetical to each other, added balance and focus to one another. If human history had as its goal the process of moral culture, that process could be achieved only through nature; and similarly, if nature was the means to human culture, her end was to be found in human action and human history. Thus, in the midst of his intense biological investigations in 1834, he noted, in a passage that would later be revised in *Nature:* "Natural history by itself has no value; it is like a single sex. But marry it to human history, & it is poetry" (*JMN*, 4:311; *CW*, 1:19). The impulse that led Emerson to condemn his age for being "retrospective" and for groping in the "dry bones of the past" (*CW*, 1:7) was therefore balanced by an impulse which led him to wide-ranging historical studies.

While the influential *Nature* tends to dominate our perspective of Emerson's work in the middle 1830s, we should not overlook his enormous amount of biographical and historical writing in this period. In 1835 Emerson delivered not only the "Biography" and "English Literature" lectures, but also the "Historical Discourse" on Concord; in 1836 he began the series entitled "The Philosophy of History." His fast pace of work was due in large part to his remarriage and settlement in Concord, and as Leonard Neufeldt has argued, it reflected his determined entry into his literary vocation.[1] But the content of that work indicates that his new vocation did not alter his focus on self-culture.

The pattern which we saw in the formulation of *Nature* was repeated in the biographical and historical writings of 1835 and 1836. Just as Emerson moved from an abstract theory of nature during his ministry to an actual immersion in natural history later, he moved from the theory of a "genuine" or "universal" man developed in his ministry to an actual appraisal of the men of the past. Though he grounded his speculations in historical research, he was still formulating a theory of the human ideal, using historical example to extend and confirm that theory.

His consciousness of the link between human history and his human ideal was made clear in an 1834 journal entry which begins with the question, "What is it that interests us in biography?" Great figures of history interest us because of the "silent comparison between the intellectual & moral endowments portrayed & those of which we are conscious." Such a comparison exhibits the same working of the moral sense that we saw Emerson describe in his sermons. He confirms the similarity by adding that, "as far as we accord with his judgment, we take the picture for a standard Man, and so let every line accuse or approve our own ways of thinking & living by comparison" (*JMN*, 4:256). This answer formulates Emerson's version of didactic historiography based upon the use of biographical exempla; the aim of moral culture remains the same.

The change from the abstract human ideal of the sermons to one based, at least in part, on biographical fact posed a new problem which Emerson struggled to resolve in the 1835–36 period. The struggle culminated finally in his "Philosophy of History" lectures (1836–37) and the closely related "American Scholar" (1837). The problem lay in the conflict between the historical progressivism embodied in his lecturing on science and the underlying assumption of his theory of biography, that we can turn to the past for a moral ideal. From one perspective, Emerson saw the possibility of the coming of a "brighter age"; yet he simultaneously rebelled against the drift of modern society and turned to the great men of the past as an antidote to it. He began to find a solution to this dichotomy when he inquired into the moral character of history. He was committed to the proposition that "history taken together is as severely moral in its teaching as the straitest religious sect" (*JMN*, 5:12), but he also realized the moral limitations which history revealed in even the greatest persons. "The world looks poor & mean so long as I think only of its great men; most of them of spotted reputation," he noted in 1834. But the saving fact of the situation is that these men, if they are admirable, "reflect the mind of all mankind." It is not the great man himself, therefore, who makes history moral, but rather the idea he embodies: "Each fine genius that appears is already predicted in our constitution inasmuch as he only makes apparent shades of thought in us of which we hitherto knew not (or actualizes an idea)" (*JMN*, 4:353). The shift in emphasis which this passage implies, from the great men of the past to the mind of the individual who encounters them now, begins the solution to the dichotomy of past morality and future progress which Emerson faced. The importance of the historical character or event lies in the idea it embodies, but that idea manifests itself now only in the mind of the student of history. Emerson needed to make only one more closely related intellectual move to complete a philosophy of history which was thoroughly idealistic.

He was beginning to take this step in January 1835: "The great value of Biography consists in the perfect sympathy that exists between like minds. Space & time are an absolute nullity to this principle" (*JMN*, 5:11). This doctrine of the likeness of minds, or of the "one Mind," was of course implicit in Emerson's thought from its inception; but largely owing to the combined stimuli of science and history, it was becoming the dominant idea of his thinking in the middle 1830s. The striking opening of *Essays: First Series* (1841) in fact was first recorded in an October 1836 journal entry: "There is one Mind common to all individual men" (*JMN*, 5:222). By this point, Universal Man had become Universal Mind for Emerson, and had become the foundation of his idealist system.

The importance of historical investigation to his idealism is best understood in the context of the preceding discussion of his study of science. Like the scientist, the scholar or historian seeks "the principle which classifies the facts" (*JMN*, 5:117). Like science, history reveals a "correspondent Order" of nature and mind. This correspondence suggests that "the world was made by mind like ours," a conclusion which is confirmed by the three principles history teaches:

1. The presence of Spirit
2. The antecedence of Spirit
3. The humanity of Spirit
[*JMN*, 5:168–69]

The suggestive merger of science and history, the ability to see history as a form of nature, or nature itself as having a history, consolidated two central intellectual claims on Emerson's mind. But one remaining fact needs to be reemphasized. Both science and history finally suggested a "mind *like ours*," or "the humanity of Spirit" (italics mine). Emerson's deepest excursions thus far into science, history, and metaphysics remained moral investigations, whose results were measured by the light they shed on the culture of human nature.

Idealism and Moral Aspiration

Quoting his new friend Carlyle in December 1834, Emerson wrote, "I like well the doctrine 'that every great man, Napoleon himself, is an Idealist[,] a poet with different degrees of Utterance'" (*JMN*, 4:363). As was the case with most of Emerson's widely varied sources, Carlyle seems to have confirmed and articulated what Emerson was moving toward himself. In the "Biography" lectures which began in January 1835, Emerson persistently treats the biographical subjects of his lectures as "idealists," focusing in each case on the particular capacity for moral aspiration that explains their achievement.[2] The mixture of figures—Michelangelo, Luther, Milton, Fox, and Burke—seems at first to be almost a random selection, but the range of Emerson's choice in fact adds force to his argument that a universal element accounts for all human achievement. His label for that element is "the Ideal"; it manifests itself, as he shows here, in actions, and as he later shows in the "English Literature" lectures, in language.

Emerson stresses the "Idealist" in each of the heroes of his "Biography" lectures by constantly pointing to the ways in which the aspiration for moral growth accounts for the pattern of their lives. Michelangelo, "the perfect image of the Artist," was one who "strove to express the Idea of Beauty. This was his nature and vocation. This Idea possessed his soul and determined all his activity" (*EL*, 1:100). Luther's ability to influence the actual lives of men through immaterial or spiritual means was the unique translation and expression of the ideal, and its result, as Emerson stresses, was a moral influence long outliving him. The word "ideal" runs through the lecture "John Milton" like a litany. The perfections Milton's biographers report of him make us suspect they are "ideal" portraits (*EL*, 1:150), but his embodiment of the moral sentiment was so complete that the portraits are borne out. His lifelong concern was with "ideal justice" and "ideal liberty," and his contribution, both to his age and to the nineteenth century, was his perception "of a purer ideal of humanity" and his ability "to raise the idea of Man in the minds of his contemporaries and of posterity" (*EL*, 1:146, 158, 160, 149). But we see Milton's idealism, and are able to define its nature most clearly, in his art, which seeks "to create an ideal world better than the world of experience" (*EL*, 1:162). Idealism is based on the perception, originating in man's moral sentiment, of a better world—indeed, a better race of men—than the actual. The pervasive imagery of light, rather than any verbal repetition, impresses George Fox's idealism on us. The Quaker's "inner light" becomes a symbol for the ideal, "a vital light which when observed by the mind it inhabits, not only fills the mind, but radiates outward upon all near and all remote objects" (*EL*, 1:166).

Even Edmund Burke, the *"philosophical politician,"* can be seen as yet another embodiment of the ideal. The tool of Burke's success was his power as an orator, and oratory was the area in which he exemplified idealism most clearly. Certainly Emerson's longstanding love for that form of expression moved him to include Burke among his subjects, particularly since Burke exemplified the highest form of oratory. Even though Burke rose to eloquence "only rarely" in Emerson's view, his speeches were still "monuments of genius." At his best, he attained "the perfect triumph of the orator which consists in the oneness of his audience" (*EL*, 1:189, 200,

198). The combination of devotion to moral principle, an aspiring vision for humanity, and mastery of a medium through which to realize the ideal made him a hero and an idealist. Idealism, therefore, explains both the influence and the formation of Emerson's hero, signifying an aspiration for the better, a desire for continual moral progress. The "Universal Man" finds objective embodiment in the heroes of history because they lived from ideals and can thus be studied by the biographer from an ideal perspective.

The moral aspiration that accounted for the qualities of greatness Emerson found in historical figures also accounted, in his judgment, for the creation of great literature. In one sense, the creative act itself was moral, whether it took form as literature or as another art form. But the nature of the creative act, and the related principle of form in literature, demanded further exploration, and this exploration led to the "English Literature" lectures of 1835–36.

The theory of organic form, which Emerson began to put forward in these lectures, is well known, although the relation of this aesthetic theory to his philosophy of history has received little attention.[3] Both theories spring from the same root, the doctrine of the one mind. History is, for Emerson, essentially the process of that mind expressing itself in human action, whereas literature is the process of that mind expressing itself in literary form. History, in this sense, is the macrocosmic expression of mind, while literature is its microcosmic expression.

The basis of literary expression is in language, in the act of naming, and here also is the spiritual foundation of literary form. Thus Emerson offers a theory of language early in the series: "All language is a naming of invisible and spiritual things from visible things. The use of natural history is to give us aid in supernatural history. The use of the outer creation is to give us language for the beings and changes of the inward creation." The act of naming thus bridges the gap between spirit and nature, making nature the tool of spirit. But if the source of language is spiritual, so is its end. Thus Emerson argues that "the aim and effort of literature in the largest sense" is "nothing less than to *give voice to the whole of spiritual nature* (*EL*, 1:220, 226). Given this source of language and this purpose for literary expression, the theory of organic form necessarily follows.

The "English Literature" lectures have a format similar to that of the preceding "Biography" series, being composed of biographical and interpretative commentaries on selected authors, arranged in a generally chronological order.[4] Yet Emerson sets the tone for his own researches by commenting on the mistaken notion that literature "is easily to be distributed into epochs by order of time, or into departments by the mere form of the composition." The study of literary history is rather the contemplation of "the striving . . . of the great national mind, now under the opening and progressive force of one Idea, . . . opposed by or blended with another" (EL, 1:231). The equivalence is clear between the pattern of moral aspiration which constitutes the idealism of a great man and the "progressive force of one Idea" out of which literature is born. Emerson's underlying purpose is thus to sketch the progress of the universal mind in its attempts at expression.

The two lectures on Shakespeare are central to this purpose, for Emerson sees him as the author who most nearly approaches the status of universal man: "To analyze the powers of such an individual is to analyze the powers of the human mind." Shakespeare's universality arises from the fact that he "possesses the power of subordinating nature for the purposes of expression beyond all poets," and he thereby most completely fulfills the poet's task of "convert[ing] the solid globe, the land, the sea, the air, the sun, the animals into symbols of thought" (EL, 1:289–92). This process of conversion, based, as we noted earlier, on the power of language to bridge the natural and the spiritual, is the means by which the "one Idea" is manifest. While from one perspective this is an aesthetic process, it is ultimately a religious one; its final goal is the "vision of all being we call Reason," a term which Emerson defines further: "We speak of it generally as the mind's Eye. It is the Reason which affirms the laws of moral nature and thereby raises us to a region above the intellect" (EL, 1:296–97). If it is hard to distinguish between Emerson's descriptions of spiritual enlightenment and creative artistry, the reason is that, for him, they are distinctions without a difference. As he comments in his working notes for the lectures, literature is "the Second Religion" (JMN, 12:49).

If the creation of literature is directed by the force of a universal idea seeking expression, then the form of expression must also follow that idea. The form of a work will unfold, in other words, from its inner logic, not from any standards imposed from without. It is "false doctrine" to believe that there is "something else in style than the transparent medium through which I should see new and good thoughts" (*EL*, 1:215). There is an appropriate similarity between the "transparent" style of good literature, and the human feeling of "transparency" Emerson associates with moments of inspiration. He sees this same facility as allowing content to dictate form in Shakespeare's blank verse. Commenting on the difficulty of writing such verse in English, Emerson sees most of it as "mere metrical prose" which is "turned laboriously by cutting off syllables and substituting worse words, into verse." In contrast, we sense that Shakespeare's thought "first took body in this melodious form, that the sentence was born Poetry" (*EL*, 1:308). The difference lies in the sense we have of a structure dictated by inner necessity rather than outer convention.

Despite the close connection he posits between creativity and religious vision, and the emphasis he lays on inspiration as an artistic tool, Emerson rejects the idea that Shakespeare's poems, or any great art, are "rhapsodies cast forth at a heat." They are rather the result of "the union of many parts each of which came solitary and slowly into the mind." Composition, the unification of individual parts, is therefore essential to the aesthetic process, but even composition is a natural process, "the most powerful secret of Nature's workmanship." As an example, Emerson turns to his beloved art of oratory. The orator's creation may seem to be the most spontaneous of all forms of art, but in fact, "every link in this living chain he found separate: one ten years ago; one last week; some in his father's house or at his first school; some of them by his losses; some in his sick bed; some through his crimes" (*EL*, 1:317, 318). Emerson's explanation of the orator's skill, which is an analogue for all literary and artistic creation, reflects his consciousness of his own developing practice as an artist. His process of daily journal keeping, and of indexing and organizing journal material into lectures, and then essays, served a double purpose. The moment of insight was preserved, so that the connection of the individual and the universal mind was maintained, while the demand for unity, implied by the concept of the one mind, was satisfied through careful composition.

"The Philosophy of History"

Nature was the culmination of Emerson's scientific thinking, as we saw in the preceding chapter, and was also a further extension of the ideas of language and literary expression he offered in the "English Literature" series (see, for example, *EL*, 1:220, 289–90). Both of those themes, as well as the central idea of the expression of the one mind in history, are woven into the lecture series Emerson began just after the publication of *Nature*, "The Philosophy of History." His working notes for the series confirm that the idea of a unified world soul or spirit was still his dominant concern:

> There is one soul
> It is related to the world
> Art is its action thereon
> Science finds its method
> Literature is its record
> Religion is the emotion of reverence it inspires
> Ethics is the Soul illustrated in human life
> Society is the finding of this soul by individuals in each other
> Trades are the learning the soul in nature by labor
> Politics is the activity of the soul illustrated in power
> Manners are silent & mediate expressions of Soul
> [*JMN*, 12:163; see also *EL*, 2:181]

With some minor rearrangements and additions, this is the outline of the lecture series as Emerson presented it. What is notable is the comprehensiveness of the series. Here Emerson would make the first of several attempts over the next years to present a unified and comprehensive philosophical program. We may balk at calling the series systematic, remembering the commonly accepted wisdom about Emerson's not being a "systematic" thinker. But as the publication of the lectures of the late 1830s demonstrates, he was moving steadily toward a synthesis of his ideas in one unified philosophical statement. Each of the lecture series, beginning with "The Philosophy of History," has the quality of comprehensiveness and ultimately lends that quality to *Essays: First Series.*

Emerson's journal entries and working notebooks for the series suggest a clear sense of direction, and the result is a series much more tightly knit than has been recognized. Rusk, in fact, sees the lectures merely as a loose collection of explorations of a theme, and portrays Emerson as the developing poet whose mind could not be bounded by dry logic and systematic reasoning. Such a description does not do justice to "The Philosophy of History." While not rigidly systematic, the lectures are not "too poetical to submit to logic" (*Life*, p. 247), and they do reveal a structure very closely related to their argument. It is, in fact, through careful attention to the structure of the lectures that we can understand them thematically.

The twelve lectures in the series fall into two large groups of six each, dividing after the sixth lecture, "Religion." These groups present different views of the same process of spirit expressing itself in history. The first six lectures represent the major means of expression available to the individual, and thus deal with the process of history from the perspective of the individual. Science, fine and useful arts, literature, politics, and most importantly, religion are the vehicles through which the individual can act universally, participating in the ongoing expression of the one mind. The last six lectures take the perspective of society as a whole regarding these forms of expression. Emerson's major concern in these lectures is to present the social manifestations of human expression, that is, to see individual expression as it contributes to existing social forms and processes. All the forms of society—professions, manners, ethics, political reform, and social intercourse itself—are based upon the prior need of the individual to find a form of expression that will actualize the generic soul within him.

It is no accident, therefore, that the first group of lectures ends with "Religion," the individual's highest and most universal form of expression. Similarly, the second group, and the series as a whole, concludes with "The Individual," the most important manifestation of spirit in society. A paradoxical tension is thus established in the series: the first half, devoted to means of individual expression, culminates in "Religion," which demands the extinction of the individual in the universal; the second half, devoted to the social forms created through expression, culminates in the individual. Thus, in "Religion," Emerson argues that "the antagonist nature to this Universal mind is the Individual, the Personal"; the result is "the perpetual conflict between the dictate of this Universal mind and the present wishes and interests of particular persons" (*EL*, 2:84). But in "The Individual," he can confidently assert that "the best work of society is the formation of the Individual" (*EL*, 2:174). The apparent paradox is the result of the different perspectives taken in the two halves of the lectures, and is ultimately resolved in Emerson's familiar distinction between the private and the universal self. "The Philosophy of History" leaves us with a view of the individual whose most important form of expression lies in the surrender of self.

The first group of lectures can be seen as analyses of forms of expression, in which expression is portrayed as a process of the return of the individual to an underlying unity. Scientific classification, which is discussed in "Humanity of Science," ultimately reveals itself to be a searching for ever larger and more comprehensive classifications for known facts—a process, in other words, of reaching from discrete facts to a unified law. The reluctance "to make many classes or to suppose many causes," the tendency to reduce all phenomena "to a few laws, to one law," is labeled "the tyrannical instinct of the mind." Emerson's recent immersion in scientific classification is of course the basis of this insight, but he sees in it a law of nature also, and thus a fundamental principle for all human intellectual expression. The tendency toward unity in the mind is matched by "a parallel unity" in nature "which corresponds to this unity in the mind, and makes it available" (*EL*, 2:23, 25).

With this basis established in "Humanity of Science," Emerson goes on to show that other forms of thought and expression, various though they may be, also resolve themselves into expressions of unity. The paired lectures "Art" and "Literature" are concerned with forms of expression which Emerson portrays as mirror opposites: "Whilst Art delights in carrying a thought into action, Literature is the conversion of action into thought." Yet different though they may be in this respect, both gain their power through their ability to bring together artist and audience, or author and reader. Both literature and art, at their best, provide the medium through which the creator and the perceiver can participate in the one mind being expressed, so that the poet or writer becomes an "organ" of "the divine Spirit" (*EL*, 2:55, 65).

If other forms of expression rely upon an individual surrender to unity, religion consists entirely of such a surrender and thus underlies all expression. Religion is the manifestation of the unifying spirit within man, universally present in all men: "Of this pure Nature within him every man is at some time sensible. Language cannot paint it with his colors; it is too subtle. It is undefinable; immeasurable, but we see plainly how it lies all around us. We see plainly that all spiritual being is in man." It is this spiritual presence in man which, as "the Universal Mind," wars against "private benefit" or "petty advantage" to create "the moral discipline of life." When the private self is surrendered, and virtue is the result, religion manifests itself as "the accompanying emotion, the emotion of reverence which the presence of the Universal mind always excites in the individual" (*EL*, 2:85, 84).

The fact that religion underlies each of the forms of expression Emerson discusses reminds us that expression is a means of self-culture. Although we might at first think the perceiver of a work of art, or the reader of literature, to be the one pursuing cultivation, the creator of such art, as the expresser of the universal mind, is similarly engaged in self-cultivation. Emerson's continuing insistence that self-culture is really Self-culture, that the formation of the soul necessitates a surrender to the generic soul, can thus be seen in his analyses of human expression. The equation of expression with cultivation is important to his theory of history, and suggests the close association of history and culture that made "Human Culture" the topic of his next series of lectures.

Paradoxically, when Emerson focuses upon the individual and his tools of expression, as in the first six lectures, the result is a stress upon the negation of the individual. But when he begins to examine society, it is the individual who is constantly present. His theory of society begins, however, with the assertion that "it is this generic nature common to all the individuals which makes society possible." What the lens of society allows us to see is that "beside this generic nature every man has an individual nature." The most fundamental expression of that individual nature is the ethical life, described as "the law whereof all history is but illustration" (*EL*, 2:99–100, 144). Though it is the law of history, though it underlies the very nature of existence, the central task of a code of ethics is to reveal to us the individual. So closely associated is the law of history with the individual that "Self-Trust" emerges as "the one maxim which makes the whole Ethics of the Mind." By self-trust, Emerson means "a perception that the mind common to the Universe is disclosed to the individual through his own nature" (*EL*, 2:151). Such a definition does not minimize the importance of the universal mind, but it emphasizes the importance of the individual in the workings of that mind.

The final lecture in "The Philosophy of History" is primarily concerned with refining this doctrine of individualism by stressing that "all history exists for the Individual." The idea, which would also serve as the cornerstone of the "Human Culture" lectures, was that of the "progress" of the individual: "I look therefore at the result of all the great agencies we have looked at in turn to be the education of the observer—of the private man. He takes them all up in his progress into himself." Such individual progress is especially important when we realize that it is not merely one form of progress —it is the only real progress possible. The final point to be made, therefore, in his analysis of society, is that "progress is not for society. Progress belongs to the Individual" (*EL*, 2:173–76).

Such a realization bridges the apparent gap between Emerson's faith in the "progressive" and his sense of the failings of society. "We are confounded," he notes, "by the discord between our theory and the actual world" (*EL*, 2:176), but the discord is the result of trying to make a doctrine for the individual into a doctrine for society. The theory which attributes growth or progress to the individual, a doctrine which would find its fullest statement in "Human Culture," will make no claims about the progress of society. Culture, therefore, stands as the theory which can preserve the possibility of progress, even in the face of the falsity and injustice of all human societies.

Culture, Society, and the Scholar

"The Philosophy of History" might have ended Emerson's writing on man in society, for the time being, had he not, on June 22, 1837, received a belated invitation to deliver the Phi Beta Kappa Oration

at Harvard the following August. "The American Scholar," which
he called "the topic which not only usage, but the nature of our
association, seem to prescribe to this day" (*CW*, 1:52), became
Emerson's "most famous speech."[5] Illness, business matters, and a
lack of inspiration seem to have postponed work on the address
through much of the summer, and three weeks before delivering it,
Emerson complained to his brother William, "We cannot get any
word from Olympus" for the address (*L*, 2:94). In fact, the word he
was to give to the Phi Beta Kappa chapter at Harvard was one he
had long been developing. The extensive examination of the genesis
of the address provided by Merton M. Sealts, Jr., reveals that "most
of its basic ideas about the scholar and his relation to society had
already been worked out in discernible stages over the preceding
three years."[6] The most prominent among the sources is, as we
might expect, "The Philosophy of History" lectures, which not only
stood close in time to "The American Scholar," but provided a
framework of thought easily adaptable to the new topic. In those
lectures he had sketched a theory of social man which included a
treatment of literature and of the professions. The composition of
"The American Scholar" was in one sense a process of applying this
theory to the actual position of the man of letters in society. Emerson's application was achieved with particular success, however,
largely because of its stylistic brilliance and the skillful structural use
of the motif of the universal man, depicted as the "old fable" whose
doctrine is "ever new and sublime; that there is One Man,—present
to all particular men only partially, or through one faculty"
(*CW*, 1:53). Whether Emerson had a specific source in antiquity
is questionable;[7] the important point is that the idea of the "One
Man" has its roots deep in the "genuine man" of his early preaching,
and the idea of the one mind which had dominated his lecturing
most recently.

The address opens with the concept of the one man as an assertion of metaphysical unity, which Emerson quickly qualifies in a
survey of the actualities of social life. The original unity of man is
balanced against the lack of unity we encounter among men: "The
state of society is one in which the members have suffered amputa-
tion from the trunk, and strut about so many walking monsters,—
a good finger, a neck, a stomach, an elbow, but never a man"

(*CW*, 1:53). This is one of Emerson's more striking and effective metaphors, because it graphically exploits the analogy of society and the human form which the fable of the one man had suggested, establishing a tension in the essay between unity and individuality, as between man and his individual faculties. The definition of the scholar as "Man Thinking" serves as a point of reference for this tension throughout the essay, because the definition itself combines both the individual and the universal aspects of the scholar's role. "Thinking," from the point of view of society, is part of the "distribution of functions" necessary to society, and is therefore a unique task which sets the scholar apart from other men performing other functions (*CW*, 1:53). Yet, at his best, the scholar is not an individual, but "man" in the universal sense of the term. When the scholar can express the universal man through the proper exercise of his individual task of thinking, he is fulfilling his office.

There is an irony in the role of the scholar, however, arising from the reaction of society to the proper exercise of his function as the delegated intellect. Even though he performs an essential task—perhaps the most essential task—in society, his place is not an easy one. Emerson notes that one of the scholar's basic problems is "the state of virtual hostility in which he seems to stand to society, and especially to educated society," and his resulting "poverty and solitude" and "loss and scorn." In other words, the scholar who does act universally, transcending his isolated individuality to express the concerns of mankind, finds himself rejected by society. For society is essentially a conservative force, and the true scholar will reject "the ease and pleasure of treading the old road, accepting the fashions, the education, the religion of society." Yet the compensation for these losses is the scholar's knowledge that he is "exercising the highest functions of human nature" (*CW*, 1:62). Even if the scholar is rejected by society, he is eventually accepted by mankind, for the demands of society and the needs of individual men are often at odds.

Thus, while the scholar, in acting the part of man, often isolates himself socially, this superficial isolation is offset by the deeper unity he achieves with the universal mind of all men. "He [the scholar] then learns that in going down into the secrets of his own mind, he has descended into the secrets of all minds." Such an achievement is the scholar's success, exemplified in Emerson's depiction of the interplay between an orator and his audience:

The orator distrusts at first the fitness of his frank confessions,—his want of knowledge of the persons he addresses,—until he finds that he is the complement of his hearers;—that they drink his words because he fulfils for them their own nature; the deeper he dives into his privatest secretest presentiment,—to his wonder he finds, this is the most acceptable, most public, and universally true. The people delight in it; the better part of every man feels, This is my music: this is myself.   [CW, 1:63]

The implication of this discovery that the scholar fulfills and expresses the nature of all men is that all men are, in their better moments, "scholars," or thinkers. Thus Emerson brings the address full circle at this point, returning to the concept of the unity of man, but only after having incorporated into the concept the elements that give the scholar a unique individuality. When he goes on to argue that "self-trust" is the sum of the scholar's virtues (CW, 1:63), he extends the universality of the role, in keeping with his description of self-trust as "the whole Ethics of the Mind" (EL, 2:151) only a few months earlier in "Ethics." The scholar's highest characteristic, therefore, is precisely the same as the universal ethical quality available to all men.

Yet even with this assertion of man's essential unity, Emerson remains painfully aware that this unity is not realized in the day-to-day affairs of men. Their sense that their common nature has never fully realized its potential is often manifested in the most unequal and unjust of social arrangements. The men who see in the poet or the hero "their own green and crude being—ripened" are therefore "content to be less, so *that* [the hero] may attain to its full stature." Metaphysical equality ironically manifests itself in social inequality. But the hope for man lies in a revolution—perhaps a political revolution, but certainly a revolution in man's self-conception which must precede any social reform. Emerson uses "culture" as the term to denote such a revolution:

This revolution is to be wrought by the gradual domestication of the idea of Culture. The main enterprise of the world for splendor, for extent, is the upbuilding of a man. Here are the materials strown along the ground. The private life of one man shall be a more illustrious monarchy,—more formidable to its enemy, more sweet and serene in its influence to its friend, than any kingdom in history.   [*CW*, 1:65–66]

By the "domestication of the idea of Culture," Emerson means the process by which each individual will come to take the universal man within him more seriously. Some light is shed on this idea in a journal entry of April 1837, where two concepts of "culture" are revealingly contrasted:

Culture—how much meaning the Germans affix to the word & how unlike to the English sense. The Englishman goes to see a museum or a mountain for itself; the German for himself; the Englishman for entertainment, the German for culture. The German is conscious, & his aims are great. The Englishman lives from his eyes, & immersed in the apparent world.

[*JMN*, 5:303]

The difference, of course, is that for Emerson's Englishman, culture is a thing apart from the self, while it is the very process of the self in progress for the German, whose best representative would be Goethe.[8] When "culture" does come to represent the unfolding of the self, it becomes "domesticated," as he put it in "The American Scholar."

The address hinges, to a large extent, on the idea of culture, for therein lies the hope that the primal unity of Man can be restored to a society of fragmentary men. Emerson's concluding look at both this present age and its possible future reflects his hope in the increasing culture of man, and his conviction that "the age of Revolution" (*CW*, 1:67) is the most desirable of times for any man. Such a conviction makes necessary a fuller treatment of a philosophy of "Human Culture."

VI

The Theist

The Paradox of Achievement

In discussing Emerson's yearly lecture series in the late 1830s and early 1840s, Rusk leaves the impression that there is little more than superficial variation from one set of lectures to another (*Life*, p. 261). One of Emerson's remarks lends some credence to this view. In March 1838, after completing the "Human Culture" lectures, he wrote Frederic Henry Hedge, then in Maine, that he had completely ceased his duties as a preacher, and went on to discuss the activity which had come to replace his preaching—his lecturing:

> The notes I collect in the course of a year are so miscellaneous that when our people grow rabid for lectures as they do periodically about December, I huddle all my old almanacks together & look in the encyclopedia for the amplest cloak of a name whose folds will reach unto & cover extreme & fantastic things. Staid men & good scholars at first expressed mirth & then indignation at the audacity that baptised this gay rag bag English Literature, then Philosophy of History, then Human Culture, but now to effrontery so bottomless they even leave the path open.   [*L,* 2:121]

Emerson's tone here is one of humorously exaggerated self-deprecation, but the issue he raises is important. Is there more than a superficial difference between the lecture series, or is Emerson merely shuffling the same cards to disguise a game that changes little from year to year? Do individual series of lectures therefore deserve treatment as artistic and intellectual entities? The editing and publication of the lectures in the early 1960s have made the problem more pressing by providing the reader with texts of the lecture series, and thus stressing their unity, while also suggesting the great use Emerson made of the lectures in his literary essays and underscoring the essential continuity of his thought in this period. But despite the lectures' eventual use in the essays, the lasting effect of their publication will be the recognition that Emerson's thought is best revealed not in individual lectures, but as it emerges from an entire series, each part of which is constructed to advance the central theme of the series as a whole.

The "Human Culture" lectures offer the best opportunity to examine this problem, and, in fact, they demand that it be faced. They follow the "Philosophy of History" lectures, which were precedent setting in their establishment of a format that would be followed in succeeding lectures. Many similar themes are discussed in the two series—vocation, the arts, the development of intellect, to name a few—and Emerson's essential philosophical premises are constant. "Human Culture" is, in other words, close enough to "The Philosophy of History" to raise the methodological problem of uniqueness. But what might be taken for superficial changes are, I will argue, important clues to Emerson's development, and conclusive indications that the nature of his lecture series rewards their treatment as artistic and intellectual entities. Their similarities to one another only provide a consistent backdrop against which subtle, though important, changes can be noted.

Emerson had offered a theory of history with very little actual use of the word "history"; but when he set himself the task of constructing a theory of culture, he used "culture" and related words repeatedly in a variety of contexts. The power of the word is explained in part by its association with another of Emerson's familiar terms, "the ideal." Whatever similarities it had to other key terms in Emerson's vocabulary, the manifold presence and evolving definition of the word "culture" make this lecture series unique. "Human Culture" does, like "The Philosophy of History," ultimately aim to present a complete theory of human potential, but the concept of culture serves as a lens to offer new perspectives and new dimensions to the question of human potential.

Emerson argues that "the basis of Culture is that part of human nature which in philosophy is called the Ideal." Such a definition raises an even larger question about the nature of the ideal itself, which Emerson goes on to answer in terms which echo *Nature:*

A human being always compares any action or object with somewhat he calls the Perfect: that is to say, not with any action or object now existing in nature, but with a certain Better existing in the mind. That Better we call the Ideal. Ideal is not opposed to Real, but to Actual. The Ideal is the Real. The Actual is but the apparent and the Temporary.

The definition appeals to human nature's almost universal tendency toward restlessness, a trait he would link directly with a potential for betterment. What remains unclear in the definition, and what would become increasingly unclear for Emerson in the late 1830s and early 1840s, was the nature of the "certain Better existing in the mind." The implication of this passage is that the "Better" is an entity directly intuited by the mind, which surpasses all "Actual" objects and events in comparison. If this interpretation is valid, Emerson might, in other moods, have called this entity the universal mind, the one, or God. He does, in fact, go on to say that "in character the mind is constrained ever to refer to a moral Ideal which we call God" (EL, 2:217–18).

There is an alternative interpretation of this idea of the better, however—one which may not be exclusive of the first interpretation, but which does change the emphasis of the definition significantly. When Emerson offers the example of art, among several others, as an illustration of the function of the better, this alternative becomes clearer: "The great works of art are unable to check our criticism. They create a want they do not gratify. They instantly point us to somewhat better than themselves." Emerson's language in this instance leads us to believe that our sense of the better is not the product of a direct knowledge of an entity against which we measure all other experiences, but rather the result of a dissatisfaction with the present which is not necessarily based on a definable standard of comparison. A "want" is created in this case by the unrealized potential of an actual work of art, not by any mental comparison with our sense of a perfected entity. Culture based upon this form of a quest for the better involves a large element of the merely negative, rather than the positive experience of an ideal. That this was not Emerson's settled opinion of the ideal is suggested by the example of science: "In Nature it is no otherwise. No particular form of man or horse or oak entirely satisfies the mind. The physiologist sees ever floating over the individuals the idea which nature never quite successfully executes in any one form" (*FL*, 2:217). The metaphor or the image of the ideal "floating" over the form of the actual seems to specify, in this case at least, that the better has more definite grounding than mere dissatisfaction with the actual.

Whichever view of the nature of the better one takes—and Emerson's thought seems to be in transition on this issue—there remains a stress on the dynamism of the soul. The element of the "progressive" that Emerson had called "essential to a true theory of nature & man" (*JMN*, 5:182) is at the basis of this definition of culture, for the continual striving of the soul for betterment is in fact progressive. There is no better definition of the active soul, which Emerson valued so highly, than this description of the progressive moral nature of man in the "Introductory" lecture: "The fruit of this constitutional aspiration is labor. This aspiration is the centrifugal force in moral nature, the principle of expansion resisting the tendency to consolidation and rest. The first consequence of a new possession is a new want. The first fruit of a new knowledge is a new curiosity." Just as the moral nature of man is dedicated to "the principle of expansion," Emerson argues that "the instinct of the Intellect is progress evermore." This emphasis on dynamism, expansion, and progress means that man must assume a future-oriented stance to realize his potential fully. As he puts it, "In a true and ingenuous mind the appeal is always being made to the future" (*EL*, 2:218, 254, 303). The unresolved question of the "Human Culture" lectures, therefore, is not whether progress is the proper state of the soul, but what the basis of the progress really is.

This distinction between a process of culture based on an intuition of the perfect, and one based instead on a dissatisfaction with the imperfect, is important, and it takes us to the heart of the question of the optimism and pessimism in Emerson's thought. The familiar difference between the optimistic and self-confident "early" Emerson and the skeptical and pessimistic "late" Emerson, established largely by Whicher, is now almost axiomatic. The most notable shift in Emerson's thought comes between *Essays: First Series* (1841) and *Essays: Second Series* (1844), and Whicher takes "Circles" as a transitional essay in this change.[1] The "Human Culture" series is an essential part of Emerson's earlier Transcendental optimism because of its stress on the human ability to pursue the better, and thus presumably to draw closer to the ideal. The problem, however, is whether the pursuit of the better actually leads us closer to the ideal. In "Circles," parts of which are based on the "Human Culture" lectures, Emerson would call the ideal a "flying Perfect," arguing that it forever receded before the questing grip of man (*CW*, 2:179). While in "Human Culture" he does not go this far, it is evident that all the elements of such an assertion are present in his initial definition of culture as a striving for the better, and his observation that the fruit of new knowledge is curiosity. Although a philosophy that insists on a human capacity for betterment is optimistic, one which tinges that betterment with a recognition of ultimate frustration has its edge of pessimism.

Whicher has attributed Emerson's fading optimism to his loss of faith in the means of improvement available to the individual. Arguing that Emerson found a "fatal flaw" in *"all* the means of culture," he notes his "acquiescence in the irremediable waywardness of the divine uprush of soul."[2] While Whicher's analysis perceptively notes the basic problem of the unreliability of the experience of divinity, other causes for this despair are suggested by the "Human Culture" lectures. The real problem was less the unreliability of the means of culture than the paradox of achievement itself. Emerson found the experience of divinity to be elusive at this point, not because man lacked the means to search it out, but rather because, in the course of this search, man discovered that the goal had receded before him. The process of the search thus altered its conditions. Such a realization is indeed a tragic one, and Whicher is largely correct in portraying Emerson's career as a deepening battle against tragedy, and in arguing that "his view of life can properly be called tragic."[3] But the element of tragedy which Emerson faced cannot at its inception be thought of as a tragedy of limitation. Emerson's problem in the late 1830s took a different form. He did not dwell on the realization that man's capacities are too limited to achieve the goals he sets for himself, but rather glimpsed the more disturbing notion that the nature of existence is such that achievement cannot yield satisfaction. Emerson's later skepticism took increasing account of the capriciousness of the presence of the divine and reveals a growing hunger for such experiences. But that skepticism was rooted in the deeper question of achievement itself; it was an indictment of the universe as well as of the self.

Emerson begins the concluding lecture of the series with a quotation, repeated from *Nature* (*CW*, 1:25), that summarizes the paradox of achievement: " 'What we know is a point to what we do not know' " (*EL*, 2:358).[4] From one perspective, this idea offers the hope of continual progress in thought, and makes the ideal of the active soul a possibility. But from another equally valid perspective, it suggests the ultimate frustration of a quest for the unachievable. By the winter of 1837–38, Emerson was poised between these two perspectives—unswervingly dedicated to progress, but unavoidably beginning to recognize its limitations. The idea of culture was the point from which he reexamined his previous positions, and his sustained treatment of the idea brought the underlying question of optimism into clearer focus.

The Redefinition of Discipline

In the "Human Culture" lectures, Emerson argues that culture is dependent upon a certain internal harmony and proportion in man himself. That proportion, the result of the proper relation among his senses and faculties, creates a spiritual harmony which parallels the harmony of the physically healthy body. "Proportion certainly is a great end of culture" (*EL*, 2:226), and is based on the correct judgment and measurement of the forces competing for man's attention and the right relation of man's senses and faculties.

Emerson's concern with the harmony of the human faculties is most clearly revealed in the structuring metaphor of the lecture series as a whole, the human anatomy, which is suggested by the titles of the lectures themselves. Since the "scale" of culture is man himself, Emerson uses the image of the body to suggest the range of senses, faculties, and qualities that must be balanced in the process of culture. The second lecture of the series, "The Doctrine of the Hands," offers a theory of employment, encompassing both the benefits of manual work as a profession and the more universal benefits attainable from the daily labor that every individual must perform. "The Head" offers a theory of "the Culture of the Intellect" (*EL*, 2:246), "The Eye and Ear" explores the doctrine of beauty, and the heart is used to emphasize the necessary qualities of love and sincerity in "The Heart" and "Being and Seeming." These five lectures sketch a basic image of the ideal man, a figure rarely mentioned directly in this lecture series, but one who underlies the entire doctrine of individual growth. "Human Culture" uses that idea metaphorically—not as a philosophical doctrine but as an assumed ground plan for the lectures.

The reference of the editors of the lectures to this "anatomical group" (*EL*, 2:209) might suggest that the final lectures on abstract qualities—"Prudence," "Heroism," and "Holiness"—do not readily fall into the overall anatomical scheme of the earlier lectures in the series. In fact, the final lectures actually refine and extend the structuring metaphor of the lectures by suggesting the image of man in action. It should be remembered that Emerson's idea of a universal man is not static, that the first and last requirement for human greatness is moral action. With that in mind, it is easier to understand the function of the final lectures: they present the image of man established in the earlier lectures exhibiting the moral virtues that make him a universal symbol. Each lecture presents one of the forms that moral action can take, forms which must be exhibited in harmonious proportion. Just as an individual must balance his head with his heart, he must also balance his prudence with heroism, and his heroism with holiness. Moreover, these three lectures complete the image of the genuine man in another important way, representing "successively higher states of the soul" (*EL*, 2:340). The image of man, once completed in physical terms, is repeatedly raised to a higher spiritual level in the concluding lectures, until it reaches its highest plateau in the state of holiness.

Emerson's stress on balance and proportion as an essential ingredient of the process of culture is itself a balancing factor of another dominant idea in the lectures, that of the growth of the soul. Emerson regarded such growth not as the result of an unnatural effort, but rather as the natural course of the soul when completely free of inhibiting factors. This "natural" growth does rely finally on the divine, for the growth of the soul is the expression of the divinity of man. Emerson's sense of the fusion of the human and the divine finds powerful expression in the following sentences, which carry different emphases but do not contradict each other: "His own Culture,—the unfolding of his nature, is the chief end of man. A divine impulse at the core of his being, impels him to this" (*EL*, 2:215). Culture is therefore humanistic in its expression of human nature, and religious in its dependence upon a "divine impulse."

Given Emerson's conviction that the culture of the soul is a natural process, it follows that to encourage culture, one must remove the artificial inhibitions to the progress of the soul: "The main thing we can do for it is to stand out of the way, to trust its divine force, to believe that God is in it, and only disencumber and watch its workings. All general rules respecting intellectual culture must be based on this negative principle." (*EL*, 2:255). Such a view of the culture of the soul returns to the basic organic connotation of the word "culture," for it depicts the soul's progress as natural in much the sense that we consider the growth of a plant or the development of the body of an animal natural. If there are no inhibiting factors, growth will occur. Emerson's full recognition of this implication of his idea of culture is revealed in his reliance on organic metaphors to explain human spiritual development. His desire to "unfold before you in calm degrees a natural history of the intellect" (*EL*, 2:246–47) uses the term "natural history" to establish the link between the investigation of the human mind and the investigation of nature. This suggestion is made more explicit when he directly compares intellectual progress with the growth of a plant:

All our progress is an unfolding like vegetable bud. You have first an instinct, then an opinion, then a knowledge, as the plant has root, bud, and fruit. Trust the instinct to the end though you cannot tell why or see why. It is vain to hurry it. By trusting it, it shall ripen into thought, into truth, and you shall know why you believe.   [*EL*, 2:250–51]

Dealing with an essentially mysterious process, the growth of the mind, Emerson pleads for faith by referring to another essentially mysterious process, the growth and fruiting of a plant. If we can trust the processes of nature in the world around us, can we not trust the same processes within ourselves? Emerson's organic metaphor is thus polemic as well as descriptive; it does more than describe the self—it argues for a certain view of the self which must be taken as an act of faith.

Such an act of faith is best expressed in the analogy of the growth of the soul not only with the growth of an individual plant, but with the total natural landscape:

Culture in the high sense does not consist in polishing and varnishing, but in so presenting the attractions of nature that the slumbering attributes of man may burst their sleep and rush into day. The effect of Culture on the man will not be like the trimming and turfing of gardens, but the educating the eye to the true harmony of the unshorn landscape, with horrid thickets, wide morasses, bald mountains, and the balance of the land and the sea.
[*EL*, 2:216]

The passage is built around certain now familiar images: the arousal of the "sleeping" potential of man and the "education" of the eye to an existing harmony in nature. But the central image of the passage is the comparison of the garden and the wilderness as possible descriptions of human nature. This comparison goes to the heart of the problem of American identity, for it is a widely accepted fact of American literary history that the changing pattern of American attitudes toward the wilderness is a key to the American character itself. Emerson's use of the metaphor of the wilderness is striking, however, because he embraces the "unshorn landscape, with horrid thickets, wide morasses," without giving up the idea of a "true harmony" expressed by that landscape. The harmony is the product of the full expression of each of the forces of the landscape, which results in a compensatory balance. Such a conception is closely related to Emerson's organic theory of beauty and art, and by analogy, it also explains his dual concern with the expansive growth and the proportional harmony of the character. His willingness to embrace the wilderness connotes a similar willingness to embrace the self, and his preference for the wilderness over the garden symbolizes his commitment to the romantically expressive self of the Transcendentalists, rather than to the regulated self of his Unitarian predecessors and colleagues.

The contrast of the garden and wilderness as metaphors for human nature brings into focus Emerson's ultimate departure from Unitarian conceptions of culture. In general, he remained faithful to the ends of the idea of self-culture as the Unitarians preached it, but he came to differ with them on the means of achieving those

ends. The idea of "balance in character," which is closely related to
that of moral discipline, can provide us a revealing point of comparison. Emerson's concern for a balance of faculties and actions has
very clear antecedents in the similar Unitarian belief that human
moral growth requires a very delicate balance of potentially inhar-
monious factors in human nature. The most obvious of these potentially problematic factors were, as we noted previously, the demands
of the flesh and the spirit, and of reason and the affections. No
complete character could exclude any of these factors, or any other
part of human nature, but neither could any one of them be allowed
to throw the character out of balance and disturb the progress of the
moral life. Thus "prohibition," "obedience," "sacrifice," and "self-
denial" were the terms to which the Unitarians turned to express
their conviction that "discipline" was an indispensable characteristic
of the religious life. After reading the "Human Culture" lectures,
one is tempted to agree with Whicher that, by 1838, Emerson had
completely rejected discipline as a means to moral progress, for what
is immediately memorable in the lectures is his stress on the dynamic
and expansive self, and his view of a religious life based on positive
acceptance rather than self-denial. Referring directly to "Human
Culture," Whicher argues that "at the outset, he appears to have
hoped for much from a course of ascetic self-discipline," but the
unreliability of the results of such discipline led him to revise his
views entirely: "As it turned out, however, the drill and inspiration
had little relation to each other; health remained an unpredictable
miracle. For this reason the theme of preparatory asceticism in time
virtually dropped out of his thought; it simply did not work."[5] But,
in fact, the term "discipline" and related concepts appear at key
points in the "Human Culture" lectures. The central role of discipline in *Nature* is carried forward in these lectures as an under-
current which gives balance to the more obvious stress on progress
and expansion. This discipline, however, is one of exertion rather
than denial:

The only motive at all commensurate with his force, is the ambition to
discover *by exercising* his latent power, and to this, the trades and occupa-
tions men follow, the connexions they form, their fortunes in the world,

and their particular actions are quite subordinate and auxiliary. The true culture is a discipline so universal as to demonstrate that no part of a man was made in vain.   [*EL*, 2:215]

In this passage, Emerson associates the exercise of human power, or the expression of individual talents, with "a discipline" which is "true culture." Similarly, when he refers to "the higher discipline of the heroic," or "the discipline of Prudence" (*EL*, 2:229, 325), he is suggesting an exertion of the human soul, not a contraction of it. Even when he uses terms such as "self-denial" to explain the process of culture, it is within the context of human progress:

Another of the austere laws of intellectual culture resulting from the same unconditioned allegiance to Truth, is a self-denial as harsh as that enjoined upon the Christian. He who would know thoroughly must have been mistaken and found out his error by hard experience, and to know well the secret of pleasure he must know the taste of pain. He must love defeat; he must not love victory.   [*EL*, 2:258]

Whatever austerity Emerson sees as part of culture, it is an austerity which results not from the quelling of instincts, not from caution or guardedness. It is an austerity born of the exertion of the faculties.

The concept of a necessary discipline is therefore shared by Emerson and the major Unitarian thinkers, but there is a subtle difference in the nature of the discipline they propose. The best illustration of this difference is provided by returning to the contrasting metaphors of the garden and the wilderness. It can be said that the Unitarians tended to see the growth of the soul as the cultivation of a garden, in which harmony could be maintained only by severely checking the growth of certain plants and encouraging the growth of others in a pattern imposed upon them from without. Discipline was the method that channeled the growth of the soul into such a preconceived harmony. Yet Emerson's faith in the potential for harmony in man led him to hold that any hindrance to the full expression of each facet of the soul was the only possible cause for disharmony. His resulting view of discipline was thus man's constant effort to exercise his potential fully. The wilderness itself revealed a true harmony to the educated eye, because each of its components expressed itself as fully as possible, given its potential.

Emerson's redefinition of discipline both suggests his ties to the

Unitarian thought which was his own beginning and illustrates the growing distance that his developing philosophy was creating between Unitarianism and what was coming to be known as Transcendentalism. While his reluctance to abandon the idea of discipline is clear enough, his stress on discipline is easy to overlook in our concentration on the "Transcendental" Emerson. Even so, discipline is, as he defines it, not at odds with the general direction of this thought, which is epitomized in a sentence from "Being and Seeming": "What is really good is ever a new creation" (*EL*, 2:308). As a constant encouragement to the expression of human talents and the exertion of human powers, discipline insured the continual creation of the new. New creation, far from threatening proportion of character, actually secured it.

The continuity with Unitarian thought provided by the concept of discipline was to be totally overlooked, however, in the controversy over Emerson's Divinity School Address the following summer. The controversy is a turning point, both for Emerson personally and for American intellectual history, but the drama of this clear break is not the result of a sudden turn in thought by Emerson. His position in the address is essentially a restatement of the position he presented in more detail in "Human Culture," and a clear understanding of the relation of the address to the "Human Culture" lectures will clarify what was at stake in that controversy.

The Divinity School Controversy

Emerson had little idea how prophetic his words would soon be when he remarked in "Holiness" that "a storm of calumny will always pelt him whose view of God is highest and purest" (*EL*, 2:354).[6] A little over five months later, his Divinity School Address, remarkably similar to "Holiness" in many essential respects, would raise a storm which, though not a total surprise to Emerson, would be far more turbulent than he had expected. The prevailing mood of the time is revealed in a journal entry of September 1837 in which Emerson notes his recent receipt of an invitation to speak before the Salem Lyceum on any topic of his choosing, "provided no allusions are made to religious controversy, or other exciting topics upon which the public mind is honestly divided." They had come to the wrong man, of course, and Emerson refused, saying, "I am really sorry that any person in Salem should think me capable of accepting an invitation so encumbered" (*JMN*, 5:376).

He was not, however, set on religious controversy, though he felt that he could not honestly avoid speaking his mind on any topic, however dangerously "exciting" it might be. His deep distaste for religious sectarianism was coming into conflict with his commitment to a full and free expression of his ideas. When the invitation came for him to address the Divinity School graduates, the issue could not be avoided. The letter of invitation had asked Emerson to deliver for the class "the customary discourse, on occasion of their entering upon the active Christian ministry" (*L*, 2:147), but as Emerson neared the delivery of the address, he realized that it would have to be an uncommon message, whatever the consequences. A journal entry made a week before the address tells us much about Emerson's state of mind and deserves to be quoted in its entirety:

We shun to say that which shocks the religious ear of the people & to take away titles even of false honor from Jesus. But this fear is an impotency to commend the moral sentiment. For if I can so imbibe that wisdom as to utter it well, instantly love & awe take place. The reverence for Jesus is only reverence for this, & if you can carry this home to any man's heart [,] instantly he feels that all is made good & that God sits once more on the throne. But when I have as clear a sense as now that I am speaking simple truth without any bias, any foreign interest in the matter,—all railing, all unwillingness to hear, all danger of injury to the conscience, dwindles & disappears. I refer to the discourse now growing under my eye to the Divinity School.   [*JMN*, 7:41–42]

It is plain that Emerson was aware that his views would not be universally applauded, and that he had some hesitation about embroiling himself in controversy. But the passage also reflects his underlying confidence that if he could disassociate himself from any sectrarian motives, if he could speak "simple truth without any bias, any foreign interest in the matter," any possible controversy could be overshadowed.

It is precisely this faith that was wounded in the furor over the

Divinity School Address. Whicher has rightly suggested that the speech "was involved emotionally more than he knew with this personal sense of mission," and that Emerson "was correspondingly affected by its hostile reception."[7] He was, after all, speaking to young men who were entering the profession he had tried and found wanting, who would certainly face the problems and frustrations, both professional and intellectual, that he had faced, and who, most importantly, shared the commitment to religious truth which he had found could take channels different from those most frequently recognized by the institutional church. It would have been hard, therefore, for him to remain oblivious to the hostile criticism which was so swift and vehement. Rusk quotes Emerson's uncle Samuel Ripley, himself a clergyman, on that reaction: "The whole band of clergymen . . . have raised their voice against him, with a very few exceptions; and the common people, even women, look solemn and sad and roll up their eyes . . . 'Oh, he is a dangerous man; the church is in danger; Unitarianism is disgraced; the party is broken up'" (*Life*, p. 272). Emerson was prepared to take the consequences of offending some, but he was not prepared for this. He had taken his message to an audience somewhat different from his usual, and had preached it in a somewhat special place on a special occasion, but the deepest irony of the storm over the Divinity School Address is that his message was not a new one.

As historians of the Divinity School controversy have noted, there was more than one Unitarian objection to the address.[8] Andrews Norton was most vociferous in his rage at Emerson, associating him with atheism and infidelity chiefly because of Emerson's rejection of the idea of a historical revelation in the scriptures established as divine by the miracles reported in those same scriptures.[9] Emerson could not have been more explicit in his attack on miracles, which Norton considered the indispensable foundation of Christianity and upon which he would base a life's work of biblical research. As Emerson put it, "The very word Miracle, as pronounced by Christian churches, gives a false impression; it is Monster. It is not one with the blowing clover and the falling rain" (*CW*, 1:81). He was certainly making no effort to soften his attack on a historical Christianity based on miracles, and there is evidence that he cared very little about Norton's reaction one way or another, since he had come to doubt Norton's theological position long before he even resigned his pastorate at the Second Church. Nor had Emerson hesitated to express his doubts about miracles in the Unitarian pulpit long before this address. In a letter to Carlyle after the controversy, it is not surprising to see him display a determination to continue this mode of thought:

Let us wait a little until this foolish clam[or] be overblown. My position is fortunately such as to put me quite out of reach of any real inconvenience from the panic strikers or the panic struck; &, indeed, so far as this uneasiness is a necessary result of mere inaction of mind, it seems very clear to me that, if I live, my neighbors must look for a great many more shocks, & perhaps harder to bear.   [*CEC*, p. 197]

The passage indicates Emerson's own sense of the freedom his new career as an independent lecturer has given him, but since it follows his own suggestion that Carlyle delay a possible visit to New England because of this controversy, it also indicates his sense of the divisiveness his address had caused. The impatience he exhibits toward his critics—"the panic strikers and the panic struck"—is captured in his characterization of their uneasiness as the result of "mere inaction of mind." He expressed his indignation even more pointedly in a later journal entry:

In all my lectures, I have taught one doctrine, namely, the infinitude of the private man. This, the people accept readily enough, & even with loud commendation, as long as I call the lecture, Art; or Politics; or Literature; or the Household; but the moment I call it Religion,—they are shocked, though it be only the application of the same truth which they receive everywhere else, to a new class of facts.   [*JMN*, 7:342]

This was not, however, Emerson's only reaction to the controversy over the Divinity School Address—largely because Andrews Norton's cry of "Infidel!" was not the only critical reaction from the Unitarians.[10] A problem different from the miracles question was bothering other Unitarians, a problem which grew from Emerson's assertion that "the soul knows no persons" (*CW*, 1:82). Henry Ware, Jr., the most outspoken of this group, was concerned with the pantheistic tendencies of Emerson's thought, and answered his address with a sermon of his own, *The Personality of the Deity*, which he preached at the Divinity School on September 23, 1838. He had written Emerson soon after the delivery of the Divinity School Address to express his concern about his theological positions, and Emerson's reply to Ware exhibits concern, genuine respect, and a desire for conciliation consistent with the full expression of his own opinion (L, 2:146–50). Had all of Emerson's critics followed Ware's tone and procedure, the controversy would at least have been less damaging to the feelings of those involved. After delivering his answering sermon in September, Ware again urged Emerson to respond. It was a mannerly invitation to debate, but Emerson could only say of himself that "there was no scholar less willing or less able to be a polemic." Yet he also noted, in a phrase which is less than a disclaimer but somewhat conciliatory, that "if it [Ware's sermon] assails any statements of mine perhaps I am not as quick to see it as most writers" (L, 2:167, 166).

Emerson's tone can partly be explained by his long association with Ware, and his real respect for him, despite their differing styles of ministry. Yet it is important to remember that the issue Ware raised was itself different from the miracles question, and a much more sensitive problem both for Emerson and most other Unitarians. Ware's sermon is a full expression of their concern that the abandonment of a concept of God as a "person" would have disastrous results for the Christian community. Ware, of course, expressed his concern in a logically rigorous fashion, offering six numbered reasons why the abandonment of God as a "person" is "inconsistent with just and wholesome doctrine." But the essentially emotional nature of his argument is best summarized in his opening analogy of the difference "between the condition of a little child that lives in the presence of a judicious and devoted mother, an object of perpetual affection, and of another that is placed under the charge of a public institution, which knows nothing but a set of rules." In Ware's eyes, the Christian who was asked to give up the concept of a personal God was like the orphan, left with only a lifeless set of rules for conduct. The implication was that Emerson's stance threatened to take the heart out of religion and morality by taking away the figure of a fatherlike God. Moreover, by removing the heart from religion, such a doctrine "puts in jeopardy the virtue of man."[11] To Emerson, who had staked so much on man's moral nature, who had, in fact, recently offered two eloquent lectures on the necessity of the "heart" in moral development, this criticism must have struck home.

Strictly speaking, there is some truth to Emerson's mild disclaimer that Ware's sermon did not assail any of his statements in the Divinity School Address. Emerson's real concern in that address was not the personality of God, but rather the problems which arose from offering undue reverence to the person of Jesus:

In thus contemplating Jesus, we become very sensible of the first defect of historical Christianity. Historical Christianity has fallen into the error that corrupts all attempts to communicate religion. As it appears to us, and as it has appeared for ages, it is not the doctrine of the soul, but an exaggeration of the personal, the positive, the ritual. It has dwelt, it dwells, with noxious exaggeration about the *person* of Jesus.   [*CW,* 1:82]

Emerson did not explicitly go beyond this position in the Divinity School Address itself, but the fact is that Ware's critique of theology based on an impersonal God did counter a position that Emerson had been assuming gradually in the period before the address. There are several journal entries over a period of years that allow us to chart the progress of Emerson's conception of an impersonal God, but the most important statement of that position comes in the lecture "Holiness" in the "Human Culture" series. If we remember that the state of holiness represents the highest rung on the ladder of culture, the most elevated state of the soul, it will be easier to realize the importance of the Divinity School controversy to Emerson. The "Human Culture" lectures had, for the time being, summarized his thought on the most important of his themes, the development of the soul. The Divinity School Address was actually an adaptation of that thought, principally as it was expressed in "Holiness," to the particular needs of the new ministers of the church. So there was more at stake for Emerson than the one address at Harvard—he had put into that address the best of what he had accomplished thus far as "Man Thinking."

Emerson did not arrive at his conclusion that "the soul knows no persons" without a deep and persistent intellectual struggle over the nature of God. The struggle began where Emerson's theology began: with the concept of God established through the evidences of the design of the universe. As noted earlier, Emerson at one point

accepted such arguments as sufficient to establish the presence of
God in the universe, but he was troubled over the question whether
they established a code of ethics. Similarly, while he agreed that
arguments from design could prove the existence of God, he
doubted that they could prove God's providence—the quality of
devoted attention usually associated with a personal God. In a long
journal entry in 1826, he concluded: "But when all the facts accumulated in many years lend their confederated evidence to the
same result, we feel the evidence of the Div[ine]. exist[ence]. to be
indisputable, for that knowledge out of which it grows has become
one with us, and to assault it is almost to unsettle consciousness."
But he went on, later in the same entry, to add that "natural religion
would not have evidence enow to make it credible that a Divine
Providence existed and human virtue <would fail for> want <of>
support & human suffering would want consolation" (*JMN*, 3:47,
48). The distinction made here between divine existence and divine
providence was significant in that it foreshadowed Emerson's eventual conclusion that God was the least personal of entities. But more
importantly, it led him to deeper exploration of the nature of God,
the result of which was a radical assertion of the identity of God with
the human character. Thus, in a February 1830 journal entry, he asks
and answers a basic question: "What is God? The most elevated
conception of character that can be formed in the mind. It is, the
individual's own soul carried out to perfection" (*JMN*, 3:182). The
answer Emerson offers here shows that he has moved his search for
the nature of God from the outside world to the soul. His concept
of God is consistent, therefore, with his growing stress in this period
on self-trust. And though it appears that his idea of God as the "most
elevated conception of character" suggests a personal God, it is in
fact the idea which led him to the concept of a God freed from
personality.

In a journal entry of late July or early August 1832, very soon after
he had decided finally to resign his pastorate, we find the following
speculation on the nature of God: "What is God but the name of
the Soul at the centre by which all things are what they are, & so
our existence is proof of his. We cannot think of ourselves &
how our being is intertwined with his without awe & amazement"
(*JMN*, 4:33). In some respects, the passage is similar to the one

previously quoted which links God to the human character. The direction of both is to assert the identity of God and man, and to affirm the concept of the God within. But this passage goes further in its assertion that "God" is one name for an entity or phenomenon which can be known by other labels. As the power "by which all things are what they are," the idea of God takes on a ubiquitous quality that prevents its identification with the limitations usually associated with personality. A longer journal entry of May 1836 reveals Emerson's growing impatience with those who would limit God by attributing personality to him. Noting that in the most cultivated minds there is "a studious separation of personal history from their analysis of character & their study of things," he goes on to comment on the major exception to this observation: "And yet when cultivated men speak of God they demand a biography of him as steadily as the kitchen & the bar room demand personalities of men. Absolute goodness, absolute truth must leave their infinity & take form for us. We want fingers & sides & hair" (*JMN,* 5:162). Only a few weeks later, with *Nature* under way, Emerson's journal shows him surer of his impersonal concept of God, basing it on his own religious experience. For him, the point was not to worship a God who was a person, but to experience a God capable of taking his own personality, his limiting individuality, away from him. The following passage is thus consistent with the mysticism of the transparent eyeball passage of *Nature:*

A fact we said was the terminus of spirit. A man, I, am the remote circumference, the skirt, the thin suburb or frontier post of God but go inward & I find the ocean; I lose my individuality in its waves. God is Unity, but always works in variety. I go inward until I find Unity universal, that Is before the World was; I come outward to this body a point of variety.
[*JMN,* 5:177]

God as "the ocean" in which one can lose his individuality is certainly the equivalent of "the currents of the Universal Being" which "circulate through me," as he expressed it in *Nature* (*CW,* 1:10). In both cases, the power of God lies not in his personality, but rather in his all-encompassing "Unity"—a unity that transcends personhood.

As his emphasis on self-reliance and the divinity of the soul increased, the complexity of his idea of God deepened correspondingly. In the fall of 1836, some weeks after the completion of *Nature*, Emerson again asked, "And what is God?" His answer was a frank expression of bewilderment and confidence: "We cannot say but we see clearly enough. We cannot say, because he is the unspeakable, the immeasureable, the perfect—but we see plain enough in what direction it lies" (*JMN*, 5:229). The suggestion that God is a direction of the mind captures both the dynamism and the ineffable nature of God.

All of these private speculations were finding their way into public view in *Nature* and in the lectures that followed it. While no one could have expected the furor over the Divinity School Address, there is some indication that Emerson's "pantheistic" tendencies were beginning to attract attention even before that controversy. John White Chadwick, in his biography of Theodore Parker, describes a meeting of "The Friends," a group that Channing often attended, which was evidently a more moderate equivalent of the Transcendental Club. Emerson's theology was the subject of that meeting: "A week later, February 15, 1838, the subject was given by some recent lecture of Emerson's and the discussion was upon the personality of God. Parker agreed with Ripley that Emerson was too pantheistic and that his God was too much an idea."[12] The lecture, of course, would have been "Holiness," delivered first in Boston on January 31, 1838; it was a lecture which might indeed have given pause to anyone committed to a concept of God as person. Convers Francis's journal of the period confirms the notion that the doctrine of God Emerson enunciated in "Holiness" was beginning to cause a stir. Hearing the lecture in Cambridge on March 28, 1838, Francis noted that when it was given in Boston, it had "alarmed some people not a little, as certain parts of it were supposed to deny the personality of the Deity and to border close upon atheism."[13] Francis, an admirer of Emerson's, disagreed with that charge, but left the impression that a controversy was building up over the very issue Emerson faced in the Divinity School Address.

"Holiness" cannot be completely understood outside the context of the entire "Human Culture" lecture series. It is the climactic lecture of the series, followed only by the concluding summary lecture, and reflecting upon and adjusting each of the lectures before it. As we have already noted, the state of holiness is the highest of the three states of the soul that Emerson discusses in the series. While prudence and heroism are necessary qualities to the cultivated man, and natural balances for each other, holiness adds an entirely new dimension to human life. Acts of prudence and of heroism are acts of self-expression, but they are ultimately individual acts, aimed at the preservation of a separate and independent self, whether that self be wise and cautious or valiant and assertive. While prudence is "the virtue of the senses," whose aim is to bring "the external world . . . into conformity with the law of the mind" (*EL*, 2:311), heroism is "a concentration and exaltation of the Individual" which leads to his "setting himself in opposition to external evils and dangers, and regarding them as measures of his own greatness." Holiness, however, is not aimed primarily at subduing the external world, but rather at subduing the soul by striking the right balance between the universal and the individual in man. The point is not that holiness can be practiced without prudence or heroism, but that holiness gives a direction and purpose to all human activities. Emerson describes it as "the state of man under the dominion of the moral sentiment" (*EL*, 2:340), a state attained by self-negation:

The self-surrender to this moral sentiment, the acceptance of its dominion throughout our constitution as the beatitude of man, is Holiness. And as students of Human Culture, I call your attention to the fact, that, the highest state of which we have any experience, is the act of adoration, the state in which, with perfect lowliness, we aspire. It is readily thereby discriminated from Heroism.   [*EL*, 2:346]

The imagery of light and dark expresses the state of holiness, for when one begins "exploring his own consciousness," one discovers "that what light he there finds though it be faintest, is primary and causal." The result of devotion to this inner consciousness, the highest aim of culture, is enlightenment: "The moments in life when we give ourselves up to the inspirations of this sentiment, seem to be the only real life. The mind is then all light" (*EL*, 2:343, 345).

Emerson's reliance on metaphor to push back the limits of expression illustrates his conviction that language is always unequal to the task of defining God. The mystery surrounding God is the result not of an uncertainty about God's presence, but of man's inability to articulate fully his own consciousness of that presence. Again the image of light suggests the idea: "God hides the stars by day in a deluge of light. So he hides himself in the simplicity of the common consciousness." But when that consciousness desires expression, it is thwarted: "From month to month—from year to year—I come never nearer to definite speaking of him. He hideth himself. We can not speak of him without faltering. I unsay as fast as I say my words. He is, for I am: say rather, He is. But in the depth inaccessible of his being, he refuses to be defined or personified" (EL, 2:352, 353). Emerson's use of the word "personified" in conjunction with the word "defined" in this passage is a key to the basis of his concept of an impersonal God. A "person" suggests an entity capable of definition and, thus, an entity which is limited in some way. But Emerson's view of the nature of holiness, that is, of communion with God, is based, as we have seen, on the notion of "self-surrender." Holiness is the diffusion of the limited person into an unlimited, and therefore inexpressible, "Unity." To ascribe to that unity a sense of personality is to deny its essential characteristic.

It is for this reason that, in "Holiness," Emerson insists that the influx of the moral sentiment into the soul is "wholly impersonal." As he describes it, "it passes through my whole being, and I cannot think without being affected by it,—but it refers me to all the world; and is as present to every other creature, as to me." As "the most impersonal of all things," it is "the breath of the soul of the world and therefore as it passeth through us, makes us feel our unity with all other beings" (EL, 2:345, 346). It is easy to see how any of his hearers who might be resistant to pantheism would have some reservation about such a lecture, as Parker evidently did. But if the concept of a personal God, so long an essential part of the Christian tradition, was the price Emerson had to pay to remain consistent to his own experience, he was willing to pay it. And if there was an unsettled quality in his conception of God and of holiness, a sense of flux which might be disturbing to some, this was an assurance of rightness for Emerson. For security is the result of resting in an attainment, but "holiness is the undervaluing of all actual attainment, in the on-look of the soul" (EL, 2:351). The soul's "on-look," the highest state of culture, is the essential "progressive" element in Emerson's system. It is the expression of the soul's sense that, though it may not know God precisely, it knows the direction in which he lies.

While the intellectual nucleus of the Divinity School Address had been formulated in the "Human Culture" lectures, events immediately preceding the address had a significant impact on its final form. The invitation from the seniors at the Divinity School had come soon after Emerson had broken off his commitment to serve as a supply preacher for the church in East Lexington, where he preached for the last time on March 25, 1838. It was a final break with the church, and even at this time, he did not take the step lightly, despite the fact that the success of his lecturing justified it and the inclinations of his thought demanded it. Emerson was at this time "a man arguing with himself," finding a final break with his profession necessary, but still loath to take the step.[14] The force and directness of his attack on the church in the address were due at least partly to his own need to justify his decision.

But despite his own problems with the church, Emerson regarded his address to the new ministers as a heavy responsibility and presented a fervent and hopeful appeal to them. The Unitarian authorities took offense because they feared that Emerson's address would be considered an official pronouncement of the school. These institutional considerations were secondary to Emerson, who clearly hoped to use his opportunity to speak to the church's best hope, its future leaders. His final counsel to them, one which is often forgotten in light of his critique of the church, is to preserve and enliven its existing forms rather than to desert it:

The question returns, What shall we do? I confess, all attempts to project and establish a Cultus with new rites and forms, seem to me vain. . . . Rather let the breath of new life be breathed by you through the forms already existing. For, if once you are alive, you shall find they shall become plastic and new. The remedy to their deformity is, first, soul, and second, soul, and evermore, soul. A whole popedom of forms, one pulsation of virtue can uplift and vivify.   [CW, 1:92]

Emerson's threefold solution to the problems of the church—soul, soul, and soul—had been prepared by a long critique of the existing barriers to life in the church, but more fundamentally, by a memorable presentation of what he felt was the basis of the church itself, the religious sentiment which "creates all forms of worship." That sentiment makes man "illimitable" by "showing the fountain of all good to be in himself" (*CW*, 1:79). This is the fundamental notion of "the infinitude of the private man" which Emerson would later call the central theme of all his lecturing (*JMN*, 7:342), translated in this instance into religious terminology, and thus taking one of its highest forms.

The cutting edge of the address, and the element that raised the controversy, was his attack on what he called "a decaying church and a wasting unbelief" (*CW*, 1:88). Those who heard Emerson's address were close enough to the Unitarian split from New England Calvinism to maintain their conception of themselves as a party of reform. But the orthodox Calvinists had charged, and perhaps many of the Unitarians felt or feared, that their reform under the banner of reason had had its cost in piety and fervency of belief. There was a fear that the loss of Puritan dogma meant the fading of Puritan piety, and this fear manifested itself among some Unitarians in defensiveness toward the Transcendentalists' call for reform. Emerson shared this sense of the fading of religious ardor, but his hope was that a religion of intuition could restore the lost fervency. His sense of the need for restoration is clear in this reference to the end of Puritanism:

The Puritans in England and America, found in the Christ of the Catholic Church, and in the dogmas inherited from Rome, scope for their austere piety, and their longings for civil freedom. But their creed is passing away, and none arises in its room. I think no man can go with his thoughts about him, into one of our churches, without feeling that what hold the public worship had on men, is gone or going.

Emerson's discussion of this loss of faith reveals his own deep concern about the drift of his country and his age, a concern which accounts for his willingness to speak frankly to the young ministers. "Any complaisance," he notes, "would be criminal, which told you, whose hope and commission it is to preach the faith of Christ, that the faith of Christ is preached" (*CW*, 1:88, 84–85).

Speaking in this vein, Emerson echoes the doubts he had expressed about his age and society in "The Present Age" and "Holiness." While he insisted in the latter lecture that "holiness is

unattractive" (*EL*, 2:341), this conviction finds more forceful statement in the Divinity School Address. The "Law" of religion which
demands "exploration of the moral nature of man," Emerson says,
"is travestied and depreciated, . . . behooted and behowled" in the
pursuit of tradition, historicism, and decorum. The results of turning
away from this exploration as a principle of religion are disastrous:
"The pulpit in losing sight of this Law, loses all its inspiration, and
gropes after it knows not what. And for want of this culture, the soul
of the community is sick and faithless" (*CW*, 1:87–88). The "culture" Emerson finds lacking in his society is no different, at bottom,
from the willingness to "explor[e] the moral nature of man" that is
the fundamental law of religion. It is this culture which Emerson
had recently held out as the key to the growth of the soul in the
"Human Culture" lectures. Culture and religion are therefore virtually interchangeable if each is conceived in its highest sense. Even
though culture may connote a wider range of human activities, these
activities can all be comprehended as religion, when religion is freed
from its institutional and historical bondage and taken in its radical
meaning as the realization and exploration of the divinity within the
soul. If the self is indeed divine, the cultivation of the self can also
be thought of as the exploration of the nature of divinity, the pro-
foundest of religious undertakings.

The Divinity School Address is a call to arms for the battle to
make religion an exploration again, to make the church and pulpit
purveyors of culture in its highest form. As such, it gives us none of
the sense of the possible paradoxes of such exploration and achievement that we noted in the "Human Culture" lectures, alerted as we
were by a knowledge of the future turns in Emerson's thought. The
choice as he saw it for the church was stark: either tradition or
"soul," decay or progress, death or life; between such opposites there
could be no hesitation. His hope for what the church could and
might be was real enough, as this vision of the church's awakening
tells us: "It is time that this ill-suppressed murmur of all thoughtful
men against the famine of our churches; this moaning of the heart
because it is bereaved of the consolation, the hope, the grandeur,
that come alone out of the culture of the moral nature; should be
heard through the sleep of indolence, and over the din of routine"
(*CW*, 1:85). Emerson, who in a journal entry while a young student

had staked all his personal hopes on the moral nature he felt he shared with all humanity, here put his hope for humanity in the culture of that moral nature. It was a hope that, immediately at least, his own church did not repay, and a hope that would be modified, though never abandoned, in years to come.

PART THREE

From Lecturer to Essayist

VII

The Years of Transition, 1838–1840

The Question of Leadership

One of the most important results of the Divinity School controversy was its impact on Emerson's sense of vocation. He did smart
from some of the criticism, but Norton's attack seemed largely to
breed contempt in Emerson, for it represented to him the "natural
feeling in the mind whose religion is external" (*JMN*, 7:110–11). As
he later remarked, "It is plain from all the noise that there is Atheism somewhere. The only question is now, Which is the Atheist?"
But these slashes were reserved for the privacy of his journal, while
publicly he studiously ignored the controversy. He blessed his wife
Lydian for her counsel of silence: "In the gossip & excitement of the
hour, be as one blind & deaf to it," and reminded himself that it
was "a bad sign" to think of his critics (*JMN*, 7:112, 96, 118). After
speaking to him during the controversy, Convers Francis found him
"perfectly quiet amidst the storm."[1]

Beneath his lofty stance of public composure, however, Emerson
was undergoing an immensely important struggle. Norton's attack
had brought into clearer focus the fact that there was a new movement afoot, one which was growing in importance, and that Emerson was a leader, if not the leader, of it. The movement, of course,
came to be known as Transcendentalism. While Emerson had long
before sensed the existence of this movement with positive eager-
ness, and had even seen his own part in it, he stubbornly resisted
being cast as its leader or spokesman. The reasons for his resistance
can be found partly in the nature of the Transcendental movement,
but also in Emerson's own complex and fragile sense of his mission
and vocation.

The fact that controversy erupted over a doctrinal issue in Christian theology suggests that the new movement was perceived by the public, and by its critics, as religious in nature. But in fact, it was simply that the public's nerve ends seemed rawest over theological issues because of years of such controversy in New England. The public was attuned to religious controversy, the ministry felt a duty to publicize its differences, and the vehicles of publication were well established. Clearly, however, Transcendentalism was also a literary movement in many important respects, especially since a large part of its appeal to youth seemed to be aesthetic in nature. Finally, it was a political movement, whose religious and aesthetic roots also implied a commitment to profound change in the structure of society. Emerson, in his own way, shared in all three of these sides of the movement, but he relished leadership in none of them. If his temperament inclined him in any direction it was toward a literary leadership, as his promotion of Carlyle's reputation in America suggests.. But even that was more a rare demonstration of personal loyalty than a public act.[2] He accepted editorship of the *Dial*, for instance, only after all avenues of escape were closed, and then only out of duty.[3] He desired even less to enter into a debate with Harvard's leading theologians. Most importantly, he felt that he could not allow himself to be forced into a role as leader of a group or sect with political overtones. Politics were distasteful to him on a temperamental level, a necessary evil at best, and the constant social responsibilities of the political leader, like those of a minister, were inimical. In short, he feared that the demands of the Transcendental movement, a movement whose existence had been amplified in the public consciousness by Norton, might well swallow him up.

Thus the most unsettling thing for Emerson about the Divinity School controversy was not that he was attacked, or that he felt betrayed or persecuted, but that he feared being cast into the position of leader of a sect despite himself. This fear is reflected in certain journal entries of self-counsel in this period, in which he pleads with himself for steadfastness in his established pattern of thought and activity. One entry begins, "Steady, steady," and mentions the "hint at odium, & aversion of faces" in society. He speaks of himself in the third person as the "scholar" to begin with, but revealingly changes to first person as his emotions rise: "The vulgar think he would found a sect & would be installed & made much of.

He knows better & much prefers his melons & his woods. Society has no bribe for me, neither in politics, nor church, nor college, nor city" (*JMN*, 7:60). The irony here is that, in many ways, the Divinity School Address and its reaction fulfilled Emerson's earlier ambition for oratorical greatness. It was a blow, he felt, for the progressive; it was an eloquent expression of his key ideas; it gained him a larger audience; and it was even beginning to make his opponent Norton look the worse.[4] He had not realized, however, that the cost of this success would be high, both in the public attention focused on him and in the attendant demands that would be made on him. "I hate to be defended in a newspaper," he wrote in late September 1838, for "as soon as honied words of praise are spoken for me, I feel as one that lies unprotected before his enemies" (*JMN*, 7:95). That sense of vulnerability is evidence of his resistance to the kind of publicity that would force him into a false position of leadership.

As a result, his journal in late 1838 reveals the pull of opposing tendencies. He records with hope such signs of a new movement in art, religion, and society as he can find, but simultaneously defines himself in static and conservative terms, stressing his detachment, his irresponsibility, and even his provincialism. In August he contemplates lectures on topics and figures "proper to this age," such as Carlyle, Wordsworth, and the rights of woman (*JMN*, 7:48). Later in October, he writes to his Aunt Mary, "I, for my part, am very well pleased to see the variety & velocity of the movements that all over our broad land in spots & corners agitate society" (*JMN*, 7:115), and later still he defends in his journal "young men who are still engaged heart & soul in uttering their Protest against society as they find it" (*JMN*, 7:155). But when he analyzes his own role, he preaches aloofness. Society does not remember, he says, "the irresponsibility of a writer on human & divine nature." That writer is "only a reporter, & not at all accountable for the fact he reports" (*JMN*, 7:71). He is not, in other words, the one who created the conditions he reports, nor should he be blamed for seeing what others ignored. His role is strictly that of a seer, although that is a potentially powerful role. In late October he composes a passage of veiled self-description, telling of the speaker whose word is "the first entering ray of light" into darkness, even "the first cry of the Revolution," but from whom society at first flees in fear and anger

(*JMN*, 7:126). But even more frankly self-analytical, and a good deal less melodramatic, is his entry a few days later, which describes his "strait & decorous way of living": "I content myself with moderate, languid actions, & never transgress the staidness of village manners. Herein I consult the poorness of my powers. More culture would come out of great virtues & vices perhaps, but I am not up to that" (*JMN*, 7:131). The passage hints at Emerson's feeling that many of his personal relations lacked intensity, and it also suggests the reticence that made him shy away, guiltily at times, from larger roles of public leadership. Its tone of recrimination mixed with self-justification echoes earlier passages of self-analysis concerning his doubts about the public nature of the ministerial vocation. The same uneasiness he felt about parish duties he felt again, in a different context, about his role as the leader of the Transcendental movement. Part of his hesitation was plainly a matter of temperament; another part, however, was a reaction in defense of what he considered the necessary detachment and objectivity of vision of the thinker, whom he had publicly defined as the scholar in 1837. The scholar must carefully preserve the balance between truth and action, between past and future. Emerson was clearly battling, as Sherman Paul has noted, "to make self-culture itself a social good."[5]

Faced on the one hand with Norton's public challenge over issues that deeply concerned him, and on the other with a growing nucleus of young intellectuals who looked to him for both friendship and leadership, his reaction was to retreat, partially at least, into himself, in an attempt to preserve a necessary balance. He did not know what effect the controversy would have on the demand for his lectures, but he feared the worst for his next series, "Human Life," which he planned for December 1838.[6] He hoped that he would have an audience, not followers; he wanted to be a speaker, not a spokesman.

Emerson's shrinking away from potential leadership of the new movement was accompanied, however, by a simultaneous affirmation of his role as a lecturer and a new hope for realizing the possibilities which the lyceum offered him. If his shyness made his personal relations difficult, there was a compensating sense of communion with others which he found in lecturing. At its best, it was a process which seemed to draw speaker and listener together, dissolving the barriers of individualism between them. In August of

1838, he wrote that "in perfect eloquence, the hearer would lose the sense of dualism; of hearing from another; would cease to distinguish between the orator & himself; would have the sense only of high activity & progress" (*JMN*, 7:52). The phenomenon of speaker merging with hearer presented here as the perfection of the lecture had its roots in the doctrine of the one mind, and had been part of Emerson's aesthetic of preaching and lecturing for a number of years. But as Porte has pointed out, this sense of the lecture as a communal enterprise, as "a joint experiment or voyage of discovery" between speaker and hearer, gained particular strength in the period after the Divinity School Address.[7] Fuller's remark to Emerson that she found the best of him in his lectures is, in this context, shrewd analysis indeed. The "frigidity & labor of . . . speech" (*JMN*, 7:301) in private conversation, which he helplessly admitted, found its obverse in his attempts to make the formal exercise of public speaking into an intimate experience. "A lecture is a new literature," he wrote in 1839, "which leaves aside all tradition, time, place, circumstance." Its success, however, comes only when the orator "is himself agitated & is as much a hearer as any of the assembly" (*JMN*, 7:224–25). The remark reveals his desire to do away with the dualism of subject and object, of speaker and hearer.

Emerson had begun to develop a method of structuring the lecture series, as we saw in examining "The Philosophy of History" and "Human Culture," but in 1838 and 1839 that sense of structure seemed less immediately important to him than the freedom the lectures could offer. "There is a limit to the effect of written eloquence," he wrote in 1838. The real "miracles of eloquence" were rather the product of "the man who thinks on his legs" (*JMN*, 7:41). Emerson did not, of course, abandon structure and literary form for the extemporaneous, as the written texts and working notes of his subsequent lectures show. But he did come to have higher hopes for the lecture event. We sense this hope in a note from the fall of 1839, just before his lecture series "The Present Age," that all a "true orator will ask" can be found in a lyceum, "for here is a convertible audience & here are no stiff conventions that prescribe a method." Because "everything is admissible" the orator "may dare to hope for ecstasy & eloquence" (*JMN*, 7:265).

The ideal of speaker merging with hearer that the lecture seemed to promise was one version of a larger aesthetic pursuit that would eventually lead to Emerson's essays. Even during 1838–39, when he was still enamored of the lyceum, he had one eye on a collection of essays,[8] and the lectures of this period came to be the basis of it. In a revealing remark on reading in November 1838, he recorded the feeling of the reader in perfect understanding of an author who "sees no reason why he should not continue the sentence—[overleap] that invisible barrier & [continue] the sentence" (*JMN*, 7:161). Writing, of course, was more elusive because of that invisible barrier, but the reader's sensed unity with the author—his sense, in fact, of being able to exchange places with the author and compose through read-ing—was for Emerson the most complete aesthetic experience. The lyceum, which offered unique possibilities for intimacy between artist and audience, was an appropriate proving ground for the growing aesthetic that the *Essays: First Series* would later seek to embody.

Human Culture and "Human Life"

Part of Emerson's strategy for stability and continuity after the summer and fall of the Divinity School controversy was to fashion the "Human Life" lectures as an extension of the "Human Culture" lectures. The connection between the two series is close indeed, in that "Human Culture" sets forth an argument for the necessity of the growth of the soul, and "Human Life" attempts to describe the process of that growth as it manifests itself in the various stages of life. The metaphor of the body which controls "Human Culture" by calling attention to the parts of man which require growth is now replaced by a more complex symbolic structure, a view of the soul as it evolves through the cycle of life. We thus see "the outset of the pupil Man, his early teaching, the discipline of the affections, the sallies of the intellect, the antagonism that appears always to the unfolding of the soul," and in the last four lectures ("Tragedy," "Comedy," "Duty," and "Demonology,") "the shades of the pic-ture," which help define the directions the soul takes (*EL*, 3:103). Within this larger framework, Emerson also makes use of other structural techniques which show an increasing command of his genre. He pairs certain lectures in the sequence for complement and contrast: "Home" precedes "The School," and "Tragedy" and "Comedy" are paired, as are "Duty" (the laws of spirit) and "Demonology" (the apparent exceptions to it). The use of various narrative voices in the lectures is reminiscent of the "Orphic poet" ending in *Nature*. He assumes the voice of a lover (*EL*, 3:42, 59) and of one who prefers his thoughts to love (*EL*, 3:43), of a young man in protest against society (*EL*, 3:95–97) and of an older man apologizing for his "mature philosophy" (*EL*, 3:53–54). In addition, there is a careful internal structuring of individual lectures that is closely akin to the numbering of points in a sermon. We are given, for example, three functions of the soul, five teachers of the soul, or four qualities of genius. Each of these techniques, further refined and modified, would be used in *Essays: First Series*.

The choice of the cycle of life as the major structuring metaphor was especially relevant to Emerson at this time, for his journals suggest a consciousness of his own aging.[9] "After thirty," he notes in September 1838, "a man is too sensible of the strait limitations which his physical constitution sets to his activity. The stream feels its banks, which it had forgotten in the run & overflow of the first meadows" (*JMN*, 7:71). Later in November, he repeats an observation made in 1835: "After thirty a man wakes up sad every morning" (*JMN*, 7:135; see also *JMN*, 5:77). If Emerson is lamenting here his own passing youth, that lament culminates in the midst of the "Human Life" series, where in "The Protest" he identifies "this old age" as "the Fall of Man" (*EL*, 3:89). Whicher has convincingly demonstrated the autobiographical nature of this lecture, and has given it context in Emerson's increasing concern over "the long slow ebb of his power to rise to inspiration at all."[10] But if Emerson recognized the limitations of his constitution as a source of personal tragedy, he also saw the process of aging, his own and that of others, as the symbolic revelation of the more fundamental spiritual truth of the endless nature of the quest for truth itself. Finding himself in middle age as the teacher of a youthful movement, experiencing, as purveyor of the new, the stubborn intransigence of the old, he saw in his own situation the paradox of the pursuit of truth. Although it always promised permanence, truth always demanded pursuit.

Thus youth comes to be the hero of the "Human Life" lectures, and age the villain, with Emerson using these antagonists in three senses. His own youth and approaching age form the autobiographical background of the series; the parties of young and old, which the Divinity School controversy brought into focus, are implied as an immediate point of reference; and the qualities of youth and age take on symbolic meaning in the process of culture which constitutes human life, youth representing the continuing energy for culture and age representing the surrender before the endless nature of the quest.

The problem was brought into clearer focus in July 1838 when Emerson delivered the second, and less well known, public address of that summer, "Literary Ethics." Largely ignored for years, the address has come to be recognized as a biographically revealing piece.[11] It also sheds light, I would suggest, on the central problem Emerson brought into the "Human Life" series, one which the Divinity School controversy only exacerbated. Warning the young graduates in the audience at Dartmouth not to be crushed by the weight of tradition, he argues that freshness is the only measure of great literature: "Whilst I read the poets, I think that nothing new can be said about morning and evening." But in the actual presence of nature, it is not the poets who come to mind: "No; but I feel perhaps the pain of an alien world; a world not yet subdued by the thought." Intended, and presented, as a principle of hope, the passage also has a resonance of despair. If the world is newly before us now, saving us from the vision of the past, the implication is also that the world will always be before us, unsubdued and therefore alien. Despite years of thought, "we have nothing but tendency and indication"—no true religion, or politics, or philosophy or letters or art. This "tendency and indication" is a direction of movement for the soul, promising the potential of achievement, but never satisfying it, because of the ephemeral quality of truth: "Truth is such a flyaway, such a slyboots, so untransportable and unbarrelable a commodity, that it is as bad to catch as light. Shut the shutters never so quick, to keep all the light in, it is all in vain; it is gone before you can cry, Hold. And so it happens with our philosophy" (*CW*, 1:106–8). Truth stands, in the context of this literary address, as the label for what Emerson had more generally called the ideal or the better, the goal toward which human culture aimed itself. Its impermanence thus has great implications for the process of culture itself.

The central problem of the lecture series, the fact that the ideal lacked any quality of permanence, was symbolized by the contrasting qualities of "Home," and "The School," his titles for the second and third lectures. Home implied the soul's "subjective or inward sense of stability and repose" (EL, 3:26), while the School represented its "nurture and breeding" (EL, 3:34), the factors necessary for its continual growth. The dialectical relationship of progress and stability is suggested in his description of the mind's process of expansion: "The instinct of the mind requires ever some permanent thing— permanent as itself—to be its outward object; to be its home, and as fast as one and another are seen to be impermanent and fleeting, it transfers its regard" (EL, 3:26–27). All the elements of the paradox of achievement are present in this single sentence: the continual reaching out toward a better, a permanent goal; the recognition of impermanence that follows, born of the further need for a better; and the corresponding transfer of aspiration, which begins the cycle again. But the most suggestive idea here is contained in Emerson's parenthetical aside, "permanent as itself," which establishes the principle of permanence in the mind itself.

While Emerson's articulation of this principle of permanence is striking in the series, it is accompanied by an emphasis on the continuing expansion of the soul itself. The principle of inner permanence does not, it seems, mark a boundary of the soul's expansion, for Emerson insists that "the constant progress of Culture is to a more interior life." The connotations of the word "constant" should be noted here, for they suggest that whatever else it may be, the mind's quality of permanence is not the achievable goal of culture, even when that culture is regarded as an inner delving. The complications of this problem are made clearer when Emerson remarks, in "The School," that man's eye "habitually asks or inquires" (EL, 3:31, 34). As we have seen, the eye has served Emerson as a basic metaphor for perception, but he now suggests that perception itself is a form of inquiry. The exercise of our powers leads to the demand for their further development. Later in the series, he turns to a different metaphor, the circularly expanding ripples of a pool, to suggest this constant movement of the soul: "In the procession of the soul from within outward it enlarges its circles ever like the pebble thrown into the pond or the light proceeding from an orb" (*EL*, 3:63). When he composed "Circles," he would connect the circular shape of the eye with that of the expanding concentric circle, for each of them symbolized the outward thrust from a fixed inner point that captured for him the process of the soul's growth.[12]

The presence of this polarity between permanence and growth in the intellectual fabric of the lectures results in a notable emotional tension, as Emerson stands poised between the optimism of his early years and the reserve of his later thought. The inspired confidence which he wanted to bring to his audience can be sensed from the tone of his closing paragraph, in which he apologizes for not completing his series (he canceled two lectures because of illness) by reminding his listeners that no intellectual or moral task is ever complete: "And to this progress there is no bound. It is the privilege of man, that, soar as high as he will, there is always a higher. And as in doctrine so in life. I would inspire the love of grandeur of character." But even this "privilege" of perpetual growth has its basis in a restless discontent, as he noted by asking rhetorically, "What is the reason of this uneasiness of ours? of this great Discontent?" The only antidote to that discontent is "an infinite hope," the greatest quality of genius. And that hope is the product of failure: "Genius counts all its miracles poor and short. Its own idea genius never executed" (*EL*, 3:171, 14, 84). But the enemy of genius is the surrender of hope in fatigue and frustration, in the "old age" which is "the fall of man."

The Present Moment and "The Present Age"

Emerson's recognition of the tension between progress and stability led to the renewed reflections on historical progress which he formulated in the lecture series "The Present Age" in 1839–40. While these lectures developed largely from the context of issues established in the "Human Life" series, another circumstance of their composition also influenced their character: Emerson's move toward his contemplated book of essays. The fact is that the lectures were a financial necessity for him, postponing the work he had actually begun on the essays.[13] As a result, he had a mixed attitude toward them: an initial resentment of their necessity and a quandary about a topic for them, which seems to have tempered as his involvement in the series grew, and even to have given way to a renewed hope for the possibilities of eloquence (see *JMN*, 7:265, quoted earlier).

These circumstances of composition inevitably affected the form of the lectures, which Spiller and his coeditor, Wallace E. Williams, seem to regard as an improvement over "Human Culture" and "Human Life." Not only is the historical subject "more palpable," but the lectures are "more unified," having a "topical, simple" structure (*EL*, 3:183). But Emerson pays for the simplicity of his topical structure with a loss of the imaginative force which the structuring metaphors of the body and the maturing individual gave the two previous lecture series. It seems that the more prosaic structure of "The Present Age" resulted not only from the subject matter, but from the fact that Emerson recognized the necessity of lecturing before he had a topic to present. It is also apparent that he wrote the lectures with one eye on the planned book of essays, which accounts for his heavy use of passages from the lectures in the essays (notably "Self-Reliance") and for part of the fragmentary condition of the series.

But the lectures are compelling; even those with significant portions now unavailable to us communicate forcefully a certain mental excitement arising from Emerson's sense that he was experiencing at first hand a period of immensely important social and intellectual change. His choice of title focuses on that experience by suggesting a consideration of the place of the current movement of ideas and events in history. And on one level, this is exactly what he addresses, arguing with what we can now label a degree of historical validity that the movements of the early nineteenth century can be explained as the awakening of the individual. But his title, if we take the liberty of dividing it into its two parts, also suggests the central conflict which, on a deeper level, his lectures face. "The Present," in the sense of a timeless now, forms one of the series' poles, while "Age," in the sense of consciousness of time past and passing, forms the other. The individual, independent of social forms, may be the basic fact of the modern world, but that individual must himself face his temporal nature in order to maintain his position and progress.

Emerson's concern with the issue of temporality might have been expected, given the questions of youth and age which he addressed in "Human Life," but his consciousness of his task is made explicit in an October 18, 1839, journal entry. Calling each of his series of lectures over the last five years "my creed & confession of faith," he contemplates the new series of the coming winter with this resolution: "I am to invite men drenched in time to recover themselves & come out of time, & taste their native immortal air" (*JMN*, 7:270–71). In other words, he hopes, momentarily at least, to erase the consciousness of time from the minds of his hearers. Such a desire may seem paradoxical in a series which purports to be historical in nature, but as Emerson unfolds his topic it becomes clear that the historical quality of his age revolves around the struggle against history, and against time. The worth of the individual, on which the age depends, is determined by the extent to which he can render time irrelevant. Thus the superficially historical nature of the series actually opens into one of Emerson's most prolonged analyses of the ahistorical nature of the individual soul.

We are first struck by the refinement of his earlier definition of the fall of man. It is not enough now to say that the fall consists of age, for Emerson is intent not only on defining the fall, but on remedying it. Here the fall is associated not with the natural process of aging, but with a mode of perception. In "Religion" he defines that perception through a comparison with nature, in a passage which would in part be used in "Self-Reliance": "Nature through all her kingdoms admonishes us of our fall, of a broken analogy. . . . These roses that open in July under my window make no reference to former roses or to better ones: they are for what they are: they exist with God today. There is no time to them." What he calls for is a process of living and thinking so immersed in the present that past and future, our only standards for measuring time, are irrelevant. The point may not seem notable until we consider its implications for self-culture, which are made clearer in a continuation of this passage: "Before a leafbud has burst its whole life acts; in the full-blown flower there is no more; in the leafless root there is no less. Its nature is satisfied and it satisfies nature in all moments alike. There is no time to it. So is it with the soul" (*EL*, 3:283). What is striking here, particularly given his taste for the metaphor of organic development, is that Emerson resists the implied analogy of temporal progress that the developing rose suggests. One is not to see in the leaf bud the tendency that will produce the rose, or in the root the tendency that will produce the leaf. It is a denial of teleology.

The same position, when applied to self-culture, is Emerson's attempt to answer the paradox of achievement, and the tragedy of age. The tragedy arises not from the process of growth itself, but rather from the desire of consciousness to measure that growth against some future end or goal. By denying the necessity of such a measurement, by denying, in other words, the factor of time in the process of culture, he can avoid the problem of the receding ideal. If we recall the roots of this problem in Unitarian thinking about the nature of immortality, Emerson's application of the idea to that doctrine takes on new significance. He notes that "the idea of immutableness is essentially associated" with such attributes of the soul as "truth, justice, love," and then adds that "Jesus . . . never made the separation of the idea of duration from the essence of these attributes; never uttered a syllable about the simple duration of the soul." Duration, or perhaps better, timelessness, is not a quality separable from the nature of the soul itself, and right action, which is always performed in and for the moment, is thus essentially timeless. Emerson's conclusion is that "the moment the doctrine of the Immortality is separately taught, Man is already fallen." A consciousness of time has entered his otherwise purely timeless actions. But it is necessary to remember that "the soul is true to itself, and the man in whom it is shed abroad, cannot wander from the present which is infinite to a future which would be finite" (EL, 3:277). Even the future orientation which Emerson considered an essential part of the culture of the soul is now seen to be tinged with the finite and with time. Immortality lies in the perfection of the present act.

Emerson is making a complex demand in calling for such a consciousness, for it is delicately poised between a future-mindedness that results in dissatisfaction with the present and a satisfaction with the present that could mean the end of growth. In "Education," he returns to his familiar insistence that "a sense of the Perfect accompanies, overhangs us alway." For Emerson, this sense of the perfect is worth even the high cost of being "unhappy . . . unquiet, ashamed, and always tormented by riddles we cannot expound." The solution seems to lie in a balancing of these tendencies in the mind—an adjustment of perception that preserves both a sense of the unique completeness of each momentary experience and a constant sense of a further perfect. The process, as Emerson explains it in "Tendencies," the last lecture, is dialectical: "Every man carries with him alway the vision of the perfect, and the highest actual that fulfils any part of this promise instantly exalts the Ideal just so much higher and it can no more be attained than he can set his foot on the horizon which flies before him" (EL, 3:292, 293, 313). The description makes a place for achievement, but it also leaves room for a further fulfillment, the need for which is awakened in the process of achievement itself. Each right action, in ethical terms, will be self-fulfilling, but will reveal further possible acts in its accomplishment. The key to psychological balance in the process is thus to concentrate on the moment itself; to look to the past is to invite deadening satisfaction, while to look to the future is to invite tragic frustration.

To regard the present moment both as fulfilling in itself and as one part of a continuing process requires that it be seen as potential. To the extent that one holds the moment to contain limitless possibilities, one preserves its eternal quality, for it is no longer bound either to the restriction of the past or to some rigid future goal. In the broader context of society, in Emerson's view, such openness is the most important quality of the present age, for the young have cultivated not only an openness lacking in previous generations, but a positive taste for the infinite, or a "love of the Vast": "The age is characterised by a certain yearning or aspiration which has given a new element to poetry and is called the Feeling of the Infinite." Finding its roots in German philosophy and noting its presence in English romanticism, he also senses that this yearning "finds a most genial climate in the American taste." It is the symptom of "the long imprisoned but now escaping Soul" (EL, 3:196), whose freedom is in part manifest in the freedom from time.

This element of the vast within the individual, the same element which we have seen as the soul and the one mind, makes a timeless consciousness possible. "Before it [the soul], Time—which usually we think the strongest of powers,—is weak." The reason is that time is the measure of the finite, but the soul is man's capacity for the infinite. The "uprise of the soul" in the modern age is evidenced by "the new consciousness of the One Mind (to which all have a potential access and which is the Creator)" (*EL*, 3:250, 214). Thus, while the character of the age may superficially seem to be the result of an explosion of democracy and radical individualism, it is in fact born of the ability of the soul to deny its identity as separate, as individual. Such selflessness is paradoxically the final criterion which Emerson proposes as a measure of the progress of self-culture:

A man's progress seems to be the continual transference of his *me*, of his egoism, back from his person, his body, his name, his circumstances, to the great soul which animates him and all, the justice, love, and beauty which are the eternal mind. In them let him aspire to live that the visits of the soul shall not be rare and interrupted but that he draw fuller inspirations of the common soul continually; then he will surmount also the fear of death, seeing that his heart is the Eternal life.   [*EL*, 3:253]

The pietistic, even mystical flavor of this insistence on the denial of ego is notable, not because it is a new element in Emerson's sensibility, but because it seems particularly intense in "The Present Age." This sensibility, of course, has existed almost from the first, along with elements of rationalism and pure aestheticism. But the emphasis on an experience that is timeless and infinite in "The Present Age" seems related to the rational dilemma of progress versus stability central to the "Human Life" series. The appeal to the mystical is given new weight as Emerson reaches the limit of the rational. He attempts not to resolve the paradox of achievement on logical grounds, but rather to insist on its irrelevance in experiential terms, assuming that experience can in some sense be freed from time. As a result, self-culture ultimately becomes self-negation, as Emerson answers one paradox with another.

But if the idea of selfless denial of the ego increased in significance in this period, it did not result in anything approaching a communitarian vision of society. Emerson's distrust of any communal avenue to reform is revealed most clearly in his later refusal to join Brook Farm, but these lectures are marked by his persistent articulation of that skepticism. The mysticism that tempers the elevation of self in his work also contributes to his denial of the efficacy of any social grouping. In this respect, he sets himself against what might be considered one of the leading tendencies of the party of the future, given the rising interest in various philosophies of association in the period.

For Emerson, however, it is "the Age of Severance, of Dissociation, of Freedom, of Analysis, of Detachment"—in short, "the age of the first person singular." Thus any association or social organization is rendered "accidental and momentary." Any question of political reform is reduced to one of ethics. Taking a position which Thoreau would later enlarge upon in "Civil Disobedience," Emerson argues that self-sufficiency "needs no crusade against the state but the simple abstinence from participating its wrong deed." Not only the state, but also the groups which would reform the state, must be treated warily, for much the same reason. The principle is simple: "Accept the reforms but accept not the person of the reformer nor his law" (*EL*, 3:188–89, 245, 260). Here Emerson's decade-long struggle with the church seems finally to have ended. He has announced not only that his own place in the church is limited, as he did in 1832, or that the church itself must be radically reformed, as he did in 1838, but that the church itself can play no essential part in the coming age of human development. He had warned in the Divinity School Address that the age required no new church, but rather a breath of new life into its existing forms. Compare that position, taken before a largely ecclesiastical audience in 1838, to the one he takes in the 1840 lecture "Reforms," before a secular audience: "Religion does not seem to me to tend now to a cultus as heretofore but to a heroic life. We find extreme difficulty in conceiving any church, any liturgy, any rite that would be quite genuine. But all things point at the house and the hearth" (*EL*, 3:263). Ironically, Emerson delivered that lecture on the evening of the day on which he had been asked to participate in the dedication of the church at East Lexington, where he had preached from 1835 to 1838. His theoretical views on the church did not prevent him from offering an address of extreme good will there, but he was careful to remind his former congregation that a church is properly a church only "when the consciousness of his union with the Supreme Soul dawns on the lowly heart of the worshipper—when the church becomes nothing and the priest nothing for all places are sacred and all persons" (*EL*, 3:330).

Emerson's loss of any vision for the church is one result of the corresponding growth of his vision of a humanity so self-sufficient that no institution can serve it. He saves his best expression of that vision for the conclusion of the final lecture of "The Present Age," a long passage portraying his genuine or ideal man. His image seems both more tangible and more democratic than that of a decade before, and perhaps because of this change, more arresting. Seeking to find peace through the external means of "arts and sciences, states and churches, books and persons, power and property," man is instead haunted by "the stern Fact, the sad Self, unrelenting, identical that he fled from." But surrendering to it, he finds the world transformed, and begins to realize

a quiet yet sublime Religion . . . whose temple shall be the household hearth and under whose light each man shall work that which his genius delights, shall possess that which he can enjoy; shall draw to him those companions that belong to him, and shall have a property in entire nature by the renouncement of all selfish and sensual aim. [*EL*, 3:314–15]

This vision is an impressive prelude to the chastened optimism of Emerson's later period. The prophetic, even utopian, strain is there in his image of the new individual in a radically changed world. But the change is reflected not in new institutions and associations, but in their absence. The church becomes the hearth, and the community becomes the family and a few close companions.

──── VIII ────

Essays: First Series

Emerson's Turn to the Essay

After noting the close of "The Present Age" in February 1840, Emerson apparently looked back to the journal entry of the preceding October in which he voiced his hope for "ecstasy & eloquence" in the lectures (*JMN*, 7:265). In a passage with close verbal parallels to the earlier one, he admits disappointment, frankly confessing, "I have not done what I hoped when I said, I will try it once more." As if exploring the reasons for this failure, he continues:

I have not once transcended the coldest selfpossession. I said I will agitate others, being agitated myself. I dared to hope for extacy & eloquence. A new theatre, a new art, I said, is mine. . . . Alas! alas! I have not the recollection of one strong moment. A cold mechanical preparation for a delivery as decorous,—fine things, pretty things, wise things,—but no arrows, no axes, no nectar, no growling, no transpiercing, no loving, no enchantment.   [*JMN*, 7:338–39]

The depth of his sense of disappointment is best revealed in his felt inability to transcend "the coldest selfpossession." Given his theory of oratorical success as the elimination of the barriers of self between speaker and hearer, this is an admission of serious failure. We may feel that anyone with such a passionate aim was bound for a disappointment, but it was exactly that passion which had fueled his intellectual productivity and secured his sense of vocation for over a decade. Now, however, his ambition for eloquence was being eroded as he fashioned an increasingly literary identity.

The reasons for this change are complex, but one important factor in the process was Emerson's growing sense of the confining nature of lecturing. Part of his reason for moving from preaching to lecturing was his belief that there were wider possibilities for expression in the lyceum than in the pulpit. But even at the height of his most creative period of lecturing, he began to feel its restrictions. In November 1838, just before "Human Life," a journal entry headed "Freedom" shows his restlessness with the mechanics of arranging the series. "Why should I read lectures with care & pain & afflict myself with all the meanness of ticket mongering," he wonders, reminding himself that his lecturing is not financially necessary. It would be better to "write & speak the beautiful & formidable words of a free man" (*JMN*, 7:136). During the next year, this attitude would grow, sharpened by what did in fact become the financial necessity of delivering "The Present Age." But he felt restricted not only by the scheduling and details necessary in arranging a lecture series, but also by a growing dissatisfaction with the lecture as a form of expression. While it promised to be a "new art," it too often degenerated into conventionalism. In the midst of "The Present Age" he wrote Margaret Fuller that his topics were beginning to sound like the titles of "Blair's sermons," and that with their "treadmill gait" they "would walk with due decorum in the columns of the Christian Register" (*L*, 2:246). This light self-mockery covered a real preoccupation with failure. He felt that his lectern had not become, as he hoped, "a pulpit that makes other pulpits tame & ineffectual" (*JMN*, 7:265), but had retained instead the cold decorum which he had hoped to avoid in the sermon.

Beneath this frustration with the lecture's conventionalism was the deeper frustration with its failure to live up to its promise as a means of communion between the artist and his audience. Emerson's early ambition for eloquence was based on this promise, which he had himself felt while hearing great preachers and orators in his youth. But he was coming to see that oratory also fell victim to "the tragedy of Art," the fact that "the Artist was at the expense of the Man." Even though he knew the necessity of expression, he also felt the truth of a remark of Thoreau: "If the man took too much pains with the expression he was not any longer the Idea himself" (*JMN*, 7:144). The painful self-exertion of creative art stymied the great promise of art: the loss of self in an expression of the one mind.

This was a particularly painful realization to Emerson, who saw lecturing as a possible compensation for the closeness he found difficult to maintain in personal relationships. "Thy love must be thy art," he wrote in 1840. "Thy words must spring from love, and every thought be touched with love" (*JMN*, 7:386). When he wrote William Emerson to tell him that his "Present Age" lectures were over, his description of them was telling: "ten decorous speeches & not one extacy, not one rapture, not one thunderbolt. Eloquence therefore there was none. As the audience however were not parties to my intention or hope, they did not complain at my failure" (*L*, 2:256). The most painful part of the failure seems to have been the distance he felt from his audience. Even to have felt that they sensed his disappointment might have been better than to suspect them of apathy and want of sympathy.

Out of the growing disillusionment with the spoken word, Emerson turned with increasing expectation toward the written word. In 1840 he returned to his planned book of essays and became heavily involved in work for the *Dial*, rather than writing a new series of lectures. His career as a lecturer was far from over, and in fact his reputation was only beginning to grow beyond the Boston area. But his quest for eloquence had largely given way to a concern for creating a vital prose style.

Emerson's developing ideas about the style of his essays were formed largely from the legacy of his ambition for the lecture. His goal was a style which would engage the reader in such a way as to transform reading into a dialogue of two minds. The feeling that the reader "overleaps that invisible barrier & continues the sentence" (*JMN*, 7:161) was what Emerson, as a writer of prose, hoped to duplicate. This desire, based partly on his reading, was sharpened by his sense of the immense difference between hearing a lecture and reading an essay. In an essay, the author's physical absence placed a new burden on the resources of language. Voice quality, eye contact, tone, rhythm, intensity—all the tools available to a skillful lecturer—had somehow to be replaced. The challenge was even greater, since even those tools had rendered the lecture less successful than Emerson hoped.

Emerson's oratorical ambition is therefore a helpful background for understanding his hope for *Essays: First Series*.[1] He sent the book to press on January 1, 1841, with the wish that "the page

be filled with the character not with the skill of the writer"
(*JMN*, 7:411). He hoped for a personal presence in the book, a
vitality that would bring him to life before his reader. While at work
on it earlier in the summer, he praised the "language of the street,"
valuing the "rattling oath" of the teamster over "a page of the North
American Review," a leading vehicle of Unitarian writing. Behind
vernacular language was the raw physical vigor of a living presence,
as his bodily metaphor indicates: "Cut these words & they would
bleed; they are vascular & alive; they walk & run" (*JMN*, 7:374).
Carlyle, Plutarch, and Montaigne were his examples of such a vitality in prose style. Even more revealing of his ambition is a journal
entry on Carlyle a few weeks later which mixes this earlier praise of
him with blame. Carlyle uses language "like a protean engine which
can cut, thrust, saw, rasp, tickle, or pulverize," but in so doing, "he
exhausts his topic. . . . He is not suggestive" (*JMN*, 7:382). A certain
balance must be kept, for the vitality which engages the reader can
also overpower him. The purpose of creating a prose with a living
presence is to call the reader to life as well.[2]

   When Emerson carried this ambition into practice in the essays,
the result was a blend of oratorical flair, confession, conversational
chattiness, and aphorism, which when it cohered was surprisingly
moving, but which always risked the danger of diffuseness. *Essays:
First Series* stands, therefore, at one remove stylistically from the
major lectures of 1837–40, much as *Nature* stands at one remove
from the sermons and early lectures. In both cases, Emerson can still
be found in the process of forging a new style, which is complete
and forceful at key points, but which has not yet fully emerged from
its oral background. Moreover, to read *Essays: First Series* with the
fresh perspective of the major lectures is to realize the extent to
which a sensitivity to such oral considerations as emphasis and tim-
ing influence their impact.

   Let me offer one example, a paragraph from "History" brief
enough for analysis, which seems representative of some of the key
elements of that style. The context of the paragraph is Emerson's
argument that the facts of history must be seen and understood
through private experience, an approach that makes all history "subjective" and ultimately transforms it into biography.

History must be this or it is nothing. Every law which the state enacts, indicates a fact in human nature; that is all. We must in ourselves see the necessary reason of every fact,—see how it could and must be. So stand before every public and private work; before an oration of Burke, before a victory of Napoleon, before a martyrdom of Sir Thomas More, of Sidney, of Marmaduke Robinson, before a French Reign of Terror, and a Salem hanging of witches, before a fanatic Revival, and the Animal Magnetism in Paris, or in Providence. We assume that we under like influence should be alike affected, and should achieve the like; and we aim to master intellectually the steps, and reach the same height or the same degradation that our fellow, our proxy has done.   [*CW*, 2:7]

The first sentence resonates with the emphatic "History must be this," and though we sense its force, we are left with a subtle choice of emphasis. Does the voice stress "must" or "this"? If we hear the emphasis on "must," the whole phrase, and the whole paragraph, assume a pleading tone, asking us to make a moral choice. "This is what *we* must make of history," it says. But if we hear the emphasis on "this," the tone is more factual and positive, closer to the announcement of an intellectual discovery than a moral exhortation. Similarly, when the next sentence ends with "that is all," we face another choice behind the flat assertion. Does "that" refer to the entire opening of the sentence, or to the closer phrase, "human nature"? Both, of course, fit, but we hear the cadence and emphasis differently when we consciously or unconsciously choose one or the other. In the same vein, we can choose to emphasize either "ourselves" or "see" in the next sentence, the first choice offering a more coolly factual assertion, and the second carrying, again, a quality of preacherly exhortation. And, in the next sentence, if "stand" is more heavily emphasized than "every," the tone is exhortative rather than factual. Both possible tones blend into the catalogue of men and events which follows, each item in which depicts some form of physical or mental violence, ranging from images of victory and martyrdom to the haunting threat of mental and emotional turmoil. Depending on the tone we have chosen, we can survey these upheavals with the cool assurance of knowing that they are not alien but a part of us and thus not to be feared, or with the tense hope that the power we see here can be converted to good with our own moral exertion. Emerson offers no consolation here, and insists that we are capable not only of any height but of any degradation of history. What he offers is a choice of psychological stances before these possibilities. That choice of stances is in turn dependent on the way we imagine the voice behind the printed page. There is a presence, but it is a suggestive rather than an aggressive one. While this particular doubleness of tone is peculiar to the paragraph in question, the process of choice required of the reader, and his resulting attempt to engage the person whose voice we hear, exemplifies the best quality of Emerson's prose.[3]

For this reason, Emerson's use of the almost isolated sentence unit, more prominent in the essays than in lectures of the same period, seems appropriate. Carlyle's well-known complaint that Emerson's paragraphs resemble "a beautiful square *bag of duck-shot*" rather than "a beaten *ingot*" (*CEC*, p. 371) ignores Emerson's willingness to pay such a price for the freedom to make sudden shifts of tone, subject, and image. Behind these shifts is the constantly changing persona of the essays, always presenting the reader a fresh challenge and a chance for fresh dialogue. By never totally committing himself to one tone or stance, Emerson preserves the suggestiveness he missed in Carlyle, and constantly holds out the possibility of what he felt to be the highest aesthetic pleasure —the merging of minds between author and reader.

Consider, for instance, this familiar paragraph from "Self-Reliance":

A foolish consistency is the hobgoblin of little minds, adored by little statesmen and philosophers and divines. With consistency a great soul has simply nothing to do. He may as well concern himself with his shadow on the wall. Speak what you think now in hard words, and to-morrow speak what to-morrow thinks in hard words again, though it contradict every thing you said to-day.—'Ah, so you shall be sure to be misunderstood.'— Is it so bad then to be misunderstood? Pythagoras was misunderstood, and Socrates, and Jesus, and Luther, and Copernicus, and Galileo, and Newton, and every pure and wise spirit that ever took flesh. To be great is to be misunderstood. [*CW*, 2:33–34]

The first sentence is witheringly satirical; the second haughtily matter-of-fact. With the image of the "shadow on the wall," Emerson introduces a tone of humor and resumes an essentially satirical pose. The next sentence is straightforward New England preaching, which leads into the imaginary objector's " 'Ah, so you shall be sure to be misunderstood.' " This dramatic interruption makes possible the rhetorical catalogue of great, and misunderstood men, leading to the clinching aphorism, "To be great is to be misunderstood."

While Emerson's style was molded by an essentially oratorical standard of aesthetic effect, it was also particularly suited to his method of composition. He worked by piecing together the journal entries he kept almost daily, and the lectures that they produced, sometimes taking long passages from either journal or lecture with little revision, sometimes revising and expanding them heavily, and almost always fusing them into a proximity with each other that itself gave them new meaning. Critics have long recognized the strengths and weaknesses of this method, but what remains to be emphasized is how completely it reinforced Emerson's strategy of frequently varying tone, image, and persona. The purpose of the journals was to preserve the mood and insight of the moment, which he seems at times to have regarded as sacred: "Happy is he who in looking at the compositions of an earlier date knows that the moment wrote them, & feels no more call or right to alter them than to alter his recollections of a day or a fact" (*JMN*, 7:315). The preservation of his varying moods in the journal made the varying tone of his essay style possible.

The risk of disunity which his style posed did not discourage him, largely because of a faith that a consistency of character would gradually provide a common strand to tie the essays together. In a journal entry of June 1839, he notes that "succession, moments, parts" are the destiny of authors, not "wholes & worlds & eternity." In answer to the worry that this raises about the inability to "sail no straight line," he appeals to the ship's "zig zag line on a hundred tacks. . . . See the line from a sufficient distance & it straightens itself to the average tendency" (*JMN*, 7:216–17). "Line" here means both the ship's course and the line of prose or verse, and when he uses the metaphor again in "Self-Reliance" (*CW*, 2:34), it refers to the pattern of daily actions that any individual's life exemplifies. Emerson's point is that the same thread of character that can make the most contradictory actions of an individual seem comprehensible from the right perspective will also smooth the sharp edges of his staccato prose. Thus "character" and the composition of prose merge in this passage from "Self-Reliance," a brief evocation of both his life and his aim as an essayist:

A character is like an acrostic or Alexandrian stanza;—read it forward, backward, or across, it still spells the same thing. In this pleasing contrite wood-life which God allows me, let me record day by day my honest thought without prospect or retrospect, and, I cannot doubt, it will be found symmetrical, though I mean it not, and see it not. My book should smell of pines and resound with the hum of insects. The swallow over my window should interweave that thread or straw he carries in his bill into my web also. [CW, 2:34]

The "web" of words is a useful metaphor for thinking of Emerson's style. It suggests the complexity of the many individual strands, the loose symmetry, and the quality of the spiral or circle which mark his prose, all of which are denials of linear logic and progression. Yet the denial of logical succession in the prose was only partial. The logic of the sermon form still underpins most of *Essays: First Series,* when we move from sentence and paragraph unit to each essay as a whole. And further, when we regard the structure of the book itself, other strategies of form are apparent. Let us look at each of these formal strategies as we move from this consideration of individual sentences and paragraphs outward to the essay and the book as a whole.

The Essay as Sermon: "Circles"

The common complaint about the inconsecutive quality of Emerson's prose is directed not only at individual sentences, but at the larger structure of entire essays. Carlyle's comment (about *Essays: Second Series*) was that the sentences were "strong and simple" but that "they did not, sometimes, rightly stick to their foregoers and their followers" (*CEC,* p. 371). James Russell Lowell escalated this complaint to refer to the coherence of paragraphs when he described a lecture appearance by Emerson in the late 1860s: "The first lecture, to be sure, was more disjointed even than common. It was as if, after vainly trying to get his paragraphs into sequence and order, he had at last tried the desperate expedient of *shuffling* them. It was chaos come again, but it was a chaos full of shooting-stars, a jumble of creative forces."[4] Lowell exemplifies the persistent attitude among some readers that Emerson seems to "get away" with disorder because of his special poetical and mystical gifts, and though he refers in this case to a lecture, his complaint can be readily understood as applying to the essays as well. But Buell's analysis of the "buried" structures of the essays raises a pertinent point: it seems that the "formlessness" in the essays, even paragraph to paragraph, is deliberate. Buell notes the persistence of Emerson's use of the "buried outline," the "careless list," and the developed but unlabeled argument, all of which suggest Emerson's conscious use of logical and sequential structure, and his corresponding battle against it.[5] The battle is not necessarily against order itself, but against its restrictive aspects. In it we see an attempt to avoid exhausting his topic in logical discourse—his complaint about Carlyle's prose—in order to preserve its suggestiveness. In this sense, then, *Essays: First Series* represents a final stage in Emerson's reaction to the sermon tradition, though like all rebellious offspring, the essays mirror certain characteristics of their parents. He had embraced the lyceum for its welcome freedom from the pulpit, and he regarded his essays as a further extension of that freedom. But much of the sermon remained in the lectures, and much of both sermon and lecture remained in the essays. The sections and subsections of which most of the essays are composed, which if not numbered are numerable,[6] remind us of Emerson's sermonic habits of composition, and his attempts to hide the structures confirm his own consciousness of that habit.

Aside from such dividing and subdividing, the strategy of moral persuasion, with its movement from a general truth to a moral stance, or from doctrine to application, is also an important aspect of the impact of the essays, the roots of which are also in the sermon tradition. "Circles" is the essay in which this debt can be most clearly traced, both formally and thematically. A pivotal essay in Emerson's transition from optimism to skepticism, it also tells us much about his movement from preacher to essayist. Moreover, its theme, the continual growth and culture of the soul, is the constant theme of his writing since his days in the ministry.

Emerson opens the essay with the image of the expanding concentric circles of "the eye" and "the horizon which it forms," adding that "throughout nature this primary figure is repeated without end" (*CW*, 2:179). As David Wyatt notes, the opening sentence- is a "microcosm" of the entire essay, in which Emerson captures the central act of the individual's continual outward expansion into nature.[7] The circle is thus "the highest emblem in the cipher of the world" (*CW*, 2:179). James M. Cox has noted the play on "cipher," used here to mean both letter or emblem and zero,[8] which further suggests the tension of the essay. On the one hand, the world promises a richness of meaning, waiting to be deciphered; on the other, we see only its absence.

When Emerson introduces his next image, based on a quotation attributed to Augustine, that tension is extended: "St. Augustine described the nature of God as a circle whose centre was everywhere, and its circumference nowhere."[9] The image prepares us for metaphysical and theological speculation, and suggests the paradox at the foundation of the lecture. The poles of the paradox, the "everywhere" and "nowhere" of God, return us to the double possibility of the abundance or absence of meaning suggested by the pun on "cipher."

If we approach "Circles" from its homiletical context, this quotation serves as Emerson's "text," while the rest of the essay explores its meanings or "doctrine," and its "application" to the moral life. That part of the paradox which asserts that God's "circumference" is "nowhere" indicates that God, because unlimited by any defining circumference, is infinite. That God's "centre" is "everywhere" suggests his presence in all being, including the individual soul. The earlier metaphor of the eye forming "the first circle" implies a center for that circle within the self, establishing the association of "self" and "centre." The "God within" is later made explicit in the pronouncement, "We learn that God IS; that he is in me; and that all things are shadows of him" (*CW*, 2:183). The suggestive and epigrammatical quality of the quotation makes it well suited for an Emersonian text, and though he does not attempt elaborate exegesis of it, he does form the essay around its two suggestions: the idea that the essence of divinity is to overcome potential outer barriers, or to have no circumference, and the corresponding idea that God is within every soul, or "centered" everywhere.

The two-part division of the essay, which Buell suggests is indicated in the phrases "There are no fixtures in nature" and "There are no fixtures to men,"[10] can also be taken as the two-part division of the "doctrine" section of the essay-sermon, in which Emerson explores the two implications of his text. In the first section (CW, 2:179–82), he argues for the impermanence of all outer barriers to growth, and thus for the potentially divine ability to resist outer restraints. His appeal, once again, is to the example of God: "Permanence is but a word of degrees. Our globe seen by God, is a transparent law, not a mass of facts. The law dissolves the fact and holds it fluid" (CW, 2:179). The essential word "transparent," long Emerson's favorite, illumines the whole passage. Rather than seeing nature as an opaque mass, and therefore a barrier, God sees through it. We are taken back here to the earlier image of the eye and the horizon with the new insight that it is the ability of the eye to see the horizon as "transparent" that makes the drawing of a further circle possible.

The section proceeds by asserting the impermanence of even such great vision as is displayed in the art of classical Greece, with Emerson using the fact of the physical decay of the artifacts to suggest the impermanence of the art as well. The lesson is positive, however, for "new arts destroy the old." Here we see again Emerson's recognition that impermanence is the price of new vision. When the law is applied to humanity, the circle image is given its most direct application: "The life of man is a self-evolving circle, which, from a ring imperceptibly small, rushes on all sides outwards to new and larger circles, and that without end." The use of the circle to describe man carries with it the implication that man is Godlike, since God has also been envisioned in terms of a circle. Like God, man must resist any final circumference, and "[burst] over that boundary on all sides" (CW, 2:180–81).

In the second part of the doctrine section (CW, 2:182–84), Emerson turns from the impermanent barriers of the soul to its divine center. "There are no fixtures to men" he explains, "if we appeal to consciousness," and he explains this fact with a new metaphor for the soul: "Every man supposes himself not to be fully understood; and if there is any truth in him, if he rests at last on the divine soul, I see not how it can be otherwise. The last chamber, the last closet, he must feel, was never opened; there is always a residuum unknown, unanalyzable. That is, every man believes that he has a greater possibility." By introducing the image of a final closet or chamber in the soul, Emerson extends the symbolic power of his circle image, for what the circle and this final closet have in common is that they are both perfectly enclosed geometrical spaces. In using the circle to portray the soul's growth, Emerson suggested a centrifugal expansion, with the circle as the perimeter which we must surpass to affirm our power and extend our vision. But in this image of the last chamber, Emerson presents us with a barrier we seek to break not out of, but into, one which continually recedes before our efforts to penetrate it. The image of centrifugal expansion is replaced by an image of centripetal recession, in a way that suggests an inner core of the soul which perpetually contracts before our inner delving. The connection of this "last chamber" with God is confirmed in the phrase "if he rests at last on the divine soul," but the qualifying "if" should be stressed here, for the tone of the essay is more tentative than these affirmations of boundless human power might suggest. The moments of divine presence, which are always potentially available, are balanced by moments of absence. "Alas for this infirm faith, this will not strenuous, this vast ebb of a vast flow! I am God in nature; I am a weed by the wall." But the affirmative side of this ebb and flow—"I am God in nature"—again confirms the possible heights to which we can rise. Emerson describes the growth of the consciousness of identity with God as idealism, the stance by which the mind subsumes all nature. First we are tempted "to play with [idealism] academically"; then we find "in the heyday of youth and poetry that it may be true, that it is true in gleams and fragments"; and finally we realize "that it must be true" when we find it "ethical and practical." In this final confirmation of the primacy of idealism, "we learn that God IS; that he is in me; and that all things are shadows of him" (*CW*, 2:182–83). The passage is worth repeating because it culminates the movement of the entire first part of the essay, fusing the emphasis on the nature of God, suggested by the Augustinian text, and on the nature of man, suggested by the circular images. The last closet of the soul is God, and the continual expansion of the life of man beyond existing boundaries is made possible by God as well.

With the meaning of the text established, Emerson begins a series of applications of it, arranged on a discernibly ascending scale of importance from conversation through literature, religion, nature, and ethics.[11] "Conversation," his first application, "is a game of circles," because each new speaker whom we encounter "emancipates us from the oppression of the last speaker, to oppress us with the greatness and exclusiveness of his own thought, then yields us to another redeemer." In each case, we are taken beyond the limits of the speaker, and we also expand our own previous limits. Literature, a second area of application, "afford[s] us a platform whence we may command a view of our present life." By seeing ourselves as if from a distance in the reflection of literature, we gain an opportunity for further cultivation. The value of the poet is that "he smites and arouses me with his shrill tones, . . . and I open my eye on my own possibilities." Emerson introduces his next category of application, religion, by stressing that "we have the same need to command a view of the religion of the world," one which allows us to see beyond the merely personal element in Christianity. Emerson still has the issues of the Divinity School controversy in mind here; he insists that despite the great "claims and virtues of persons . . . the instinct of man presses eagerly onward to the impersonal and illimitable." The veneration of Jesus' person therefore is a limiting element in existing Christianity. Emerson even offers a Pauline text to clinch his point: "Then shall also the Son be subject unto Him who put all things under him, that God may be all in all" (*CW*, 2:184–86). The God who, in this Scripture, is elevated over the Son is the God within available to every soul.

After conversation, literature, and religion, Emerson moves to "the natural world," which "may be conceived of as a system of concentric circles," and he reminds us from time to time that "this surface on which we now stand, is not fixed, but sliding." The sense of animated nature to which he alludes suggests that "this chemistry and vegetation, these metals and animals, . . . are means and methods only,—are words of God, and as fugitive as other words." These facts of nature should always lead the scientist to the "higher fact" of "Omnipresence," the realization that all things "proceed from the eternal generation of the soul." This rising scale of applications ends with ethics: "The same law of eternal procession ranges all that we call the virtues, and extinguishes each in the light of a better." Thus the norms of ethical behavior change as each situation is seen from a greater height. Prudence, for example, may be only a "deduction" from grandeur, or debt may be preferable to prompt repayment. Caution against an evil may in fact place one in "the power of the evil" (*CW*, 2:186). There is no fixed point in nature, and there is likewise none in ethics—"no virtue which is final" (*CW*, 2:187)—so the individual is continually challenged to seek a higher mode of action.

Just as *Nature*'s ascending scale of uses rises to "Discipline," the ascending scale of applications of the doctrine of "Circles" rises to "virtue" or ethics. In *Nature* Emerson broke his ascending scale after "Discipline" to raise the "noble doubt" of idealism, and in "Circles" he breaks the series of applications after ethics to raise another doubt, one which we have seen growing in the lecture series leading up to *Essays: First Series*. He puts the doubt in the voice of a skeptical reader: "And thus, O circular philosopher, I hear some reader exclaim, you have arrived at a fine pyrrhonism, at an equivalence and indifferency of all actions" (*CW*, 2:188). The query refers most directly to the preceding argument that there is no permanent form of virtue, but its implication is even deeper: there is no permanence. Pyrrho taught that truth was unattainable, and in one sense, Emerson's entire essay has taught the same thing: "the moral fact of the Unattainable, the flying Perfect, around which the hands of man can never meet."[12] Emerson has voiced his own deepest doubt through his imagined skeptical reader, and must now try to answer that doubt.

The fact "that there is no end in nature," Emerson notes early in the essay, is "at once the inspirer and condemner of every success" (*CW*, 2:179). Until now, he has preached only the inspirational side of that fact. Faced with responding to the idea that impermanence also condemns every action, he offers a paragraph notable both for what it says and for what it does not say. We should first notice that the question posed by his skeptical reader is logical in tone, implying that Emerson is a "circular philosopher" not only because of his imagery, but because his arguments finally circle back upon themselves, making what Emerson proposes as a reason for continual moral effort into an equally good reason for moral sloth. Emerson's response, in logical terms, amounts to a shrug of the shoulders, though its impact is much greater because of his tone. "I am not careful to justify myself," he begins, shifting the tone away from that of logical debate. He follows with a personal observation:

I own I am gladdened by seeing the predominance of the saccharine principle throughout vegetable nature, and not less by beholding in morals that unrestrained inundation of the principle of good into every chink and hole that selfishness has left open, yea, into selfishness and sin itself; so that no evil is pure, nor hell itself without its extreme satisfactions.

[CW, 2:188]

You may see the world as evil, he seems to say, but you may also see it as good, as I do. His vision of good is based largely on the presence of the moral law "inundat[ing]" man at every opportunity, but it also has a certain logical subtlety, disguised in its more casual tone. Even hell can have "its extreme satisfactions," based as it is on the self. The remark is best understood in the context of an earlier one in "Self-Reliance"—"if I am the Devil's child, I will live then from the Devil" (*CW*, 2:30)—where the idea of self is elevated above any notion of right or wrong. If "hell" is seen as such an exertion of pure selfishness, it at least preserves a certain vitality and integrity, and it carries with it the seed of powerful virtue when selfishness is replaced by Self-reliance. What this stance does is to turn the paradox back on the skeptic. If you can find an element of evil (indifference or condemnation) even in that which inspires the good, Emerson implies, I can as easily find an element of good (growth or potential) in extreme evil. Seen negatively, to strive for improvement implies existing imperfection, but seen positively, the recognition of imperfection implies the potential for improvement. Emerson thereby forces at least a draw in the argument.

At this point, he begins a remarkable passage which, seen by itself, appears to be a declaration of philosophical irresponsibility:

But lest I should mislead any when I have my own head, and obey my whims, let me remind the reader that I am only an experimenter. Do not set the least value on what I do, or the least discredit on what I do not, as if I pretended to settle anything as true or false. I unsettle all things. No

facts are to me sacred; none are profane; I simply experiment, an endless
seeker, with no Past at my back.   [*CW*, 2:188]

Seen in the context of "Circles," the passage is less an Emersonian
credo than a rhetorical stance assumed for this particular context.
On the surface, it continues the tone of disclaiming involvement in
any logical debate, and the reference to "whim" again echoes "Self-
Reliance," with its stance of determined inconsistency. ("I would
write on the lintels of the door-post, *Whim*" [*CW*, 2:30]). But in
that very stance, Emerson implies his final answer to his skeptical
reader. Unable to eliminate the possibility that one might look on
the unachieved as a cause for indifference, Emerson demonstrates
his own choice in the matter, seeing the unachieved as a cause for
activity—an approach which has, at least, equal logic on its side. But
the choice to be made here is moral; the question is how to live; and
by offering an example of moral posture in his image of the "experimenter" and "endless seeker," Emerson addresses the question more
directly than logic would have allowed. His evasion of the issue thus
becomes his answer to it.

   This exemplary moral stance is the highest ethical application of
the doctrine of "Circles," and the remainder of the essay explores
it in detail. Emerson finds, in the next paragraph, "some principle
of fixture or stability in the soul," an "eternal generator" from which
the constant generation of circles proceeds. This "central life,"
another manifestation of the ideal or the God within, provides a
sense of stability because it is "superior to creation . . . knowledge
and thought." In other words, it provides a standard by which
growth can be measured. Without it, "this incessant movement and
progression, which all things partake, could never become sensible
to us." But even this principle changes, for that "central life" continually "labors . . . [to suggest] to our thought a certain development, as if that which is made, instructs how to make a better." The
conclusion, expressed in a familiar organic metaphor, summarizes
the burden of Emerson's final application of the doctrine of "Circles" to life: "Thus there is no sleep, no pause, no preservation, but
all things renew, germinate, and spring" (*CW*, 2:188).

   The essay ends, following the sermon pattern, with an increasing
pitch of emotion, centering around the metaphor of germination

and birth and its opposite, age. Adopting the symbolic associations he had developed in "Human Life," he identifies "old age" as "the only disease": "We call it by many names,—fever, intemperance, insanity, stupidity, and crime: they are all forms of old age: they are rest, conservatism, appropriation, inertia, not newness, not the way onward." In this moral stance, Emerson merges a number of the concerns developed over the course of his lecture career. To live "onward" is to recognize the irrelevance of the past, remembering that "the past is always swallowed and forgotten; the coming only is sacred." This present-mindedness is also the key to the most central moral achievement for Emerson, self-forgetfulness: "The one thing we seek with insatiable desire, is to forget ourselves, to be surprised out of our propriety, . . . to draw a new circle." When we act from the self without consciousness, we cross the line between selfishness and Self-reliance. The soul grows not by calculation but "by abandonment" to a divine center, "superior to knowledge and thought" (*CW*, 2:188–90).

The Voices of *Essays: First Series*

Despite the benefits he gained from it, Emerson's use of the essay as his genre exacted one important cost: his volumes of essays are rarely read in total, because the individual essays in them stand too readily on their own. The later *Representative Men* is the most likely to overcome this tendency because the overall scheme of the book is more readily apparent, and more clearly demands to be taken into account. But similarly, in *Essays: First Series,* there is a general organization which is lost when the essays are read separately. More importantly, there is a cumulative effect which arises not only from the thematic organization of the volume, but also from a complex interplay of different voices within it. We are accustomed to associate such a manipulation of voice with the use of persona in fiction and poetry, but Emerson also uses it in the essay, and it is his use of this device that ultimately compels us to regard his essays as art, rather than philosophy or theology, and to associate them with the poem rather than the treatise.

Since the general pattern of the book helps us understand the interplay of voices, we should first take note of it. Here a remark by Bishop, aimed at Emerson's prose in general, is helpful. All of the essays, he writes, are "a display of the whole Soul in its several distinguishable manifestations."[13] In *Essays: First Series,* however, Bishop's remark needs to be modified to reflect the idea that the soul is in process. The thematic center of the book is the culture of the soul, as exemplified in its outward expansion, and the organization of the essays reflects that culture.[14]

Emerson regarded self-culture as the progress of the potential divinity within to its concrete manifestation in moral action. In the dialectic of growth, this action became part of the fact of nature which could then reinforce further inner growth as it was comprehended by the individual. Thus the choice of "History" to begin the volume is a recognition that fact, or nature, as it is manifested in human action, is one (not the sole) starting point for the process of culture, but only if this fact is internalized by the realization that the acts of other minds are in reality the acts of one mind, which also subsumes the self. History quickly yields to "self," therefore, in "Self-Reliance," which stresses the primacy of "the aboriginal Self" (*CW,* 2:37) in both history and self-culture. The next essays, "Compensation" and "Spiritual Laws," place the actions of the self in the context of transcendent laws; and their ethical focus emphasizes the necessary outward movement to moral activity that is confirmed in the next four essays, which are explicitly concerned with the forms of activity of the self: "Love," "Friendship," "Prudence," and "Heroism." Just as it is transitional in Emerson's career, "Circles" is transitional in the structure of *Essays: First Series.* Its depiction of the outward unfolding of the soul closes the part of the book concerned with that process, but its focus on the intellectual aspects of that growth initiates a dialectical turn back from the world of action to the inner world of perception. This turn is further explored in the last two essays, "Intellect" and "Art." The soul's perception, born of its necessary interaction with the world, translates that action into intellectual truth, which nourishes the soul. Because "Art" touches upon both the comprehension and the creation of art, it is pivotal, reminding us that just as comprehension of art nurtures growth, growth leads to expression. If we remember that artistic expression is a historical act, in fact one of the most important acts in the fabric of history, then we can make a circular return to the beginning of the book again, with its stress on the effect of history on the soul. Some critics have already noticed that the best instances of Emerson's individual paragraphs and essays have a "spiral" quality about them.[15] That same quality exists in the structure of *Essays: First Series* as a whole, standing as a formal mirroring of the process of the soul's culture. The outer world is internalized in the self, the self enters that world in action and expression, and the comprehension of action and expression as forms of history once again leads to an internalization of the outer world.

This abstract pattern becomes apparent only gradually to the reader, who is much less likely to be immediately affected by this portrayal of the growing self's interaction with the world than to be struck by encounters with the concrete self who is speaking in the essays. But that self, however concrete, is also elusive because of the variety of forms it takes. Emerson counterpoints the abstract pattern of the growth of the self with a wide range of stances and attitudes —one is tempted to say, characters—which are designed to exemplify the various possibilities of the self. If the doctrine of self-culture is based on a conviction of the potential of the self, these voices dramatize the nature of that potential.

Emerson offers what can be taken as a clue to his artistic procedure in the first essay, "History," when he refers to Proteus as an appropriate symbol of the ever-changing but ever-constant self: "What else am I who laughed or wept yesterday, who slept last night like a corpse, and this morning stood and ran? And what see I on any side but the transmigrations of Proteus?" (*CW*, 2:18). Just as life has its Protean qualities, Emerson's prose is built around a similarly Protean display of moods, voices, and characters. Perhaps the most notable of these voices is one which I will label the "Orphic" voice, the essential medium of Emerson's ideas, and the unifying backdrop against which the other voices are displayed. Bronson Alcott's "Orphic Sayings" are usually remembered as the focus of ridicule by critics of the *Dial*, because of their tendency to overblown vapidness;[16] but even Alcott, on those instances when he had his material in control, could use that peculiar style effectively. Emerson, however, was able to realize more consistently the qualities of detached authority, tinged with an aura of mysticism, that Alcott hoped to achieve in his use of the form. The following passage from "Compensation" is a representative example of the Orphic voice, used here by Emerson to establish the primacy of the soul in the compensating balances of nature.

There is a deeper fact in the soul than compensation, to wit, its own nature. The soul is not a compensation, but a life. The soul *is*. Under all this running sea of circumstance, whose waters ebb and flow with perfect balance, lies the aboriginal abyss of real Being. Essence, or God, is not a relation, or a part, but the whole. Being is the vast affirmative, excluding negation, self-balanced, and swallowing up all relations, parts and times, within itself. Nature, truth, virtue are the influx from thence. Vice is the absence or departure of the same. Nothing, Falsehood, may indeed stand as the great Night or shade, on which, as a background, the living universe paints itself forth; but no fact is begotten by it; it cannot work; for it is not. It cannot work any good; it cannot work any harm. It is harm inasmuch as it is worse not to be than to be. [*CW*, 2:70]

The passage is marked by its quality of proclamation, a tone of authoritative pronouncement, best exemplified in the brief sentence "The soul *is*. " Yet the very authority and emphasis which are given to this simple assertion suggest to the reader a depth of meaning not readily apparent, and add an important edge of mystery to the pronouncement. With this mood established, Emerson continues to make assertions of fact that are increasingly cosmic in their significance. From the soul we move to "the aboriginal abyss of real Being," and then to "Essence, or God," and these are finally contrasted with "nothing . . . the great Night or shade, on which, as a background, the living universe paints itself forth." While this passage is somewhat unique in the cosmic quality of its terms, it does exemplify the voice to which Emerson repeatedly turns to make necessary assertions of fact and to advance central arguments. In this case, for instance, he demonstrates the Platonic position that evil is privation, rather than any independent force, which is a necessary step in his argument that there is no compensating cost for virtue. This Orphic voice is closely associated with Emerson's preaching, taking from the sermon the air of authority and techniques of exposition.

At its best, Emerson's Orphic voice culminated in aphorism. The impression of divine wisdom compressed into a few words punctuates the prose, often providing a striking opening which can then be developed further or a concluding thrust which the preceding prose has prepared. In "Friendship" we are caught by the almost brutal frankness that opens one paragraph: "I do then with my friends as I do with my books. I would have them where I could find them, but I seldom use them" (*CW*, 2:126). In "Intellect" the quick answer to an opening question is impressive: "What is the hardest task in the world? To think" (*CW*, 2:196). In "Spiritual Laws" we find the direct simplicity of another opening remark: "What a man does, that he has" (*CW*, 2:83). Such examples abound, giving support to the description of Emerson's prose as aphoristic, not only because he uses the sentence as his basic unit of expression, but also because he consciously works for the compressed nub of meaning to illumine key passages. The liveliness of the aphorism, its ability to engage the reader aggressively, makes it a particularly useful complement to the otherwise detached nature of the Orphic voice.

In general, we may associate Emerson's prose with the detached authority of the Orphic voice, and with a formality which is necessarily part of such detachment. But, in fact, that formality is belied by Emerson's repeated return to a colloquial tone, as necessarily casual and direct as the Orphic voice is formal and detached. If he used the divine pronouncement effectively, it was in part because he balanced it with the homely metaphor and the vernacular phrase. "Compensation," an essay particularly rich in examples of the colloquial voice, contains a depiction of the law of compensating balance as "this back-stroke, this kick of the gun." Later, Emerson compares the self-revealing quality of an expressed opinion to "a thread-ball thrown at a mark, [whose] other end remains in the thrower's bag." The principle that the entire universe is present in every part of itself is expressed graphically by the observation, "If you see smoke, there must be fire" (*CW*, 2:60–64). Referring to Greek literature in "History," Emerson compares the Greeks to "a gang of great boys with such a code of honor and such lax discipline as great boys have" (*CW*, 2:15). And in "Prudence" he summarizes the need to face the unappealing facts of life with the remark, "If we walk in the woods, we must feed musquitoes" (*CW*, 2:133). Such examples are among the most readable parts of Emerson's prose, but their value is enhanced by their tendency to make the more abstract ideas, which we associate with the Orphic voice, vividly practical. This colloquial Emerson sometimes gets pushed aside because of the temptation to set off Thoreau or Whitman as examples of writers whose language is more richly symbolic than Emerson's because more closely grounded in reality. Emerson's own remark about Thoreau's style, though it seems to admit the point, is in fact too self-deprecating when we remember his own facility with the vernacular: "In reading him, I find the same thought, the same spirit that is in me, but he takes a step beyond, and illustrates by excellent images that which I should have conveyed in a sleepy generality" (*J*, 9:522). It was precisely this ability to recognize and respond to vividly natural language, which can also be noted in his love of the conversation of his farmer neighbors, that accounts for his persistent return to the colloquial to reinforce his points. While his Orphic voice represented the divine potential of the human mind, his colloquial voice assured the role of nature in that potential. The cold detachment of the infinite is warmed, therefore, by the familiarity of the commonplace.

The Orphic and the colloquial voices were strategies of discourse based on a variation of an expected author-reader relationship. There was a point to be made by the speaker of the essay, who was addressing the reader directly and straightforwardly. But Emerson introduced into his essays other voices which had an essentially dramatic nature, and some of the most memorable moments in his essays occur when the direct relation between the author and reader is either subtly or emphatically complicated by a dramatic interlude. Such drama often involves the direct introduction of dialogue into the essays, which is most recognizably dramatic, but it can also consist of a sudden portrayal of an idea or attitude by the speaker of the essay, a pose or stance which is assumed to bring some abstraction to life.

Because such dramatic interludes usually have a rhetorical point, they often take the form of a debate or interchange of opposing views. The imagined objection of the skeptical reader who accuses Emerson of Pyrronhism in "Circles," discussed earlier in the chapter, is a good example. More explicitly dramatic is the lengthier discussion, reported in "Self-Reliance," with the adviser "who was wont to importune me with the dear old doctrines of the church." Emerson in this case uses his adviser's caution to his own advantage. The warning his adviser gives him, that to live "wholly from within" may in fact be to follow promptings "from below," only gives him the opportunity to demonstrate the extent of the risk he is willing to take for self-reliance: "If I am the Devil's child, I will live then from the Devil" (CW, 2:30). To take such a risk emphasizes further the depth of the underlying conviction that to live from within is in fact to rely on the divine. Later in the essay, there is a similar interlude, in which the other member of the dialogue is not explicitly quoted, but used instead as the audience of an extended dramatic monologue: "O father, O mother, O wife, O brother, O friend, I have lived with you after appearances hitherto. Henceforward I am the truth's." The passage continues at length as a monologue, but the friend or relative who is addressed is almost palpably before the reader: "If you can love me . . . If you cannot . . . If you are true. . . ." And the dramatic quality of the passage peaks near the end with a question that appears to be a direct response to the reaction of the intended hearer: "Does this sound harsh to-day? You will soon love what is dictated by your nature as well as mine, and if we follow the truth, it will bring us out safe at last" (CW, 2:41–42). Couched as advice to the reader (the passage begins, "Say to them . . ."), it is also a device for bringing to life the force of will, and sometimes the heavy cost, that is demanded by the commitment to self-reliance.

More often, however, the dramatic interludes are briefer pauses which punctuate a developing argument. In "Friendship," Emerson emphasizes the ephemeral quality of human relations with this confession, directly addressed to a friend:

I cannot deny it, O friend, that the vast shadow of the Phenomenal includes thee, also, in its pied and painted immensity,—thee, also, compared with whom all else is shadow. Thou art not Being, as Truth is, as Justice is,—Thou art not my soul, but a picture and effigy of that. Thou hast come to me lately, and already thou art seizing thy hat and cloak.
[CW, 2:116]

The passage gains force not only by giving us the sense that we have intruded on a conversation ("I cannot deny it . . ."), but by suggesting the concrete immediacy of a social visit in the image of the "hat and cloak," a somewhat humorous deflation of the otherwise formal language of the passage. But there need not be the implied presence of dialogue to provide a dramatic situation, as the following passage from "Intellect" (the beginning of which was noted earlier) demonstrates: "What is the hardest task in the world? To think. I would put myself in the attitude to look in the eye an abstract truth, and I cannot. I blench and withdraw on this side and on that. I seem to know what he meant, who said, No man can see God face to face and live" (CW, 2:196). The action portrayed here, metaphorically depicting the activity of thought, is entirely solitary, but as in the other examples, it offers a living image of an abstract idea.

Such solitary portrayals of self, breaking through and enlivening intellectual discourse, help to form a different mode of voice for Emerson, falling between the explicitly dramatic interlude and the variation of voice in the context of discourse (the Orphic and colloquial voices). This can be appropriately labeled the "assertive" voice, because it is usually a departure from discourse for the purpose of emphasis, and it consists of an extreme assertion of the self. It is often strident, though at times merely whimsical; yet it is always intended to be slightly unsettling to the settled. One well-known passage from "Self-Reliance," previously noted, exemplifies this assertive voice well: "I would write on the lintels of the door-post, *Whim.* I hope it is somewhat better than whim at last, but we cannot spend the day in explanation" (CW, 2:30). The passage calls to mind, intentionally, the image of a youth that we half suspect of irresponsibility. He is, after all, writing where he should not be. But our ultimate reaction is different, because the impetuousness, the energy, and the justifiable impatience of youth make a stronger appeal to us than any discomfort we might feel about proprieties having been violated. But the passage does cut two ways, raising the very reservations that it tramples through sheer boldness. Those reservations are aggressively called out by the assertiveness of the passage, because calling them out makes them visible, and thus vulnerable to the stronger appeal of freedom.

Emerson's prose constantly cuts in this fashion, using assertiveness to overcome distance between the speaker and reader. Later in "Self-Reliance" he demonstrates his wary skepticism about "great" men: "A great man is coming to eat at my house. I do not wish to please him: I wish that he should wish to please me. I will stand here for humanity, and though I would make it kind, I would make it true" (*CW*, 2:35). Clearly he flirts with belligerence in this stance, with the remark "I do not wish to please him," and though he qualifies that assertion later, it gains our attention and gives the passage the edge of tension that makes it come alive. Similarly, when he discusses the necessity of inspiration in "Art," his tone becomes dramatically aggressive: "Away with your nonsense of oil and easels, of marble and chisels: except to open your eyes to the masteries of eternal art, they are hypocritical rubbish" (*CW*, 2:212–13). The force of this tirade against the tools of art somehow sharpens the effect of the veneration for "eternal art."

One final mode of voice, complementing the others discussed above, needs also to be recognized, one which can be thought of as an "evangelical" voice and is closely associated with the methods of the sermon. The essays contain many passages of explicitly direct exhortation to the reader, maintaining the quality of religious authority associated with the Orphic voice, but also incorporating a quality of highly charged emotion which we associate with Emerson's dramatic interludes, and the directness which we associate with his colloquial voice. It is the voice of the preacher pleading with his congregation, or the teacher seeking to inspire his students. Near the beginning of a paragraph in "Spiritual Laws," Emerson bursts out with the exclamation, "O my brothers, God exists," and thus launches an extended passage of what can best be termed pastoral pleading:

There is a soul at the centre of nature, and over the will of every man, so that none of us can wrong the universe. . . . The whole course of things goes to teach us faith. We need only obey. . . . For you there is a reality, a fit place and congenial duties. Place yourself in the middle of the stream of power and wisdom which animates all whom it floats, and you are without effort impelled to truth, to right, and a perfect contentment.

[*CW*, 2:81]

The appeal of the passage is its depiction of the effortless attainment of "a fit place" and "a perfect contentment," but that promise is based on the implied but unstated effort necessary for a surrender of the will. One must undergo a struggle to cease struggling, and this exhortation is intended to inspire and facilitate that struggle. In carefully secular terms, Emerson has restated the traditional Christian paradox of the willed surrender of the will, the essay becoming in this instance a secularized version of the sermon. Later in the essay, the same point is again stressed in evangelical tones: "Let us acquiesce. Let us take our bloated nothingness out of the path of the divine circuits. Let us unlearn our wisdom of the world. Let us lie low in the Lord's power, and learn that truth alone makes rich and great" (*CW,* 2:93). Here the repetition of the exhortative "Let us" accumulates power as the passage builds, reinforced by the *l* alliteration and by increasingly intense and paradoxical assertions: we are "bloated nothingness"; we must "unlearn our wisdom." The final sentence is explicitly, even conventionally, pastoral. In "Compensation" we find, rather than an exhortation, an extended lament: "We cannot part with our friends. We cannot let our angels go. . . . We are idolators of the old. We do not believe in the riches of the soul" (*CW,* 2:72). And in "Friendship" exhortation is mixed with an element of chastisement:

He only is fit for this society [friendship] who is magnanimous. . . . Let him not intermeddle with this. . . . Treat your friend as a spectacle. Of course he has merits that are not yours, and that you cannot honor, if you must needs hold him close to your person. Stand aside; give those merits room; let them mount and expand. [*CW,* 2:123]

Emerson's preacherly tone should not be considered a monotone, as we can see from these examples. Partly because of the resources of the nineteenth-century sermon, and of course because of his mastery of that form, his evangelical voice can have a surprising variety, and an equally surprising vitality, even in a day when the sermon has lost much of its influence.

To end this consideration of Emerson's use of voices in the essays by again referring to the sermon form only emphasizes an essential continuity in his early career. In some respects he was a rebel, but the attempts to read his career in those terms take us only so far. He rejected tradition when it hindered him, but in fact relied on it heavily as the foundation for the very real innovations he made in thought and expression. We cannot finally understand the innovations without fuller recourse to those foundations.

Continuity in Emerson's Career

To remind ourselves that Emerson was a preacher is inevitably to portray him as a somewhat traditional figure. Whatever the content of his doctrine, the preacher is invested with an aura of conservative authority which is absent from our conception of the poet or philosopher. It is hard, in America, to be a rebel and a preacher; hard not to be a rebel if a poet. The appeal of Emerson's career has thus centered around his leaving the ministry, because that gesture affirms the rejection of authority that not only was a central part of his message, but is in many ways our national mythos. That this view of Emerson's career must be qualified we can conclude from the continuities of both form—sermon to lecture to essay—and content —the pursuit of self-culture—that his journals and lectures reveal.

But if to adjust our focus on the younger Emerson is to strip him of some of his rebellious appeal, it is also to acquit him of the later abject surrender that such an appeal inevitably implies. It is plain that the Emerson of the middle 1840s was a more temperate, some would say conservative, man. If too much emphasis is given to an intemperate early Emerson, only some dramatic break can account for his change. Depending on the reader's perspective, that is either a break away from the somewhat naïve opinions of his youth or, more drastically, a breaking of the personality of his youth, a defeat and surrender to the forces against which he rebelled. In the first case we undervalue the achievement of his youth, and in the second we do injustice to his later career.

The importance of Emerson's connection with the tradition of liberal theology represented by New England Unitarianism is thus essential to a just portrait of his career. Because he was nurtured in a tradition which affirmed human potential, he could reject confining and damaging barriers, but could stand on firm ground to do so. He could rebel without being a rebel, for his revolutionary gestures were affirmative ones, and were not without precedent. Certainly he challenged his own tradition, but those Unitarians who parted ways with him had to do so at a certain expense to the liberalism that had sustained them. Emerson made them, finally, show their cards, for he argued from their premises, extending their own assumptions. If we understand this continuity in his early career, we can more readily see why Emerson's youth is less a story of defiance, and his age less a story of surrender, than we might otherwise believe.

To stress continuity is not, however, to deny tragedy in his career. The outlines of that tragedy were clear enough even in the late 1830s, when his reputation as spokesman for the optimistic Transcendentalists was only beginning to be established. Yet it was less a tragedy of failure than one of wanting too much, of being unable to accept progress instead of perfection, but of clinging still to the hope of progress. What must be seen is that he continued to cling to that hope in his later career. Even "fate" he would tenaciously try to render merely a means to that progress. If we continue to need a rebellious Emerson, if we must continue to search out revolutionary ancestors to support us now, we must at least allow Emerson the justice of a courageous old age. If we recognize that continuity, then the continuity of his entire career and his religious tradition seems to be an inescapable conclusion as well. It is to recognize his rebellion as an affirmation, both of his tradition and of the promise of the future.

Notes

Introduction

1. Harold Bloom, "The Freshness of Transformation: Emerson's Dialectics of Influence," in *Emerson: Prophecy, Metamorphosis, and Influence*, ed. David Levin (New York: Columbia University Press, 1975), p. 135.

2. Joel Porte, "The Problem of Emerson," *Harvard English Studies*, 4 (1973), 85–90.

3. Frederic Henry Hedge, "Memorial Address," in Joseph Henry Allen, *Our Liberal Movement in Theology* (1892; rpt. New York: Arno Press, 1972), p. 212.

4. The major studies are Arthur C. McGiffert, Jr., *Young Emerson Speaks* (Boston: Houghton Mifflin, 1938); Kenneth Walter Cameron, "History and Biography in Emerson's Unpublished Sermons (A Report of Progress and of Research Possibilities)," *Proceedings of the American Antiquarian Society*, 66, pt. 2 (1956), 103–18; and Wesley T. Mott, "Emerson and Antinomianism: The Legacy of the Sermons," *American Literature*, 50 (Nov. 1978), 369–97.

5. James E. Cabot, *A Memoir of Ralph Waldo Emerson*, 2 vols. (Boston: Houghton Mifflin, 1888), 1:152.

6. Howard Mumford Jones, *Belief and Disbelief in American Literature* (Chicago: University of Chicago Press, 1967), p. 57.

7. See, for example, Gay Wilson Allen, "A New Look at Emerson and Science," in *Literature and Ideas in America: Essays in Honor of Harry Hayden Clark*, ed. Robert Falk (Athens: Ohio University Press, 1975), pp. 58–78; and Merton M. Sealts, Jr., "Emerson on the Scholar, 1833–1837," *PMLA*, 85 (Mar. 1970), 185–95.

8. Conrad Wright, Preface to *A Stream of Light: A Sesquicentennial History of American Unitarianism* (Boston: Unitarian Universalist Association, 1975), p. v.

9. For examples of this trend in scholarship see William Hutchison, *The Transcendentalist Ministers: Church Reform in the New England Renais-*

sance (New Haven: Yale University Press, 1959); Conrad Wright, *The Liberal Christians: Essays on American Unitarian History* (Boston: Beacon Press, 1970); Daniel Walker Howe, *The Unitarian Conscience: Harvard Moral Philosophy, 1805–1861* (Cambridge: Harvard University Press, 1970); and Lawrence Buell, *Literary Transcendentalism: Style and Vision in the American Renaissance* (Ithaca: Cornell University Press, 1973). The trend is assessed in my essay "Unitarian Historiography and the American Renaissance," *ESQ: A Journal of the American Renaissance*, 23 (2nd quarter 1977), 130–37.

10. Porte, "The Problem of Emerson," p. 89.

11. Stephen E. Whicher, *Freedom and Fate: An Inner Life of Ralph Waldo Emerson* (Philadelphia: University of Pennsylvania Press, 1953), pp. 69–71, 74–119; Jonathan Bishop, *Emerson on the Soul* (Cambridge: Harvard University Press, 1964), pp. 187–202.

1. American Unitarianism

1. Henry Ware, Jr., *The Personality of the Deity: A Sermon Preached in the Chapel of Harvard University, September 23, 1838* (Boston: James Munroe, 1838). The sermon is republished with an introduction in Kenneth Walter Cameron, "Henry Ware's *Divinity School Address:* A Reply to Emerson's," *American Transcendental Quarterly*, 13 (Winter 1972), 84–91.

2. Wright, *The Liberal Christians*, p. 39. See also Hutchison, pp. v–viii; and Buell, *Literary Transcendentalism*, pp. 5–7.

3. *The Works of Henry Ware, Jr., D.D.*, 4 vols. (Boston: James Munroe, 1846), 4:288. Hereafter cited as Ware, *Works.*

4. Howe's study of the "Unitarian conscience" stresses the convergence of theology and moral philosophy among the Unitarians.

5. *The Works of William Ellery Channing, D.D.* (Boston: American Unitarian Association, 1875), p. 15. Hereafter cited as Channing, *Works.*

6. For discussions of Unitarian theological polemics see Clarence Faust, "The Background of Unitarian Opposition to Transcendentalism," *Modern Philology*, 35 (Feb. 1938), 297–324; and Hutchison, pp. 12–21.

7. See Conrad Wright, "The Election of Henry Ware: Two Contemporary Accounts Edited with Commentary," *Harvard Library Bulletin*, 17 (July 1969), 245–78.

8. The history of American Arminianism is traced in Conrad Wright, *The Beginnings of Unitarianism in America* (Boston: Starr King Press, 1955).

9. See Perry Miller, " 'Preparation for Salvation' in Seventeenth-Century New England," in *Nature's Nation* (Cambridge: Harvard University Press, 1967), pp. 50–77; and Norman Pettit, *The Heart Prepared: Grace and Conversion in Puritan Spiritual Life* (New Haven: Yale University Press, 1966), pp. 86–124. Howe (pp. 116–20) suggests that doctrines of preparation are "antecedents of the Liberal doctrine of character cultivation," but notes that evangelical revivalism is also a response to the "tension . . . between preparation and predestination" in Calvinist thought. My discussion of Unitarian doctrines of salvation is indebted to Howe's section "Unitarian Conversion," pp. 116–20.

10. Howe, p. 118.   11. Ware, *Works*, 2:262, 264.

12. Ibid., pp. 267, 269.   13. Ibid., p. 270.

14. Joseph Stevens Buckminster, "Regeneration," Nov. 18, 1804, Buckminster Papers, Boston Athenaeum. Quoted by permission of the Boston Athenaeum.

15. William Henry Channing, *The Life of William Ellery Channing, D.D.* (Boston: American Unitarian Association, 1887), pp. 74, 75. Hereafter cited as Channing, *Life*.

16. Ware, *Works*, 3:410, 417.

17. Joseph Stevens Buckminster, "Self Dedication to the Service of Christianity," May 1810, Buckminster Papers, Boston Athenaeum. Quoted by permission of the Boston Athenaeum.

18. *Extracts from Sermons by the Late Rev. John Emery Abbot, of Salem, Mass., with a Memoir of his Life, by Henry Ware, Jr.* (Boston: Wait, Greene, 1830), p. 47. Hereafter cited as Abbot, *Sermons*.

19. Channing, *Life*, p. 238.

20. See in particular Channing's sermon "The Moral Argument against Calvinism," in *Works*, pp. 459–68.

21. Abbot, *Sermons*, pp. xxiii–xxiv, 63.

22. Channing, *Works*, p. 14.

23. Joseph Stevens Buckminster, *Sermons* (Boston: Carter and Hendee, 1829), p. 241. Hereafter cited as Buckminster, *Sermons* (1829).

24. *Sermons by the Late Rev. J. S. Buckminster, with a Memoir of His Life and Character* (Boston: John Eliot, 1814), p. 286. Hereafter cited as Buckminster, *Sermons* (1814).

25. Ralph Waldo Emerson, "Literary Intelligence," *Dial*, 3 (Jan. 1843), 387.

26. The self-conscious and introspective Channing has been discussed from another perspective, which stresses the political turmoil of the slavery issue. See Andrew Delbanco, *William Ellery Channing: An Essay on the*

Liberal Spirit in America (Cambridge: Harvard University Press, 1981).

27. Channing, *Life*, pp. 74–75, 76.

28. Ware, *Works*, 3:292.

29. Buckminster, *Sermons* (1829), pp. 303, 241.

30. Ware, *Works*, 3:101, 4:306.

31. Buckminster, *Sermons* (1814), p. 286.

32. Ware, *Works*, 4:330, 331.   33. Channing, *Works*, p. 384.

34. Ibid., p. 369.   35. See Howe, pp. 151–73.

36. Ware, *Works*, 3:275–76.   37. Channing, *Works*, p. 14.

38. Howe, p. 116.

39. Channing, *Works*, pp. 402, 404.

40. For example, see Ware's "The Example of Our Lord," in *Works*, 4:140–152; and Channing's "The Imitableness of Christ's Character," in *Works*, pp. 310–16.

41. Buckminster, *Sermons* (1829), p. 264.

42. Ware, *Works*, 3:102.

43. Channing, *Works*, p. 311.

44. Buckminster, *Sermons* (1829), p. 278.

45. Channing, *Works*, p. 313.   46. Ware, *Works*, 3:211.

47. Faust, pp. 297–324.   48. Ware, *Works*, 4:139.

49. Channing, *Works*, p. 15.

50. Buckminster, *Sermons* (1814), p. 263.

51. Channing, *Works*, pp. 172, 175.

52. Ware, *Works*, 2:296.

53. Buckminster, *Sermons* (1829), p. 307.

54. Buckminster, *Sermons* (1814), p. 279.

55. Channing, *Works*, p. 347.

56. Ware, *Works*, 4:375, 2:297.

57. Howe, p. 167.

58. In addition to Emerson's "Pray without Ceasing" (*YES*, pp. 1–12), see the concluding part of Ware's *On the Formation of the Christian Character* (*Works*, 4:283–391), and his sermon "Sources of Moral Weakness and Moral Strength" (*Works*, 3:187–201), in which he recommends moderation, promptness of action, faith, and prayer as positive steps toward moral growth. See also Channing's "Daily Prayer" (*Works*, pp. 493–96).

59. Buckminster, "Regeneration." Quoted by permission of the Boston Athenaeum.

60. Channing, *Works*, p. 291.   61. Ware, *Works*, 4:296.

62. Ware, *Works*, 4:144.   63. Ware, *Works*, 4:296.

64. Ware, *Works*, 3:96, 98.   65. Channing, *Life*, p. 233.

2. Emerson's Ministry

1. See Alan Heimert, *Religion and the American Mind: From the Great Awakening to the Revolution* (Cambridge: Harvard University Press, 1966), pp. 159–79, 208–20; and J. William T. Youngs, Jr., *God's Messengers: Religious Leadership in Colonial New England, 1700–1750* (Baltimore: Johns Hopkins University Press, 1976), pp. 120–37. As Youngs notes, the Awakening had the support of most New England ministers.

2. Wright, *The Liberal Christians*, p. 42. For accounts of Ware's ministry in Boston, see John Ware, *Memoir of the Life of Henry Ware, Jr.*, 2 vols. (1846; rpt. Boston: American Unitarian Association, 1890), 1:101–16 (hereafter cited as Ware, *Memoir*). See also Chandler Robbins, *A History of the Second Church, or Old North, in Boston* (Boston: John Wilson and Son, 1852), pp. 130–37. As John Ware notes, Henry Ware felt that "among his earliest duties" was the formation of "a personal acquaintance with all the members of his parish and their families" (*Memoir*, 1:109). For Ware's ministry at Harvard, see *Memoir*, 2:88–126; and Conrad Wright, "The Early Period (1811–1840)," in *The Harvard Divinity School: Its Place in Harvard University and in American Culture*, ed. George Huntston Williams (Boston: Beacon Press, 1954), pp. 54–58.

3. Wright, *The Liberal Christians*, p. 42.

4. Robbins, p. 132.

5. On the founding of the Harvard Divinity School, see Wright, "The Early Period."

6. Howe, p. 106. See Ware, *Memoir*, 2:112–15, for a description of the composition and reception of the volume.

7. Ann Douglas, *The Feminization of American Culture* (New York: Knopf, 1977), p. 160.

8. Ware, *Works*, 2:175–200. Walter Harding lists two copies of this work in Emerson's library in *Emerson's Library* (Charlottesville: University Press of Virginia, 1967), p. 292. Buell notes other relevant homiletical discussions by Ware and others in "The Unitarian Movement and the Art of Preaching in Nineteenth Century America," *American Quarterly*, 24 (May 1972), 180.

9. Ware, *Works*, 2:177.   10. Ibid., p. 179.

11. Ibid., pp. 178, 186.   12. Ibid., p. 178.

13. Ware, "Hints on Extemporaneous Preaching," in *Works*, 2:347–412 (first published in 1824).

14. Ware, *Works*, 2:356, 366.

15. Emerson graduated from Harvard in 1821 and did not dedicate himself to the ministry until Apr. 17, 1824 (*JMN*, 2:237–42). In the

interval, he kept school. An eye ailment in 1825 interrupted his Divinity studies, and he kept school again in 1826. He was not ordained until 1829, since ordination could be conferred only by an individual congregation. For information on ministerial training in this period, see Wright, "The Early Period," pp. 21–22.

16. Whicher, chap. 1–3. Jonathan Bishop specifically discusses Emerson's eye trouble, writing, "It is fair to suspect that the eye trouble was at least partly psychosomatic." Later he notes that "consumption is not merely a psychosomatic disease," but adds, "It cannot be accidental that his illnesses oppressed him most as he prepared and began to practice the duties of the ministry, and left him for good only when he brought himself to abandon it" (pp. 167–71). Despite Bishop's caution, and his qualifications of these statements, his study clearly leaves the impression that Emerson dreaded his vocation to the point of serious physical illness, but was too timid to resign it. Such an impression obscures the pleasure Emerson did take in many of his ministerial duties, especially preaching, and seriously overdramatizes his displeasure with the ministry.

17. Henry James, *Partial Portraits,* ed. Leon Edel (Ann Arbor: University of Michigan Press, 1970), p. 7.

18. Sealts, "Emerson on the Scholar, 1833–1837," p. 186.

19. Mary S. Withington, "Early Letters of Emerson," *Century,* 26 (July 1883), 457.

20. Ibid., p. 456.

21. Channing, *Works,* pp. 220–32. See also Conrad Wright, *Three Prophets of Religious Liberalism: Channing—Emerson—Parker* (Boston: Beacon Press, 1961), pp. 19–22, for a discussion of the impact of this lecture on Emerson.

22. For an informative discussion of the different directions of Emerson's and Hawthorne's careers, see Leonard Neufeldt, " 'The Fields of My Fathers' and Emerson's Literary Vocation," *American Transcendental Quarterly,* no. 31 (Summer 1976), pp. 3–9.

23. Henry Whitney Bellows, *A Discourse Occasioned by the Death of William Ellery Channing, D.D., Pronounced before the Unitarian Societies of New-York and Brooklyn, in the Church of the Messiah, October 13, 1842* (New York: C. S. Francis, 1842), p. 12.

24. Wright, *The Liberal Christians,* pp. 41–61.

25. Ware, *Works,* 2:178.

26. Ibid., 4:276–77. Ware left the church gradually, beginning in 1828. He did not cut his ties with the church until his position at Harvard was secure and his health had improved. See Ware, *Memoir,* 2:8–31.

27. Ware, *Works,* 4:278.

28. James, p. 17.

29. Edward W. Emerson records some favorable reminiscences of Emerson's pastorate by some of the parishioners, and suggests that the young of the congregation were particularly moved by his preaching. "Those of a more conservative and less imaginative temperament," he adds, "were not altogether pleased" (*Emerson in Concord* [Boston and New York: Houghton Mifflin, 1889], p. 38).

30. Whicher, p. 25.

31. Ralph Waldo Emerson, "Address to the Second Church," Mar. 10, 1844, manuscript b Ms Am 1280. 199 (7), Houghton Library, Harvard University. Quoted by permission of the Houghton Library.

32. Elizabeth Palmer Peabody, *Reminiscences of Rev. Wm. Ellery Channing, D.D.* (Boston: Roberts Brothers, 1880), pp. 280–81.

3. Emerson's Preaching

1. Buell, *Literary Transcendentalism*, p. 107.

2. Buell has discussed the Transcendentalist departure from doctrine to "figurative" truth (ibid., pp. 108–23).

3. Peabody, pp. 365–66.

4. Ralph Waldo Emerson, "[A True Account of the Soul]," manuscript sermon b Ms Am 1280. 215 (56), Houghton Library, Harvard University. Quoted by permission of the Houghton Library.

5. Whicher argues that Stewart was the major influence on Emerson in this regard (p. 15), but Porte finds that Price was the more significant. See Porte, *Emerson and Thoreau: Transcendentalists in Conflict* (Middletown, Conn.: Wesleyan University Press, 1965), p. 69.

6. Bishop, p. 66. See also Porte, *Emerson and Thoreau*, p. 68.

7. Bishop, p. 67.

8. *JMN*, 2:6. The editorial symbols < > are used by the editors of *JMN* to indicate a cancellation in the manuscript, and the symbols ↑ ↓ are used to indicate an insertion.

9. Channing, *Works*, p. 384.

10. Ibid., p. 293.

11. *L*, 1:257. Kenneth Walter Cameron has shown in his study of Emerson's reading, based on charging lists at Harvard and the Boston Athenaeum, that by 1830 Emerson was well under way in serious reading of Coleridge and other "modern" writers, as well as hosts of classical and other secular authors. See Cameron, *Ralph Waldo Emerson's Reading: A Corrected Edition* (Hartford: Transcendental Books, 1962).

12. Buell, *Literary Transcendentalism*, p. 105.

13. Emerson's use of the imagery of the eye and vision has had previous critical attention, notably in Sherman Paul, *Emerson's Angle of Vision* (Cambridge: Harvard University Press, 1952), pp. 71–84.

4. The Naturalist

1. William Charvat, "A Chronological List of Emerson's American Lecture Engagements," *Bulletin of the New York Public Library*, 64 (Sept. 1960), pt. 1, pp. 492–96.

2. James, p. 12.   3. Charvat, p. 492.

4. Ibid., p. 496.   5. Bishop, p. 146.

6. For a discussion of the importance of Emerson's first European trip, see Joel Porte, *Representative Man: Ralph Waldo Emerson in His Time* (New York: Oxford University Press, 1979), pp. 37–54.

7. For the major study of science in Emerson's thought in the period before *Nature*, see Harry Hayden Clark, "Emerson and Science," *Philological Quarterly*, 10 (July 1931), 225–60. Clark's views are confirmed by the publication of the early lectures in G. W. Allen, "Emerson and Science," pp. 58–78. Other important commentaries on Emerson's view of science in this period can be found in Joseph Warren Beach, *The Concept of Nature in Nineteenth Century English Poetry* (New York: Macmillan, 1936), pp. 336–43; *Life*, pp. 187–89; Kenneth W. Cameron, *Emerson the Essayist* (Raleigh, N.C.: Thistle Press, 1945), pp. 224–27; Paul, pp. 208–20; and Bishop, pp. 45–59. Rusk (*Life*) and Bishop particularly note the importance of Emerson's observations in Paris. Porte's discussion of Emerson's use of nature for moral purposes is also relevant to this discussion: see *Emerson and Thoreau*, pp. 68–92.

8. Clark, p. 228.

9. Coleridge's primary influence was not in science, but rather in his dialectical theory, which had a significant impact on Emerson's sense of form. For a thorough discussion, see Barry Wood, "The Growth of the Soul: Coleridge's Dialectical Method and the Strategy of Emerson's *Nature*," *PMLA*, 91 (May 1976), 385–97.

10. Ralph Waldo Emerson, "[Reason and Revelation]," manuscript sermon b Ms Am 1230. 215 (92), Houghton Library, Harvard University. Quoted by permission of the Houghton Library.

11. Emerson had mentioned the lecture in the fall of 1823 as a model of eloquent preaching (*JMN*, 2:160). The oration is published in Channing, *Works*, pp. 220–32.

12. Wright, *The Liberal Christians*, pp. 22–40.

13. Channing, *Works*, pp. 224, 226.

14. Ibid., pp. 224, 223.

15. William Paley, *Natural Theology* (1802; rpt. New York: Sheldon and Co., 1875), chap. 1, "State of the Argument," pp. 5–8.

16. Ralph Waldo Emerson, "[Christianity Confirms Natural Religion]," manuscript sermon b Ms Am 1280. 215 (43), Houghton Library, Harvard University. Quoted by permission of the Houghton Library.

17. Rusk refers to Emerson's developing theory of nature as a "hazy vision of evolution" (*Life*, p. 189), but Beach argues that what Emerson accepted in the late 1820s and early 1830s was a version of the "scale of being" philosophy, not a version of evolutionary theory in what came to be known as the Darwinian sense. See Beach, pp. 330–33.

18. Carl F. Strauch, "The Year of Emerson's Poetic Maturity: 1834," *Philological Quarterly*, 34 (Oct. 1955), 353–77. "Poet," "naturalist," and several other vocational terms can be subsumed under the larger label "scholar," as discussed in Sealts, "Emerson on the Scholar, 1833–1837."

19. One important immediate source of the influence is Sarah Austin's translation, *Characteristics of Goethe, from the German of Falk, Von Muller, &c.*, 3 vols. (London: Effingham Wilson, 1833). This long work seeks to portray the many-sided nature of Goethe, and discusses his work in botany and in the theory of color.

20. As Whicher and Spiller note, the arrangement of this lecture from the manuscript leaves is to an extent conjectural.

21. Cameron, *Emerson the Essayist;* Whicher, p. 52; Bishop, p. 9; Richard P. Adams, "Emerson and the Organic Metaphor," *PMLA*, 69 (Mar. 1954), 121, 122.

22. Thomas à Kempis's *Imitatio Christi* is the best known of all Christian devotional books. Jeremy Taylor's *The Rule and Exercises of Holy Dying* is labeled by Helen White the "most famous" of the class of English devotional books dedicated to "a treatment of the whole problem of the Christian life." See White, *English Devotional Literature (Prose), 1600–1640*, University of Wisconsin Studies in Language and Literature, no. 29 (Madison: University of Wisconsin Press, 1931), pp. 163–64. Emerson knew the work well and entered it in his "Catalogue of Books Read, 1819–1824" (*JMN*, 1:399). Henry Scougal, the least known of this group of writers, was a Scottish divine and author of *The Life of God in the Soul of Man* (1677). Emerson's most extended comments on these devotional writers are contained in a letter to his wife's cousin, Elizabeth Tucker, of Feb. 1, 1832, offering her suggestions for reading. He recommends, in order, Thomas à Kempis, Scougal, Taylor, Fénelon, and significantly, Ware's *On the Formation of the Christian Character*, which he considered part of the devotional tradition (*J*, 2:459).

23. Howe, p. 107.

24. White, p. 12.

25. Cranch's caricatures are published and discussed in F. DeWolfe Miller, *Christopher Pearse Cranch and His Caricatures of New England Transcendentalism* (Cambridge: Harvard University Press, 1951). One of the drawings is published in *Emerson's Nature: Origin, Growth, Meaning,* ed. Merton M. Sealts, Jr., and Alfred R. Ferguson, 2d ed., enlarged (Carbondale: Southern Illinois University Press, 1979).

26. Bishop, pp. 15, 11. For the following discussion of the transparent eyeball experience, I am much indebted to Merton Sealts.

27. The early reviewer is Francis Bowen, who argues that Emerson "turns and aims a back blow at the universe, which he has been leading us to admire and love." See the *Christian Examiner,* 21 (Jan. 1837), 375, rpt. in Sealts and Ferguson, p. 83. Porte argues that Emerson's idealism signifies "a simple denial of the inherent worth of matter and sense experience" (*Emerson and Thoreau,* p. 63). It should be noted that Porte's interpretation of Emerson is in general more sympathetic in his later *Representative Man.*

5. The Humanist

1. Neufeldt, pp. 3–9.

2. For earlier treatments of these lectures see John O. McCormick, "Emerson's Theory of Human Greatness," *New England Quarterly,* 26 (Sept. 1953), 307–9; Edmund G. Berry, *Emerson's Plutarch* (Cambridge: Harvard University Press, 1961), pp. 89–90; and Gustaaf Van Cromphout, "Emerson and the Dialectics of History," *PMLA,* 91 (Jan. 1976), 55–57.

3. For analyses of Emerson's aesthetics, see Norman Foerster, "Emerson on the Organic Principle in Art," *PMLA,* 41 (Mar. 1926), 193–208; Vivian C. Hopkins, *Spires of Form: A Study of Emerson's Aesthetic Theory* (Cambridge: Harvard University Press, 1951); and Charles R. Metzger, *Emerson and Greenough: Transcendental Pioneers of an American Aesthetic* (Berkeley and Los Angeles: University of California Press, 1954).

4. See Hopkins, pp. 107–10, for an analysis of the lectures. Emerson's working notes and outlines for the series are in his notebook "L Literature" (*JMN,* 12:33–55).

5. Bliss Perry, "Emerson's Most Famous Speech," in *The Praise of Folly and Other Papers* (Boston and New York: Houghton Mifflin, 1923), pp. 81–113.

6. Sealts, "Emerson on the Scholar, 1833–1837," p. 193.

7. In the Centenary edition of Emerson's *Works,* Edward Waldo Emerson attributes the fable to Plato's *Symposium* and Plutarch's *Morals* (*W*, 1:417). More recently, Sacvan Bercovitch has argued against the plausibility of these sources, suggesting instead that Empedocles was the source Emerson had in mind. See Bercovitch, "The Philosophical Background to the Fable of Emerson's 'American Scholar,'" *Journal of the History of Ideas,* 28 (Jan.–Mar. 1967), 123–28.

8. Emerson's "Journal C" for 1837 contains many references to Goethe in the spring of that year. See especially *JMN,* 5:300, 313–14, 316–17.

6. The Theist

1. Whicher, pp. 94–105.

2. Ibid., pp. 91–92.

3. Ibid., p. 109.

4. There is a textual problem with the final lecture since the manuscript is not preserved, and the text cited is actually that of "The Senses and the Soul," *Dial,* 2 (Jan. 1842), 374–79. This quotation, however, can also be found in an 1827 entry in Emerson's journals (*JMN,* 6:64), ascribed to Bishop Butler.

5. Whicher, pp. 85–86.

6. The comment goes back even further than the "Holiness" lecture to a May 1836 journal entry (*JMN,* 5:163).

7. Whicher, p. 73.

8. Hutchison, pp. 68–82; Wright, *Three Prophets of Religious Liberalism,* pp. 29–32.

9. Andrews Norton, "The New School in Literature and Religion," in *The Transcendentalists: An Anthology,* ed. Perry Miller (Cambridge: Harvard University Press, 1950), pp. 193–96.

10. Norton's initial reaction was expanded in his 1839 pamphlet, *A Discourse on the Latest Form of Infidelity,* partially reprinted in P. Miller, *The Transcendentalists,* pp. 210–13.

11. Ware, *The Personality of the Deity,* in Cameron, "Henry Ware's *Divinity School Address,*" pp. 8, 6, 16. Pagination cited is that of the original edition (1838), which is preserved in Cameron's reprint.

12. John White Chadwick, *Theodore Parker: Preacher and Reformer* (Boston and New York: Houghton Mifflin, 1901), p. 85.

13. Joel Myerson, "Convers Francis and Emerson," *American Literature,* 50 (Mar. 1978), 27–28.

14. Wright, *The Liberal Christians,* p. 49.

7. The Years of Transition

1. Myerson, "Convers Francis and Emerson," p. 29.

2. One can best get a sense of Emerson's work on Carlyle's behalf by reading the correspondence between them, and Joseph Slater's introduction to it (*CEC*, pp. 3–63).

3. Joel Myerson, *The New England Transcendentalists and the "Dial"* (Rutherford, N.J.: Fairleigh Dickinson University Press, 1980), pp. 74–76.

4. Hutchison, pp. 85–93.

5. Paul, p. 185. Paul discusses the challenge of Brook Farm and other communitarian movements to Emerson's philosophy at this time (pp. 183–96).

6. See his letter to William Emerson (*L*, 2:162).

7. Porte, *Representative Man*, p. 137.

8. On Aug. 31, 1838, worried that the Divinity School controversy would rob him of his lecture audience, he wrote, "If they will not hear me lecture, I shall have leisure for my book which wants me" (*JMN*, 7:60). Linda Allardt, one of the *JMN* editors, has called attention to plans for a book of essays in "Notebook F. No. 1" (*JMN*, 12:75, 81), and there is mention of it in a letter of Lidian Emerson in October 1837. See Eleanor M. Tilton, "Emerson's Lecture Schedule—1837–1838—Revised," *Harvard Library Bulletin*, 21 (Oct. 1973), 285–86.

9. Porte stresses Emerson's problem with aging as part of the general problem of "The Fall of Man" at this period. See *Representative Man*, pp. 174–76.

10. Whicher, p. 103.

11. See Merton M. Sealts, Jr., "Emerson on the Scholar, 1838: A Study of 'Literary Ethics,'" in Falk, pp. 40–57; and Porte, *Representative Man*, p. 139.

12. This concept in "Circles" will be discussed more fully in the next chapter. See also Paul's discussion of Emerson's use of circular imagery (pp. 98–99).

13. On July 4, 1839, Emerson wrote to Carlyle that he had "three essays nearly done, and who knows but in the autumn I shall have a book?" (*CEC*, p. 243). But in August he wrote his brother William, "I see plainly I shall have no choice about lecturing again next winter" (*L*, 2:218), because of financial difficulties. For more details, see Linda Allardt's discussion of the composition of *Essays: First Series* (*JMN*, 12:xxv–xxviii).

8. Essays: First Series

1. Emerson published the book under the title *Essays*, adding "First Series" in later editions after he had published *Essays: Second Series* (1844). For the sake of clarity, I have used the later title.

2. See Bishop (pp. 143–61) for discussion of Emerson's technique of reader engagement. See also David M. Wyatt, "Spelling Time: The Reader in Emerson's 'Circles,'" *American Literature*, 48 (May 1976), 140–51.

3. Bishop has discussed the importance of tone in the essays from a different perspective, arguing that Emerson's tone often suggests a war within the self (pp. 128–43).

4. *The Complete Writings of James Russell Lowell*, Elmwood Ed., 16 vols. (Boston and New York: Houghton Mifflin, 1904), vol. 2, *My Study Windows*, p. 396. For a recent discussion of Lowell's attitude toward Emerson, and of the whole problem of the "poetic" quality of Emerson's prose, see Brian M. Barbour, "Emerson's 'Poetic' Prose," *Modern Language Quarterly*, 35 (June 1974), 157–72.

5. Lawrence Buell, "Reading Emerson for the Structures: The Coherence of the Essays," *Quarterly Journal of Speech*, 58 (Feb. 1972), 58–69.

6. See Bliss Perry, *Emerson Today* (Princeton: Princeton University Press, 1931), p. 25, for comments on the easy divisibility of Emerson's essays. Perry offers no examples, but the divisions which I will offer show what he means. In each case, these divisions can be further subdivided. "Self-Reliance" falls into four major parts: (1) the necessity of self-reliance, (2) two obstacles to self-reliance (conformity and consistency), (3) the source of self-reliance, and (4) four areas of application. "Compensation" also has four major parts: (1) the fact of compensation, (2) examples of the law of compensation, (3) the moral consequences of compensation, and (4) conclusion and peroration. "Intellect" falls into three major parts: (1) the intellect receptive, (2) the intellect constructive, and (3) the intellect as process. For some other examples of divisions and subdivisions of essays, see Buell, "Reading Emerson for the Structures."

7. Wyatt, p. 143.

8. James M. Cox, "R. W. Emerson: The Circles of the Eye," in *Emerson: Prophecy, Metamorphosis, and Influence*, ed. Levin, p. 68.

9. *CW*, 2:179. As Joseph Slater has pointed out, the quotation, somewhat altered, is from John Norris, *An Essay towards the Theory of the Ideal or Intelligible World* (London, 1701–4). See the informational note, *CW*, 2:253–54.

10. Buell, *Literary Transcendentalism,* pp. 160–61, quoting *CW,* 2:179, 182.

11. Buell, *Literary Transcendentalism,* pp. 160–61.

12. *CW,* 2:179. Emerson discussed Pyrrhonism earlier, in "The Present Age" (*CW,* 3:292), and in "Spiritual Laws" (*CW,* 2:81), and a similar objection was raised in "Compensation": "The thoughtless say, on hearing these representations,—What boots it to do well? there is one event to good and evil; if I gain any good, I must pay for it; if I lose any good, I gain some other; all actions are indifferent" (*CW,* 2:70). For commentary on the query and Emerson's response to it in "Circles," see Bishop, p. 142; and Harold Bloom, *Figures of Capable Imagination* (New York: Seabury, 1976), pp. 53–64.

13. Bishop, p. 79.

14. Porte notes the "figures of ascension" in *Essays: First Series* (*Representative Man,* pp. 176–77), finding that the vision behind these figures carries over into "The Poet" of *Essays: Second Series.* It should also be remembered that Emerson was employing a principle of "polarity" or contrast in structuring the book, pairing off contrasting essays. This is discussed by Paul, pp. 117–18, and by Buell, *Literary Transcendentalism,* pp. 161–62.

15. See David F. Finnigan, "The Man Himself: Emerson's Prose Style," *Emerson Society Quarterly,* no. 39 (2nd quarter 1965), 13–15, for a discussion of spiral form in Emerson's style at the paragraph level; and Hopkins, p. 3 and elsewhere, for a discussion of the place of the spiral in his aesthetic theory.

16. For a discussion of the critical reaction to Alcott's "Orphic Sayings," see Joel Myerson, " 'In the Transcendental Emporium': Bronson Alcott's 'Orphic Sayings' in the *Dial,*" *English Language Notes,* 10 (Sept. 1972), 31–38. The term "Orphic" has generally been associated with Emerson's poetry and poetics. See Bloom, *Figures of Capable Imagination,* pp. 67–88; and R. A. Yoder, *Emerson and the Orphic Poet in America* (Berkeley and Los Angeles: University of California Press, 1978), pp. xi–30.

Index